Election of the Lesser Son

Election of the Lesser Son

Paul's Lament-Midrash in Romans 9—11

David R. Wallace

Fortress Press
Minneapolis

ELECTION OF THE LESSER SON

Paul's Lament-Midrash in Romans 9—11

Cover design: Alisha Lofgren

Library of Congress Cataloging-in-Publication Data

Print ISBN: 978-1-4514-8295-9

eBook ISBN: 978-1-4514-8751-0

The paper used in this publication meets the minimum requirements of American National Standard for Information Sciences — Permanence of Paper for Printed Library Materials, ANSI Z329.48-1984.

Manufactured in the U.S.A.

This book was produced using PressBooks.com, and PDF rendering was done by PrinceXML.

Μετὰ εὐχαριστίας εἰς πολλοὺς οἰκτιρμοὺς αὐτοῦ

Contents

Abbreviations

Ancient Works

'Abot R. Nat   'Abot de Rabbi Nathan

Abr.   Philo, *Abraham*

Aj.   Sophocles, *Ajax*

Ant.   Josephus, *Antiquities*

Aen.   *Aeneid*

1 En.   *1 Enoch*

1QH   Thanksgiving Hymns (Qumran Scroll)

1QS   Rule of the Community (Qumran Scroll)

1-2 Esdr.   1-2 Esdras

2-3 Apoc. Bar.   Syriac, Greek *Apocalypse of Baruch*

b. San.   Babylonian Talmud *Sanhedrin*

B. Bat.   Bablyonian Talmud *Baba Batra*

Disc.   Epictetus, *Discourses*

Inst.   Quintillian, *Institutio Oratoria*

Jub.   *Jubilee*

LXX	*Septuagint*
Med.	Marcus Aurelius, *Meditation*
Mor.	Plutarch, *Moralia*
MT	Masoretic Text
m. Sanh	Mishnah *Sanhedrin*
Ps. Sol.	*Psalms of Solomon*
Rep.	Plato, *Republic*
Rhet.	Aristotle, *Rhetoric*
Rom. Hist.	Cassius Dio, *Roman History*
Sir.	Sirach
Spec. Laws	Philo, *Special Laws*
Suet.	*Life of the Caesars*
T. Naph.	Testament of Naphtali
t. Sanh.	Tosefta tractate Sanhedrin
y. Ketub	Jerusalem Talmud *Ketubot*
y. Ned.	Jerusalem Talmud *Nedarim*
War	Josephus, *Jewish War*
Ws	Wisdom of Solomon

Modern Works

AB	Anchor Bible Commentary Series
ABD	Anchor Bible Dictionary
ABR	*Australian Biblical Review*

ANRW	*Aufstieg und Niedergang der römischen Welt*
AsSeign	*Assemblies du Seigneur*
BSac	*Bibliotheca Sacra*
BAGD	*Greek-English Lexicon of the New Testament and Other Early Christian Literature*, 2nd ed.
Bib	*Biblica*
BTB	*Biblical Theology Bulletin*
CBQ	*Catholic Biblical Quarterly*
DPL	Dictionary of Paul and his Letters
EDNT	Exegetical Dictionary of the New Testament
ExAud	*Ex auditu*
GTJ	*Grace Theological Journal*
JBL	*Journal of Biblical Literature*
JETS	*Journal of the Evangelical Theological Society*
JSNT	*Journal for the Study of the New Testament*
JSNTSup	Journal for the Study of the New Testament: Supplement Series
JSOT	*Journal for the Study of the Old Testament*
TDNT	*Theological Dictionary of the New Testament*
LCL	Loeb Classical Library
LSJ	Liddell, H.G., R. Scott, and H.S. Jones, *A Greek English Lexicon*
NIB	New Interpreter's Bible
NICNT	New International Commentary on the New Testament

NIDNTT	New International Dictionary of New Testament Theology
NovT	*Novum Testamentum*
NovTSup	Novum Testamentum Supplements
NTS	*New Testament Studies*
PSBSup	*Supplements of the Princeton Seminary Bulletin*
PRSt	*Perspectives in Religious Studies*
PTR	*Princeton Theological Review*
SBLDS	*Society of Biblical Literature Dissertation Series*
ScEccl	*Sciences ecléciastiques*
SNT	Studien zum Neuen Testament
TDNT	*Theological Dictionary of the New Testament*
TynBul	*Tyndale Bulletin*
TZ	*Theologische Zeitschrift*
WBC	Word Biblical Commentary
WD	*Wort und Dienst*
WUNT	Wissenschaftliche Untersuchungen Zum Neuen Testament
ZNW	*Zeitschrift für neutestamentliche Wissenshaft und die Kunde der älteren Kirche*
ZTK	*Zeitschrift für Theologie und Kirche*

Acknowledgements

I am humbled and honored to participate in interpreting God's revelation to Paul in Romans 9–11. The time and effort involved has been considerable and rewarding. I wish to thank my wife, Hillary, for her support, and also my children, Jonathan, Victoria, Valerie, Joshua, Michael, and Nathan for their patience. It is important to recognize Siegfried Schatzmann, Bruce Corley, and John Taylor for taking time to review the manuscript and for their words of encouragement. And I am especially grateful to Neil Elliott at Fortress Press for his guidance in strengthening and polishing this work.

David Wallace
November 18, 2013

Introduction

When the topic of God's election of Israel is raised in theological discussion, references to Romans 9–11 most often accompany the conversation. This passage is recognized for its emphasis on the sovereignty of God—for example, that God's will and reason for choosing Jacob rather than Esau is not known—and for its defense of God's faithfulness even though Israel has rejected God's Son. Yet significant aspects of Paul's argument in Romans 9–11 have been overlooked, leaving the reader puzzled as to why God chooses Jacob over Esau or how God can *impartially* elect Israel, yet give *priority* to Israel ("first to the Jew and then to the gentile"; 1:16). And what complicates a more clear understanding of these theological issues in Romans 9–11 is a lack of precise delineation of Paul's integrated form and style, such as his parallel thought rhymes and poetical structures (e.g., 9:30—10:3 and 11:11-24). A fresh analysis of Romans 9–11 is needed that answers these theological concerns and gives adequate attention to his literary form and style. This volume accomplishes this goal by interpreting the biblical text of Romans 9–11, section by section, explaining Paul's understanding of God's reason for electing the lesser son and how this election reveals God's compassionate heart and mind for Israel and his plan for the nations. In addition, the results of this study lead to a better understanding of Paul's purpose in writing his letter as well as contributing to a better understanding of the letter as a whole.

Need

To be more specific, when Paul opens the body of the Letter to the Romans, he confidently expresses that his "gospel is the power of God unto salvation to all who believe" and qualifies this statement with the phrase "first to the Jew and then the gentile" (1:16). It seems that here Paul emphasizes God's priority in choosing Israel. Yet in the following passage, Paul restates this priority—"first to the Jew first and then the gentile" (2:9-11)—stressing that God does not show favoritism. This raises a logical problem—how can God give priority to Israel and, at the same time, be impartial in his selection? A clear answer is needed, and a careful analysis of Romans 9–11 appropriately resolves this paradox.

In addition, when Paul narrates God's election of Jacob, he supports this decision with a quote from the prophet Malachi: "Jacob I loved, Esau I hated" (Rom 9:13; Mal 1:2-3). On the surface, it seems that Paul stresses God's sovereignty, implying that the mind of God is not known in his choosing Israel. Yet Paul's argument in Romans 9:6-29 and in the rest of the section, 9:30—11:32, is that the single characteristic in his election of Jacob was that God chose the son in the "lesser," or humble position. This insight has not been appropriately emphasized in scholarship, and it is a central truth in understanding Paul's main theme of humility in his letter, both in his relationship with the Roman church and also in his expectation from the believers so that his outreach to Spain is successful.

What has further complicated a better understanding of God's character in his election of Israel, as well to the answer to the above issues, is that Romans 9–11 is a difficult passage to interpret. This is due to Paul's combination of form and style of argument in a manner unlike his contemporaries. The insight at the heart of this work is that Paul integrates an Old Testament literary form—the lament—with an exegetical style of argumentation best known from later rabbinical materials—the midrash—in order to reach a primarily *gentile* Christian audience. His overall arrangement of lament elements—address (9:1-5), body (9:6—11:32), and formal praise (11:33-36)—shows Paul's participation in interceding for his people, revealing the heart of God. But rather than use poetry or song for the body of the lament, 9:6—11:32, Paul uses a midrashic style of argument, interpreting and applying Torah to meet the contemporary needs of his audience (incorporating primary and secondary texts, key words, thought rhymes, commentary, final thematic verses, etc.). In his first two distinct and interrelated midrashic forms, 9:6-29 and 9:30—10:21, Paul narrates in balanced logical sequence God's faithful and merciful intervention in Israel's history, preparing the recipients of his letter for a didactive and literary climax that reveals God's plan for the nations in 11:1-32. I call Paul's unique combination a "lament-midrash" and in subsequent chapters will be concerned with how each form shapes Paul's argument.

Since Paul's argument is tightly integrated, analyzing one particular section of the passage calls for an analysis of the whole. Yet no one volume on Romans has yet carefully identified Paul's forms or traced the cumulative meaning of the argument. For example, almost all of the works on Romans 9–11 are limited to published dissertations which, more recently, focus on the background texts that influenced Paul's thought, or they focus on some form of rhetorical analysis.[1]

---

1. For example: Pablo Gadenz, *Called from the Jews and from the Gentiles: Pauline Ecclesiology in Romans 9-11* (Tübingen: Mohr Siebeck, 2009); Johann D. Kim, *God, Israel, and the Gentiles: Rhetoric and Situation in Romans 9-11* (Atlanta: SBL, 2000); Francis Watson, *Paul, Judaism, and the Gentiles: A Sociological Approach* (Cambridge: Cambridge University Press, 1998); John Lodge, *Romans 9-11: A Reader-Response Analysis* (Atlanta: Scholars Press, 1996); Richard Bell, *Provoked to Jealousy: The Origin and Purpose of the Jealousy Motif in Romans 9-11* (Tübingen: Mohr Siebeck, 1994); James Aageson, *Paul's Use of Scripture* (1983); Elizabeth E. Johnson, *The*

The numerous articles and chapters written on Romans 9–11 analyze a certain verse or passage, but rarely the whole of Romans 9–11. The long list of Romans commentaries are primarily written for resource purposes, and the one-volume works do not work through each section of the argument but seek out particular passages based on a theme or view.[2] These works provide invaluable insight and rich understanding, but a one-volume work is needed that explains the biblical text, section by section, giving attention to Paul's literary forms and meaning, leading to a clear perspective of God's faithful and *merciful* character in his impartial election of Israel, the son in the *humble* position.

Several other contributions are made in this work. First, Paul's intercessory experience "in" Christ is evidenced not only in the opening section, 9:1-5, but throughout the argument, revealing God's compassionate decision in election. Second, this work makes evident Paul's literary use of the names "Israel" and "gentiles" as a reference to "works" and "faith" without compromising the theme of God's impartiality to both Jew and gentile, 10:12, and without limiting Paul from warning Christian gentiles about the consequence

Function of Apocalyptic and Wisdom Traditions in Romans 9-11 (Atlanta: Scholars Press, 1989); Folker Siegert, *Argumentation bei Paulus, Gezeigt an Röm 9-11* (Tübingen: Mohr, 1985); Paul Dinter, *The Remnant of Israel and the Stone of Stumbling in Zion according to Paul* (1980); H. L. Ellison, *The Mystery of Israel: An Exposition of Romans 9-11* (Grand Rapids: Eerdmans, 1966); and Johannes Munck, *Christ & Israel: An Interpretation of Romans 9-11*, trans. Ingeborg Nixon (Philadelphia: Fortress Press, 1967).

2. For example: J. R. Daniel Cook traces and explains the subject of resurrection throughout the letter in *Unlocking Romans* (2008); Neil Elliott interprets Romans in light of an imperial context in *The Arrogance of Nations: Reading Romans in the Shadow of Empire* (Minneapolis: Fortress Press, 2008); David Wallace reexamines Romans against the imperial imagery from Virgil's *Aeneid* in *The Gospel of God: Romans as Paul's Aeneid* (Eugene, OR: Pickwick, 2008); Andrew Das argues for a gentile audience in *Solving the Romans Debate* (Minneapolis: Fortress Press, 2007). P. J. Bekken analyzes the letter in light of Deuteronomy 30:12-14 in *The Word is Near You: A Study of Deuteronomy 30:12-14 in Paul's Letter to the Romans in a Jewish Context* (New York: Walter de Gruyter, 2007); Richard Bell investigates Paul's theology of Israel in *The Irrevocable Call of God: An Inquiry into Paul's Theology of Israel* (Tübingen: Mohr Siebeck, 2005); and Daniel Chae focuses his study on Paul's self-awareness in *An Apostle in Paul as Apostle to the Gentiles* (1997).

of pride, 11:18-22. This is an important distinction that contributes to the meaning of "all Israel" near the end of Paul's argument, 11:26. Third, Paul's various poetic structures, such as a balanced chiasm in 9:30—10:3 and a larger poetic structure in 11:10-24 (a *hapax legonomenon*), are precisely delineated. Fourth, this analysis supports the view that Romans 9–11 is one of three relevant sections of the letter, neither an addendum nor a climax, that leads the reader to the practical admonitions in the final chapters of the body of the letter.

Method

Since this effort requires a section-by-section examination of Romans 9–11, gleaning relevant information from the vast amounts of secondary literature written about Romans demands selectivity. Information from exegetical works and theological themes are not discussed topically but according to the passage at hand. In other words, this book guides the reader through Paul's arguments, focusing on Paul's emphasis on God's *character* in election in Romans 9–11, and points out the distinctive contribution of the particular passage at hand in relation to the overall argument and purpose of the letter.

For example, themes such as the law and righteousness are not discussed in detail except when these themes occur, but since "law" and "righteousness" are central themes in Romans 3 and in Romans 9:30—10:3, both sections are explored with respect to the meaning in Romans 9:30—10:3.[3] Similarly, the insight gained in this book concerning the character of God in election, 9:6-18, furthers an understanding of the practical issues in chapters 14–15, but a lengthy dialogue about the "weak" and the "strong" is not given. Theological

---

3. For the purpose of reducing visual clutter, whenever possible, commas are used to bracket scriptural citations for a Romans passage. Parentheses are used for other biblical books and for Romans citations when commas distract from readability.

implications that do relate to the rest of the letter are usually discussed at the end of each section. In summation, this author respects the contributions of the wide range of approaches (e.g., socio-historical, rhetorical, etc.), but chooses an eclectic approach to elucidate the text's meaning within the bounds of form, thematic coherence, and Pauline theology.

This work is not an exhaustive commentary nor a critical evaluation of the extensive materials written about Romans; rather, this work provides a fresh approach with research and support to engage the scholar and to guide the biblical studies student in understanding Paul's message of God's compassionate heart and mind in his election of Israel.

Overview

Chapter 1 analyzes Romans 9:1-5 in light of Paul's intercessory petition. Chapter 2 focuses on Paul's first midrashic form—God's faithfulness for Israel, 9:6-29. This section of Paul's argument begins the body of Paul's lament and clarifies the nature of God's character in election. He narrates a reversal—the inclusion of the gentiles—hinting at the hardening of Israel. Chapter 3 analyzes the second midrashic form, 9:30—10:21,[4] and explains how Paul builds upon the previous section, 9:6-29, by narrating the Moses account with respect to Christ, leading the listener to the conclusion that faith comes by hearing the word of Christ. Chapter 4 shows Paul's juxtaposition of two identities—"remnant" Israel and "hardened" Israel—in 11:1-10, as Paul prepares the reader for the mystery revealed concerning Israel's salvation, 11:11-32. Chapter 5 then explains Paul's praise to God for his infinite wisdom, 11:33-36.

---

4. The phase "midrashic form" is used rather than "midrash" because while Paul employs elements of midrash, his cohesive sections of argument cannot be neatly categorized as rabbinical "midrash."

It is important to note that Romans 9–11 continues Paul's thought and argument from the first two sections of his letter, 1:17–5:11 and 5:12–8:39. He integrates themes from these sections into the lament-midrash of Romans 9–11, providing a solid basis for his practical admonition in the final section of the body of the letter, 12:1–15:13. This means that in writing this missive, Paul sees the importance for the Christians in Rome to have insight into God's decisions concerning Israel's salvation, particularly because of the significance the information has on their understanding of the gospel and its application. Therefore, due to the integrated nature of the content of Romans 9–11 with the rest of the letter, a discussion of relevant literary concerns—style, genre, and letter divisions—and necessary background information—Paul's identity, purpose, and audience—is needed in this Introduction to give an appropriate frame of reference for interpretation.

Literary Concerns

Three basic suppositions undergird this work: (1) God's personal revelation to Paul is the driving force behind the message of his letter; (2) Paul's primary support for his assertions come from the Old Testament; and (3) Paul employs an integrated style using a variety of forms. While scholars generally agree to these claims, there is considerable disagreement concerning the "degree" to which they are true. Thus, because of its bearing upon meaning, some clarity is important at the outset concerning Paul's general style.

General Style

In his letters, Paul ministers to people in a manner that exhibits diplomacy, depth of knowledge, and attention to detail. His choice of vocabulary shows familiarity with the customs and culture of the cities and peoples for whom his letters were written, and without compromising his convictions or message, he skillfully adapts to the needs of individual congregations. In his own words: "I become all things to all people so that by all possible means I might save some" (1 Cor. 9:22-23). Paul seeks to achieve this goal in his letters through instruction as he responds to practical issues with sensitivity and with an accomplished use of the Old Testament. In this sense, Paul's theological fight takes place in the arena of knowledge, and his intelligence, training, and commission fit well with his natural motivation to reason. His pen is a diplomatic instrument for advancing the gospel.

But more than his relational skill and competence, the revelation he receives from Jesus Christ is what drives him. After being born and raised in cosmopolitan Tarsus, Paul as a young boy earned his theological education in Jerusalem, where he studied the Torah and the traditions of his fathers. He describes his pursuit of the law as "zealous," "beyond that of his peers," and on "behalf of Israel" (Gal. 1:14f). As a young man on a journey to Damascus to carry out orders against Christians, he encountered the Person of Christ. His memorization of Torah, his view of prophecy, and his rabbinical training now make sense in light of Jesus Christ, a radical reframing of his heart and mind, a reshaping of his theology and practice. Once a persecutor of Christ, now he endures physical suffering, threats, and insults from his own people as the Spirit guides him in proclaiming his message. What was once a centripetal, inclusive focus of law and Israel, has become a centrifugal outreach as he embraces gentile culture to communicate God's grace.

This sensitivity to diverse cultures, as well as his literary skill, raises the question as to the influence of Greco-Roman rhetorical education on Paul's writing. On the surface, this may not seem to be an important issue but, when diagramming Paul's thought flow or when determining Paul's theological emphases at certain points in his arguments, awareness of a rhetorical device or the rhetorical purpose within a section can and does directly affect the meaning of a passage, especially more technical ones such as Romans 9–11. While scholars agree that Paul utilizes Greek literary devices, there is no consensus as to the precise nature and extent of use.

If Paul were formally trained in rhetoric, then the sections in his letters would show a close overlap with ancient categories,[5] but they do not. Some New Testament scholars try to force Paul's content and form into rhetorical categories that were intended for speech training, not letter writing. It is more reasonable and accurate to assume that Paul writes with general rhetorical principles in mind—that is to say, his writings do not show formal training in ancient rhetoric, but his writings do show the use of common literary techniques of his day.

For example, Paul uses diatribe[6] (a device in which the speaker speaks to an imaginary student for the purpose of instruction)

---

5. For the view that Paul may have had some formal training in rhetoric, see R. F. Hock, "Paul and Greco Roman Education," 215f. Obviously Paul utilized some of the conventions of his day for speaking in his letter writing—such as diatribe, enthymemes, and persuasive elements—but he does not follow a clear cut Greco-Roman rhetorical model as discussed in contemporary handbooks of his day: Aristotle's *Rhetorica*, Quintilian's *Institutio Oratoria*, and Cicero's *De Oratore* and *De Inventione*. See also Corbett, *Classical Rhetoric*, 1990. It may be that Paul had access to handbooks or to basic rhetorical elements in school. What is important to know about the debate about ancient rhetoric is that the discipline of rhetoric was for "speaking," and while letter writing contains similar elements to a speech, there are no clear parallels of letter writing in the first century that compare to Paul's form and style. For further reading on a favorable view of Paul's use of rhetoric: G. A. Kennedy, *New Testament Interpretation*, 10f; Stanley Stowers, *A Rereading of Romans: Justice, Jews, and Gentiles* (New Haven, CT: Yale University Press, 1994), 17f; R. D. Anderson, *Ancient Rhetorical Theory and Paul*, 278f. For a less favorable view, see J. Murphy-O'Connor, *Paul the Letter-Writer*, 79–83.

A method for applying current rhetorical theory has been developed in recent years; see Dennis Stamps, "Rhetorical Criticism of the New Testament: Ancient and Modern Evaluations of Argumentation," in *Approaches to New Testament Studies*, eds. Stanley E. Porter and David Tombs (Sheffield: Sheffield Academic Press, 1995), 129–69; and Duane Watson and Alan Hauser, *Rhetorical Criticism of the Bible* (Leiden: Brill, 1994), 101–9.

6. For the view of Romans 9–11 as a diatribe, see Changwon Song, *Reading Romans as a Diatribe* (New York: Lang, 2004), 15f.

stylistically in his letters, particularly Romans (e.g., 2:17f and 9:19-23). But since this is a common device in Greek literature and Judaism, it is more likely that Greek culture—literature, architecture, art, and philosophy—permeated the known world, including Jewish Palestine. It would be appropriate for a Pharisaic Jew, converted to Christianity, whose purpose was to *reach gentiles* throughout the world, to mix his form and style appropriately. And while Paul clearly arranges his arguments in persuasive patterns, the contents of his letters do not read like first-century missives, writings, or speeches of his day. His letters reveal his Jewish thought processes as well as Greek part-to-whole argument, with the bulk of his support from Scripture.[7] Metaphorically speaking, the Jewish Paul wears a Greco-Roman literary jacket.[8]

Paul exhibits a unique writing style, even more so in Romans 9–11. Nowhere else in his correspondences does Paul arrange his argument within a "lament" sequence nor cohesively integrate midrashic elements with as many rich allusions and quotations from the Old Testament. Not surprisingly, throughout his elaboration on God's election of Israel, he uses a mix of literary devices that require attention to Old Testament contexts and his culture. All this to say, paying attention to this literary complexity results in a better understanding of his meaning.[9]

---

7. James Aageson, "Scripture and Structure in the Development of the Argument in Romans 9-11," *CBQ* 48 (1986): 286–87.

8. It may also be important to note that while Paul's style shows some similarities to other Jewish authors, such as Philo and Josephus, his letters are quite different in logic, arrangement, and literary flow. Paul shares a philosophical approach with Philo in use of allegory and use of the Old Testament, but even a cursory reading reveals the marked differences in Paul's form and purpose.

9. This information must also be combined with related theology from his letters and what we know about him, particularly from his experiences recorded in Acts.

Genre

Paul combines lament and integrated argument to narrate God's plan for Israel.[10] The lament elements express Paul's and God's compassion for Israel. For Paul's experience "in" Christ, 9:1, gives him a perspective in which he identifies with Old Testament prophets who interceded for Israel—such as Moses, Elijah, and Isaiah.[11] Within his logical arrangement, he incorporates midrashic elements and Scriptural support leading the listener to understand the wisdom of God for Israel and the nations. A general explanation of his literary method—combining lament and midrashic argument—is given below. However, since the opening verses, 9:1-5, set the emotional tone for the lament, a closer look at Paul's participation in interceding for Israel is presented in the first chapter ("Paul's Grief for Israel"), with attention given to the thematic continuity of intercession in Romans 9–11, and in the rest of the letter.

Lament

The first and last sections (9:1-5; 11:33-36) frame Paul's arguments, forming an *inclusio*, moving the reader from grief to praise.

---

10. Paul also incorporates Greco-Roman literary devices that are common to his culture. This includes his use of citation in handling quotations, which is similar to Greco-Roman style; see Stanley, *Paul and the Language*, 291 and 360. Just as Paul uses language to communicate to publics at different levels, it may be that he utilizes rhetorical principles accordingly. More certainly, Paul refers to himself in the first person (twenty-seven times) in Romans 9–11—making his appeal personal as a Jew on behalf of other Jews; Stowers, *Rereading of Romans*, 292.
11. For Moses as a prophetic figure in Romans 9–11, see Michel Quesnel's discussion, "La Figure de Moïse en Romains 9-11," *New Testament Studies* 49, no. 3 (2003): 321–35. "David" as well could be included in the list above. For the view of David as prophet in Judaism, see Margaret Daly-Denton, "David the Psalmist: Jewish Antecedents of a New Testament Datum," *Australian Biblical Review* 52 (2004): 32–47.

Grief for Israel	9:1-5
God's election	9:6-29
Israel's failure	9:30–10:21
God's plan of salvation	11:1-32
Praise for God's Wisdom	11:33-36

Paul's content and arrangement in these chapters follow an Old Testament lament pattern of an address, body, and a final praise. In the address, the speaker establishes his right to speak, he emphasizes the covenant, and he invokes God's action on Israel's behalf. In Paul's address, 9:1-5, he establishes his right to speak and lists the covenantal gifts, but rather than evoke feelings of confidence, he prays to be cursed from Christ on behalf of his brothers. And by not directly invoking *God* to act on Israel's behalf, he builds suspense concerning Israel's outcome ("What will happen to Israel?").[12]

Typically in the body of an Old Testament lament, the speaker accuses God or others and gives reasons for the distress. The mood will shift to God's faithfulness and a turning back to God. The listener is then brought to a heightened praise for God's actions and character. But unlike the tone and arrangement of a poem or song, Paul uses logical arguments within a lament sequence to defend God's faithfulness, a topic with which Old Testament laments are ultimately concerned.[13] In the first two sections of the body of his lament, he accuses not God, but Israel for their loss, 9:6-29 and

---

12. Listening to Paul's anguish would also likely stir emotions from the non-Hebrew reader, since a lament has broad range of social and theological dimensions. However, it was unusual for a male to be presented as in literature as lamenting in this way, though permitted; see Ann Suter, *Male Lament in Greek Tragedy*, 156–80; and Karen Bassi, *Acting Like Men*, 104f. On the one hand, participation in a lament may be a way of regaining kingly or moral authority; Mark Griffith, "The King and Eye: The Rule of the Father in Greek Tragedy," *Proceedings for the Cambridge Philological Society* 44 (1998): 62f. But on the other hand, lament was scorned; see Plato, *Republic*, 3.388a–e and 10.604b–607a.

9:30—10:21, and bases his reasoning on God's character in his election of Abraham, Isaac, and Jacob. In the end, "all Israel" returns to God, 11:1-32, and Paul gives glory to God, 11:33-36.

Midrashic Elements

Generally speaking, Romans 9–11 is unique not only because of the lament elements but also because of Paul's use of parallel thought and literary devices. He follows a basic pattern of commentary with proof texts (e.g., 9:6-18), supporting his reasoning with Old Testament Scripture. In the first two major sections of the body of his lament, he ends his argument with a *testimonia*, 9:26-29 and 10:18-21. On two occasions he parallels his ideas through chiastic structures, 9:30—10:4 and 11:11-24, and he identifies himself with Old Testament prophets (e.g., 11:1-10). He expresses emotion, his own and God's (e.g., 10:1, 21). He keeps the body of the argument neatly parallel, and threads the themes of each section of the midrashic sections, 9:6-11:24, into a unified whole in the final verses of the body of his midrash, 11:25-31.

More specifically, the theme texts in a midrash are drawn from the Torah—a primary text is introduced and then explained by a secondary text. As the texts are elaborated on, key words are chosen based on the author's current context, *but most often this is done with the Old Testament context in mind.* The author of the midrash may explicitly state the key word in his discussion or he may intentionally leave the key word out, trusting that the listener will remember

---

13. Most commentaries divide the body of Paul's lament, 9:6—11:32, into three major sections but with variation. The outline of Romans 9–11 with its lament frame and argument becomes clearer as the form is explained in the following chapters. Interestingly, Gadenz compares 9–11 against the postexilic penitential prayers (Azariah's prayer, Dan. 3:26–45 LXX; Dan. 9:4-19; Bar. 1:15—3:8) according to a threefold movement: (1) acclamation of God's justice and power; (2) confession of Israel's sinfulness and culpability; and (3) supplication for God's mercy and salvation/deliverance; *Called from the Jews*, 57f (Gadenz builds upon Collin's commentary on Daniel [p. 350] as well as Goldingay's [p. 233]). See also, F. Watson's discussion of the postexilic penitential prayers in *Paul and the Hermeneutics of Faith*, 459–61.

the Old Testament verse and supply the key word—an interesting and challenging instructional method. For example, in 9:6-29, Paul utilizes the Pentateuch for his primary text—Genesis 21:12 (Rom. 9:6-7)—and his secondary text—Genesis 18:10 (Rom. 9:9), then uses other Scriptural support. "Key words"—seed, children, call, and son (σπέρμα, τέκνα, καλέω, and υἱος)—within the midrash connect thematically to the primary and secondary texts.[14]

Yet, a few problems present themselves when comparing Paul's letters to rabbinical texts. First, the parallels of rabbinic literature that scholars compare with Paul's writings come primarily from a later period, after the fall of Jerusalem (70 CE). This means that it is not certain what methods Paul's contemporaries were using. Second, Paul's arrangement and style in Romans 9–11 differ from these later midrashic forms. However, the basic methods of exegesis taught by Hillel are found consistently in Paul's thought.[15] This is not surprising, since Paul was trained by Gameliel (Acts 22:3), a grandson or son of Hillel. Generally this type of midrash exegesis had two purposes: (a) textual interpretation and (b) Torah application to contemporary needs.[16] Paul, as a Benjaminite, likely remained part of a Jewish community loyal to Torah-centered Judaism (Phil. 3:4-6), but as a missionary called to proclaim his message to the gentiles, his thought was mixed with literary devices and a keen sense for his audience's culture. Therefore, the phrases "midrashic elements"

14. Ellis finds a pattern: 9:6-7, theme and initial text (Gen. 21:12); 9:9, a second supplemental text (Gen. 18:10); and 9:10-28, additional citations (Rom. 9:13, 15, 17, 25-28) and catch words (καλέω and υἱος; Rom. 9:12, 24-26 and 27), with subordinate texts from other scripture, *Prophecy and Hermeneutic*, 155. The question as to why Paul would combine Jewish lament and midrash elements to reach the Christian gentiles is a relevant one. It would seem, though, that this would align with his purpose of engendering humility among the gentile Christians (11:17-21) for them to learn some of Paul's meaning, if help was needed, from knowledgeable Jewish Christians among them.

15. For Hillel's exegetical methods, see *t. Sanh.* 7.11; *'Abot R. Nat* [A] §37.

16. For example, Ben Sira taught wisdom to upper-class young men (Sir.51:23-28), and older students received training in advanced methods of interpretation. At age six or seven, schools taught boys the Hebrew Bible, mainly the Torah (*y. Ketub.* 32c, 4).

or "midrashic-type form" are used in this discussion rather than the technical term "midrash."

Letter Divisions

More formal in tone and style than his other letters, Paul's missive to the Romans serves as a diplomatic representative of his presence until he travels to them in person. His salutation and thanksgiving sections introduce and foreshadow the tone and content of the body of his letter. He presents his theme and content in four interrelated sections:

1:1-7	Salutation
1:8-15	Thanksgiving
1:16—15:13	Body of the Letter
1:16	Theme
1:17—5:11	Part I: Atonement through Faith
5:12—8:39	Part II: Life in Christ
9:1—11:36	Part III: God's Faithfulness to Israel
12:1—15:13	Part IV: Practical Admonitions
15:14-33	Informal Plans
16:1-24	Greetings
16:25-27	Doxology

In the final part of his letter, he communicates his agenda in a less formal tone, 15:14-33, greets the believers, 16:1-24, and gives praise to God, 16:25-27.

More specifically, the central passage in the Letter of Romans is Christ's sacrificial atonement for sin, 3:21-26, the means of salvation through faith rather than by the law (or "works"). Paul supports this theme with Old Testament passages, 4:1-25, and then shows how Christ's atonement affects the life of those who believe, 5:12—8:39: "where sin increases, grace abounds more." In his third section, 9:1—11:36, Paul illustrates how this grace principle, based on the atoning sacrifice of Christ, is worked out in the salvific plan of God for Israel—"where Israel disobeys, God's grace abounds more." In this way, the theological force of the gospel flows from Romans 3:21-26, and the elaboration of the effects of God's atonement are explained in the following chapters. Thus, the first three sections of the body of the letter provide a formal, integrated, and powerful theological platform for practical admonitions in the fourth section of the body of the letter, 12:1—15:13.[17]

17. All of the content in Paul's letter was written to the Roman believers for a specific purpose. Paul writes with authority concerning the gospel and makes clear his expectations of them in relation to his future plans. His entire message informs and reminds them of the truths of the gospel, knowing that they are able to instruct each other. While a variety of elements contribute to the formal nature of his letter, its main purpose has been mistaken for other nonrelated purposes, such as a doctrinal treatise, Anders Nygren, *Commentary on Romans* (Philadelphia: Fortress Press, 1949), 7f; a document summarizing and developing his most important themes, Günther Bornkamm, "The Letter to the Romans as Paul's Last Will and Testament," in *The Romans Debate*, ed. Karl P. Donfried (Minneapolis: Augsburg Publishing House, 1977), 27; important content in preparation for his trip to Jerusalem, M. Jack Suggs, "'The Word is Near You': Romans 10:6-10 within the Purpose of the Letter," in *Christian History and Interpretation*, ed. W. R. Farmer, C. F. D. Moule, and R. R. Niebuhr (Cambridge: Cambridge University Press, 1967), 291; and Jacob Jervell, "Letter to Jerusalem," in *The Romans Debate*, ed. Karl P. Donfried (Minneapolis: Augsburg Publishing House, 1977), 61–74; or some carryover issue from another church, Robert J. Karris, "Romans 14:1—15:13 and the Occasion of Romans," *CBQ* 25 (1973): 155–78. Paul's letter to the Romans addresses a specific situation; see Mark Reasoner, *The Strong and the Weak: Romans 14.1—15.13 in Context* (Cambridge: Cambridge University Press, 1999) and Nelio Schneider, *Die 'Schwachen' in der Christlichen Gemeinde Roms*. It is apparent that Paul expects the theology of his letter—which powerfully undergirds his words in 14:1—15:6 concerning the "weak" and the "strong"—to have continuing effect on the Roman believers' lives. He does so not necessarily to see the letter as a substitute for his work if he cannot make a personal visit to Rome or Spain (see Angelika Reichert, *Der Römerbrief Als Gratwanderung: Eine Untersuchung zur Abfassungsproblematik* [Göttingen: Vandenhoeck & Ruprecht, 2001], 77f), but because the content of his letter addresses a "pride" issue. Humility produces the kind of fruit needed to reach those who do not know Christ in Rome, the region, and the world.

Romans 9–11, then, is not an afterthought as C. H. Dodd suggests (*The Epistle of Paul to the Romans*, 160). Nor does Romans 9–11 seem to be the climax of the letter (Joseph Fitzmyer,

This structural sequence leads Paul's listeners to choose humility, a decision that he sees as necessary for his successful evangelistic outreach—in Rome and in the surrounding region, particularly Spain. His formal arrangement in the body of the letter also complements his informal discussion concerning his travel plans in 15:14-33. Of the New Testament letters of Paul, only in Romans does Paul reveal a personal motive for his zeal concerning Israel—Paul knows that when the "full number" of gentiles come to know Christ, then the Jews, his people, will become jealous and return to Christ in "full number."

Figuratively speaking, fertile "humble" soil among the Roman church results in a greater harvest of "fruit" among the nations (gentiles). So when Paul discloses his agenda concerning his upcoming trip to Jerusalem and to Spain, he demonstrates for them a real-life, practical model of the theological content that he explained in the body of his letter, 1:16—15:13;[18] he practices what he preaches. Now that an overview of Paul's style and arrangement has been discussed, a closer look at his identity, purpose, and audience is given.

General Background

Due to the abundance of interest concerning the nature and purpose of Paul's letter, and due to the lack of agreement concerning how Romans 9–11 fits within Paul's purpose in writing the letter, a

---

Romans [New York: Doubleday, 1993], 541; Krister Stendahl, *Paul among Jews and Gentiles* [Philadelphia: Fortress Press, 1976], 4; and Witherington, *Paul's Letter to the Romans: A Socio-Rhetorical Commentary* [Grand Rapids: Eerdmans, 2004], 244). However, Paul's despairing grief in 9:1-5 does seem to be the most emotionally intense moment of the letter, especially against the movement from the intimacy of Christ's love in chapter 8. Most likely, Paul focuses almost exclusively on the cross and resurrection; Günter Wasserburg, "Romans 9–11 and Jewish Christian Dialogue," in *Reading Israel in Romans: Legitimacy and Plausibility of Divergent Interpretations*, eds. Cristina Grenholm and Daniel Patte (Harrisburg, PA: Trinity Press International, 2000), 1:177–80.

18. This is quite evident concerning the Jerusalem offering with respect to Paul's use of the olive tree metaphor and his imperatives in chapter 11.

pointed discourse concerning Paul's identity, purpose, and audience is warranted.

Paul's Identity

Based on Paul's direct and indirect language in his introductory and concluding remarks, 1:1-15 and 15:14-33, Paul apparently sees himself serving in a priestly role before God on behalf of the gentiles.[19] In the opening sentence, he boldly states that he has been "set apart" for the gospel, 1:1, and in his thanksgiving section, he calls on God as his witness to assure the believers of his spiritual duty: "For God is my witness, the one whom I *serve* [λατρεύω] with my whole spirit in the gospel of his Son, that without ceasing, I remember you in my prayers at all times" (1:9). The words "set apart" (ἀφορίζω) and "serve" (λατρεύω) are commonly used in worship contexts in the Greek Old Testament.[20] Writing to a congregation he knows but has not visited, Paul communicates his desire to see them in person for the purpose of giving them a "spiritual" gift, one that accords mutual edification and humility. But even more directly than these liturgical references in his opening statements, Paul explicitly expresses his role in the concluding passages of his letter (15:15-16):

> . . . grace was given to me to be a servant of Jesus Christ unto the nations, in the priestly service of proclaiming the gospel of God in order

19. Daniel J-S Chae labels the personal concluding remarks as written under Paul's "apostolic self-awareness," and what is significant concerning this discussion is Chae's emphasis on the coherence between 1:1-15 and 15:14-21; *Paul as Apostle to the Gentiles* (Carlisle: Paternoster, 2007), 21f. Furthermore, "priestly" is a better translation than "minister" for it connotes Old Testament tabernacle or temple service; thus, the first-century context is communicated more clearly. Chae's attention to Paul's thematic parallel in the "personal" remarks is noteworthy—1:1-7 to 15:14-21, concerning apostleship and harmony with the Old Testament; 1:8-15 to 15:22-33, concerning desire for visit; and gentile inclusion, 1:16-17 to 15:7-13. However, it is worth pointing out that the *informal* nature of 15:14-33 is distinct from the *formal* nature of the thanksgiving section, 1:7-15.

20. "Set apart" and "to serve" are particularly used in Exodus through Deuteronomy, as well as in Joshua and in Daniel. The word "serve" is also meant for priestly service in a pagan context; for example, see Epictetus, *Arrian's Discourses*, 1.2.13.

that the Gentiles might become an acceptable sacrifice, being sanctified by the Spirit.

In these verses, Paul chooses Levitical terminology, such as "priestly service," "acceptable sacrifice," and "sanctified" to describe his role of proclamation.[21]

This "priestly" role is not an oversimplification of his purpose. Paul seeks to influence the attitudes of the Roman believers for spiritual service. He goes to great lengths to explain the gospel in the first three sections of his letter so that believers might make the spiritual choice of humility and not pride. After portraying God's merciful act of atonement, 1:17–5:11; after clarifying God's compassionate deliverance of the believer, 5:12—8:39; and after explaining God's merciful plan for Israel, 9:1–11:36, Paul transitions into the practical admonition section of his letter with these words: "Therefore, I beseech you, brothers, by the mercies of God to present your bodies as a living sacrifice, pleasing to God, which is your spiritual service" (12:1).[22] The transition "therefore" and the phrase "by the mercies of God" summarize Paul's message thus far, which reinforces his purpose in bringing about a holy sacrifice, a unified transformation of the Roman believers to humility. Paul continues in his use of priestly terminology, 12:2-3, by exhorting them to renew their minds for the purpose of knowing what the will of God is, what is good, "pleasing,"

21. It is this imagery of priestly service unto the Lord that is prominent in Romans. Keeping this in mind along with his concern for humility among the gentiles, it is less likely that Paul seeks to write his letter mainly for apologetic reasons. But by reinforcing the foundational truths about faith—Christ's atonement, Christ's work in the believer, and Israel's place in God's plan, in addition to specific issues concerning food laws and conscience—Paul does "pre-treat" the soil for a theological climate free of legalism and pride, something he directly addresses in other letters. For interesting discussions on this issue, see Campbell, "Determining the Gospel," 320; and James C. Miller, *The Obedience of Faith, the Eschatological People of God, and the Purpose of Romans* (Atlanta: SBL, 2000), 138f.

22. The conjunction οὖν in 12:1 refers back to the body of Paul's letter; particularly, see Peter Cotterell and Max Turner, *Linguistics & Biblical Interpretation* (Downers Grove, IL: InterVarsity Press, 1989), 190.

and "perfect," so that each person does not think of himself or herself too highly.[23]

Purpose

In the salutation, Paul pointedly states his aim—to evangelize Rome. First, in these opening lines, he foreshadows the gospel content of his letter. For example, in 1:2-3 Paul writes concerning prophetic Scripture and the Davidic Messiah—a topic he explains at length in 9:1–11:36. And in 1:4-5, he writes concerning the appointed Son of God and the resurrection—a topic he elaborates on concerning the life of the believer in 5:12—8:39. He then formally states his mission: "[Christ] through whom we have received grace and apostleship in obedience of faith to all nations on behalf of his name," 1:7, a practical hint at what will follow in 12:1—15:13. Second, in his thanksgiving section, he expresses his purpose of bringing a spiritual gift to "strengthen" Roman believers and clarifies this strengthening as (a) the mutual process of building each other up in faith, and (b) a process that will bear fruit in them and in the rest of the nations. Third, he concludes his formal opening with his obligation to "evangelize" all those in Rome, 1:15. Not surprisingly, Paul's

---

23. For comparable examples for the noun εὐάρεστος see Rom. 14:18; Phil. 4:18; Heb. 13:21 (and in the LXX, the verb εὐαρεστέω—see Ps. 55:14 and 114:9); for τέλειος, Exod. 12:5 and Deut. 8:13, Judg. 21:4. Chae understands "equality" and "inclusion" as the main subject matters of Jew and gentiles in Christ in Romans; *Paul as Apostle*, 290. But these appear to be a contemporary projection of terms since "equality" is not a word used in the Roman text. It seems more likely that Paul is concerned with (1) respecting God's order of election and at the same time (2) instructing the believers as to the nature of God in his severity (wrath) and kindness (mercy) in dealing with them. As Ernst Käsemann points out, justification—or salvation in the case of "all Israel"—in relation to Christ's sacrifice, 3:21-26, is the most important theological theme; "Justification and Salvation History in the Epistle to the Romans," in *Perspectives on Paul* (Philadelphia: Fortress Press, 1971), 60–78; see also S. Kim, *The Origin of Paul's Gospel* (Tübingen: Mohr, 1981), 357. Technically speaking, *order does not necessarily mean primacy.* Chae is quite insightful in his critical argument concerning the Jews (*Paul as Apostle*, 293–300). It might be that "self-awareness" as an apostle to the gentiles fits better within the semantic domain of Paul having the perspective of Christ, the mind of Christ.

theme for the body of his letter expresses his confidence in the gospel and its power for salvation, 1:16—to the Jew first and then the gentile.

In the sections after the body of his letter, 15:14-24 and 16:1-24,[24] Paul writes in a more personal, less formal tone concerning himself and his connections with the believers. This means that Paul's objective, which he had formally introduced in the opening sections of his letter, he now communicates in specific terms concerning himself, at the end of the letter.[25] Here Paul reminds the believers of his personal call as a "priest" in the work of the gospel among the gentiles to offer an acceptable sacrifice, an accomplishment that has had great results.[26] He elaborates on his plans by letting them know that he seeks to evangelize where Christ has not been named.

Therefore, Paul's purpose is singular: to bring about the humility of Christ in the Roman church, particularly among the gentile Christians. But because of the different people groups mentioned in 15:14-24—Macedonians and Greeks, the Christian poor in Jerusalem,

---

24. Romans 1:1-15 and 15:1-33 comprise a literary framework for the body of the letter. Paul is less formal in style and tone after the conclusion of the body of his letter. This difference helps the reader understand how Paul's travel plans fit within the purpose of his letter.

Paul exhorts the believers to strengthen them, but he does not do so in a flattering way so as to receive some benefit or to have some apostolic influence; contra Günter Klein, "Paul's Purpose in Writing the Epistle to the Romans," in *The Romans Debate*, ed. Karl P. Donfried (Minneapolis: Augsburg Publishing House, 1977), 29–43. Paul uses his natural diplomatic gifts but this should not be construed as manipulative. Paul exercises his authority as an apostle to the gentiles in order that they would take seriously his message in the body of the letter, see L. Ann Jervis's analysis in *The Purpose of Romans* (1991). See also Jeffrey A. D. Weima, "Preaching the Gospel in Rome: A Study of the Epistolary Framework of Romans," in *Gospel in Paul: Studies on Corinthians, Galatians and Romans for Richard N. Longenecker*, eds. L. Ann Jervis and Peter Richardson (Sheffield: Sheffield Academic Press, 1994), 362f. Even though this information concerning the framework of the letter demonstrates Paul's mission, it is important to see that the body of Paul's letter and its influence on the Roman believers is directly connected to his success in preaching the gospel in that region, making the body of the letter not any less important to his gospel mission than the information in his literary framework.

25. For clarity purposes, this would be something similar to a preacher finishing his theological message and, after stepping out of the pulpit, informally discussing his future plans.

26. Chae argues for the continuity of Paul's "boldness" (15:15b-21) and self-awareness of his role as a minister to the gentiles in relation to other parts of the letter (e.g., 10:20 and 1:16); *Paul As Apostle*, 32–46. Chae also diagrams the close connection between the themes in the epistolary frames of 1:1-15 and 15:14-33; ibid, 38–44.

Christians in Jerusalem, the Roman believers, the Jews in Jerusalem, and the unreached in Spain—his agenda involves a multipurpose effect. Paul makes it clear early in his letter that his aim depends on working together in faith (1:12, 17), and since the Roman believers' faith is being proclaimed throughout the known world, it is important that their faith grow without pride. In this way, the gospel will be well represented as Paul evangelizes Rome—when he is there and when he is not—and when he preaches in Spain. In other words, Paul wants fertile soil in Rome, without corrupting pride, so that a harvest of fruit can be born to the neighboring territories.[27] What is important to see is that Paul's discussion of his personal plans at the end of his letter—concerning the different people groups—demonstrates for the Roman believers the theological principles of the gospel that he just explained in the body of his letter, with reference to God's plan. In other words, Paul's gospel—Romans 1–11—*is* his strategic plan, which he expresses in behavioral terms to the church, 12:1—15:13, and which he models for them as described in his own agenda, 15:14-24.

---

27. Paul's letter does have an ambassadorial tone and nature to it. His connections with the church are not from founding, nor from exercising authority over it. Spain is a part of his mission that will involve the Roman believers and in the end will impact the Jews. In this sense, writing his letter to the Roman believers is a strategic goal, but Paul does not seek a recommendation letter, nor does he give indication to make Rome his base of operation. His purpose is "spiritual" (1:12, 12:1f) and the results he seeks are spiritual; thus Spain alone is not his "ultimate" goal. But there is much to say for the nature of sending a letter in the first century to serve as a type of "presence" and Paul's diplomacy is quite evident, which means the letter has "ambassadorial" qualities. For arguments that accent the "ambassadorial" nature of the letter, see Robert Jewett, "Paul, Phoebe, and the Spanish Mission," in *The Social World of Formative Christianity and Judaism*, eds. Jacob Neusner, Ernest S. Frerichs, Peder Borgen, and Richard Horsley (Philadelphia: Fortress: Fortress Press, 1988), 142–61; Jewett, "Romans as an Ambassadorial Letter," *Interpretation* 36, no. 1 (1982): 5–20; and Arthur J. Dewey, "Eis tēn Spanian: The Future of Paul," in *Religious Propaganda and Missionary Competition in the New Testament World: Essays in Honor of Dieter Georgi*, eds. Lukas Bormann, Kelly Del Tredici, and Angela Standhartinger (Leiden: Brill, 1994), 321–49. The fact that Paul mentions Spain at the end of his letter does not minimize his emphasis. Evangelizing Rome, Spain, and the resulting effects to the Jews are closely related.

Thus the theological content of Romans 9–11 becomes important to understanding Paul's evangelistic aim. For example, through his mission Paul actualizes the truth symbolized in the olive tree metaphor. His outreach to the world will bring about salvation to the disobedient Jews, for whom he continually grieves. After expressing confidence in the church's ability to instruct one another, and after reminding them of his priestly role, 15:14-16, he informs them of his success in preaching and living out the gospel in Macedonia and Greece. This accomplishment in Christ brings him to seek new territory where Christ has not been named—currently Spain, 15:24. He quotes Isaiah 52:15 (Rom. 15:21) to show that his work among the gentiles is a fulfillment of God's design. This response from the gentiles (as understood in light of Paul's arguments in 9–11) will cause jealousy, a catalyst for the future return of Israel. Paul warns the gentiles not to make the mistake of being prideful in their position after having being "grafted in," lest they incur the severity of God, too, 11:18-22. This is why in his final remarks, 15:24, Paul clarifies his expectation for the Roman believers to *help him* on his "way through" (διαπορευόμαι) to Spain—a sign of humility on their part—only after he enjoys their company *for some time* (ἀπὸ μέρους).[28]

Furthermore, in addition to his long-range plans, Paul communicates his immediate plans to travel to Jerusalem in service of the saints. He will bring an offering from the gentile Christians to the "poor" Jewish Christians in Jerusalem as a physical demonstration of the gospel. This sacrificial act from the gentile Christians (1) shows respect for God's order of election ("to the Jew first") and (2) affirms acceptance of God's plan for the Jews in the re-grafting of the "natural olive branches" (11:11f). Paul describes this "fruitful gift" from the gentile Christians as one of obligation, for the

---

28. It is possible that the use of "some" ("part") hints at a "full" result—see chapter 4.

gentile Christians now share in the spiritual blessings of the Jews, 15:27-28: "For if they [the Gentiles in Macedonia and Greece] share in the spiritual blessings of the nations, then they owe it to serve in their earthly needs." In keeping with the meaning of the olive tree metaphor, the engrafted branches—the gentile Christians—share in the nourishment of the root, thus they should support the natural branches—the Jewish Christians—that have been regrafted.

The connection between the olive tree metaphor, 11:16-24, and Paul's missiological purpose in writing his letter can further be demonstrated by the shared imagery in his informal remarks at the end of his letter, 15:30-32. Paul encourages the Roman believers with a word of blessing and request: he encourages them to "strive together" in prayer for his deliverance from the "disobedient" in Judah—a parallel reference to the "enemies" of the gospel, 11:28—and he encourages them to pray that his service in Jerusalem will be acceptable to the saints—a parallel reference to God's election, the "beloved on account of the patriarchs," 11:28. Thus Paul serves in a priestly role as a humble servant to fulfill God's plan, to enlist the sacrificial minds and actions of the Roman believers.[29]

Audience

While Paul has not visited the Roman congregation, he does know quite a few of the believers who meet in the house churches, 16:1-23.[30] Part of the reason that the Letter to the Romans is more

29. See Karris, "Romans 14:1—15:13", 155–78. Again, notice Paul's choice of liturgical terms: "service" (ἡ διακονία) in Jerusalem and "acceptable" (εὐπρόσδεκτος) to the saints.
30. The textual evidence shows that some ancient manuscripts lack the address to the Roman church (1:7, 15); some manuscripts leave out chapter 15 or 16 or both; and some place the final doxology, 16:25-27, in different places such as at the end of chapter 14, at the end of 15. But those offering speculative hypotheses for a shorter version of Romans offer no substantive evidence.

Accepting the integrity of the letter and accepting its author as Paul gives reason for its content and meaning to be trusted and received. Only in recent years has Pauline authorship been questioned, and such arguments lack credible support. The weight of textual evidence,

formal in topic and style than his other letters probably has more to do with his not having visited them. But it is also important to keep in mind that he does not "instruct" them as if they were immature believers or new converts. The congregation is healthy. He explains and reminds them based on the grace given to him, 15:15; he is convinced that they are full of all goodness and knowledge with the ability to instruct each other, 15:14, and their obedience to Christ is well known and their faith is proclaimed to the world, 1:8 and 16:9. While Paul is aware of and does speak to an internal issue, the attributes of the church do not point to a division or an egregious problem.

Paul planned to visit the believers in Rome at different times but was hindered. He sees this delay as part of God's plan, an opportunity to see a "harvest of fruit" among them. Paul wants to continue his partnership with them, soon and in person, 1:13-15.

Paul writes to both Jewish and gentile believers, yet it seems that the majority (the "target" group for the letter) are gentile Christians. He addresses them directly, 11:13-24, and informs them of his calling to reach the gentiles in Rome and in unreached territories—1:5-6, 13, 15:14-21. On the other hand, his use of midrash and Old Testament support, his focus on the law—6:14, 7:1, 7:4, 9:30—10:3—and his address to "all" those beloved of God in Rome, indicate a Jewish Christian readership as well.[31]

---

the thematic and tightly knit arguments in Romans, and the letter's style demonstrate Pauline authorship.

31. For the argument of an exclusive gentile audience, see the following works: Stendahl, *Paul among Jews and Gentiles*; Stowers, *Rereading of Romans*; Elliott, *The Rhetoric of Romans: Argumentative Constraint and Strategy and Paul's Dialogue with Judaism* (Sheffield: JSOT, 1990); and Das, *Solving the Romans Debate*. For the view of Paul writing to an "encoded" gentile audience, see Nanos, *The Mystery of Romans: The Jewish Context of Paul's Letter* (Minneapolis: Fortress Press, 1996). While it makes sense that Paul writes to gentile Christians, the idea of a letter to the Roman believers that would not include Jewish Christians is a logical "all gentile/no Jewish Christian" fallacy. However, the emphasis on gentile believers as the primary audience makes sense.

Historical information leads to a similar conclusion. Three primary sources give brief accounts about the situation in Rome before the time of Paul's writing his letter: the Roman historians Suetonius and Dio Cassius, and the Christian author Luke.[32] In the early second century CE, Suetonius records the account of Claudius's decision to expel the Jews from Rome in 49 CE: "Since the Jews constantly made disturbances at the instigation of Chrestus, he [Claudius] expelled them from Rome." The assumption is that "Chrestus" was misspelled in Latin and refers to "Christians." This record aligns with Luke's account (Acts 18:1-2) of Paul's meeting a Jew in Corinth named Aquila "who had recently come from Italy with his wife Priscilla because Claudius had ordered all the Jews to leave Rome." However, in the early third century CE, Dio Cassius writes about Claudius's order in this way: "As for the Jews, who had again increased so greatly that by reason of their multitude it would have been hard without raising tumult to bar them from the city, he did not drive them out, but ordered them, while continuing their traditional mode of life, not to hold meetings."[33]

Luke's account of Paul's arrival in Rome records a somewhat significant and autonomous Jewish population in Rome. Luke writes about Christian brothers inviting Paul to stay with them in Rome, even though he is guarded by a soldier. Three days after his arrival, Paul calls together the Jewish leaders in Rome to explain why he is in chains, and while they know about the Christian sect, they seemingly do not have firsthand experience with them. The Jewish leader's reply (Acts 28:21-22): "We have not received any letters from Judea concerning you, nor have any of the brothers from there communicated anything bad about you. We consider what you think

---

32. See Suetonius's work on the *Life of the Caesars*, 25.3; *Dio Cassius*, 60.6.6-7; Acts 18:2 and 28:21-22.

33. For a helpful and succinct list of the different views, see Johann Kim, *God, Israel, and the Gentiles*, 50–56. All translations are the author's unless otherwise stated.

to be worthwhile and want to listen to you, for we know that everywhere people are speaking against this sect."

Taking into consideration the accounts of Luke and Suetonius, there was an expulsion, but it is not certain whether it was due to Christians. An expulsion would mean a temporary exodus of the Jews from the city of Rome. But at the time of Paul's letter, there was a reasonable sized population of Jews. These Jews were not in close contact with Judea about Paul's situation. And the lack of personal conflict with the Christian brothers suggests that the synagogues did not encounter the Christian message or much opposition.

Thus, based on the literary and historical evidence, it seems that Paul writes to both Jewish and gentile Christians meeting in house churches, 16:1-23, with the main purpose of bringing about humility among the gentile Christians. For gentile Christians to receive such a direct address concerning the temptation to become prideful (11:17f), it would mean they were in a position that warrants such an admonition—in the majority.

Finally, it might be helpful to see Paul as writing on two levels. On one level, he writes to believers about a specific situation. In other words, the first eleven chapters prepare the theological foundation for the practical admonitions concerning the "weak" and "strong" issue in chapters 14 and 15. Here Paul applies the "full weight" of the gospel so that the Roman believers choose humility—since arrogance would limit the gospel impact in Rome and likely, in turn, the world. As a missionary, it is reasonable that he would be concerned.

On another level, Paul writes in a *formal* manner to a church he does not know "well." He has not visited them, and he expects that his letter will circulate among the house churches. The recipients live at the center of the empire during a time when Rome is in the midst of a cultural revival—in literature, art, philosophy, and law. It makes sense, then, that as an apostle who is called to preach to all peoples and "kings," he would take time to pen a didactive letter with lasting theological significance. In this light, Paul's unique, formal style has a specific, continual purpose: to combat pride for a missiological end, revealing the heart and mind of God.

1

Paul's Grief for Israel

The truth I am speaking in Christ, I am not lying; my conscience bears witness to me in the Holy Spirit that my grief is great and my anguish is unceasing. For I pray to be cursed from Christ on behalf of my brothers according to the flesh. They are Israelites who have the sonship, the glory, the covenant, the law, spiritual service, and the promises; from whom are the fathers, and from them comes the Messiah according to the flesh, who is above all God blessed into the ages, Amen.

Lament Opening, 9:1-5

Like a dark blue patch of material sewn into the middle of an ornate tapestry, Paul's expression of deep pathos, 9:1-5, arrests the attention of his listeners.[1] Only moments before he rejoiced in Christ's love, 8:34, yet here sadness fills his soul. Despite this emotional shift, Paul writes in parallel form (vv. 1-2 concern Paul's veracity and his grief, and vv. 3-4 elaborate on the reason for his grief, his fellow Israelites).

---

1. "Pathos" here is not meant in the ancient rhetorical sense; Aristotle, *Rhet.* 1.2.4—though Paul likely was aware of this basic element needed in argument. For a stronger emphasis on Paul's use of pathos, see Keck, "Pathos in Romans?" 71–96; and Anderson, *Ancient Rhetorical Theory*, 234–38.

He expresses his relationship to Christ and the Spirit concerning the veracity and reason for his grief—the nation of Israel—and includes a list of God's gifts to them, followed by a doxology.

1   The truth I am speaking in Christ, I am not lying;

    my conscience bears witness to me in the Holy Spirit

2   that my grief is great

    and my anguish is unceasing.

3   For I pray to be cursed from Christ on behalf of my brothers according to the flesh.

4   They are Israelites who have the sonship, the glory, the covenant,

    the law, spiritual service, and the promises;

    from whom are the fathers,

    and from them comes the Messiah according to the flesh,

5   who is above all God blessed into the ages, Amen.

Similar to the Old Testament prophets, Paul writes as one who has received revelation—as an Israelite moved by God to intercede on behalf of his people.[2] Yet Paul's experience seems different, for he communicates to his readers that he is "in" Christ, 9:1.

---

2. In Romans 9–11, Paul identifies with Moses (9:3; 9:15; 10:5), Isaiah (9:27), and Elijah (11:1-5). Lamenting for Israel is a common motif in the Old Testament and Judaism; Dunn, *Romans*, 524. What is significant is not so much that he relates to these men from a literary standpoint but that he has received direct revelation, too. Paul experiences God's heart on behalf of Israel, a steadfast compassion. From this perspective he rightly perceives the experiences of the Old Testament prophets as they encountered revelation. This view lessens the significance that Paul expects his attitude to be modeled here as an appropriate expression of faith—see C. E. B. Cranfield, *A Critical and Exegetical Commentary on the Epistle to the Romans* (Edinburgh: T & T Clark, 1975–79), 454—and it contrasts the idea that Paul seeks to personally defend a negative reputation with the Jews—for an "anti-Jewish" defense, see Douglas Moo, *The Epistle to the Romans* (Grand Rapids: Eerdmans, 1996), 556.

It is important to understand what is happening *to* Paul—he intercedes for his people as one brought into Christ's perspective. His midrashic arguments that follow, 9:6—11:32, build and depend upon the opening oath and prayer of lament, 9:1-5, leading to praise for God's infinite wisdom, 11:33-36. After exploring the possible meanings of Paul's phrases and key words in this lament section, 9:1-5, a brief discussion follows concerning the thematic continuity of "intercession" within Romans.

Intercessory Prayer, 9:1-5

Paul's overwhelming grief receives the focus of the first sentences (vv. 1-3).[3] He describes his feeling as "unceasing" and that he "could pray to be cursed from Christ." The degree of sacrificial love begs the question as to the source of his grief. Paul either speaks in a less sincere rhetorical manner or he speaks with genuine emotion. After having just written in detail about the intimate expression of God's love on behalf of the believer, 8:1-39, it seems odd for Paul to suddenly shift from a neumenological perspective—God's perspective—concerning creation, redemption, and Christ's intercession, to a phenomenological one—his own. It makes more sense that Paul's words follow a natural progression from Christ and the Spirit's intercession for the believer (8:26-27, 34) to God's heart through Paul interceding for the nation of Israel. In this context,

---

3. The "truth" refers to Paul's emotion in verse 2 rather than the "truth of the gospel." The absence of the article before ἀλήθειαν, the order of the words, and the content of the verse suggest that Paul is concerned about the truth of the statement he is about to make (in verse 2) rather than the 'truth of the gospel'; Cranfield, *Critical and Exegetical Commentary*, 451. The phrase ἐν Χριστῷ is to be taken with λέγω; ibid.

The conjunction γάρ can be taken in a causal sense; Paul's emotion brings him to pray, or in an explanatory sense, Paul discloses the reason for his grief. The latter interpretation makes better sense. It is also interesting that of the four oath formulas in Paul's letters (Rom. 9:1-2; 2 Cor. 11:31; Gal. 1:20; and 1 Tim. 2:7), only 9:1-2 includes all three phrases: "not lying," "in Christ," and "in the Holy Spirit."

God receives glory (9:5) and Paul's willingness to intercede is made known—his words express his experience.

Paul claims that he speaks as one "in" Christ and his conscience bears witness to him "in" the Holy Spirit, 9:1. The various interpretations for Paul's "in" phrases fall into three general possibilities: Paul makes an oath (1) by calling upon Christ and the Spirit as his witnesses; (2) in the presence of Christ; or (3) in some form of union with Christ and the Spirit.[4] Paul does employ an oath formula here—"The truth I am speaking . . . I am not lying . . ."—but to imply that he does so for argument's sake discounts the action of God within Paul. In other words, if the emphasis is on his feelings and conscience, then Paul receives the respect for his great love on behalf of Israel rather than God, and something more is needed to harmonize the paradox of Paul speaking "*in*" Christ yet praying to be cursed "*from*" Christ.

Of the possible interpretations above, the connotation of "union" expresses more accurately the mutual nature of both Christ and the Spirit working within Paul. Paul's use of the preposition in the "in Christ" phrase intends a spatial connotation.[5] He does not stand

---

4. For the view that Paul makes an oath calling upon Christ and the Spirit as witnesses, see C. K. Barrett, *The Epistle to the Romans* (London: Hendrickson, 1991), 176; Black, *Romans*, 123; John Calvin, *The Epistles of Paul the Apostle to the Romans and the Thessalonians*, eds. Ross Mackenzie, David W. Torrance, and Thomas F. Torrance (London: Oliver & Boyd, 1961), 242; and Joseph Fitzmyer, *Romans* (New York: Doubleday, 1993), 543. For "in the presence of," see Leon Morris, *Epistle to the Romans* (Grand Rapids: Eerdmans, 1988), 346; and Ernst Käsemann, *Commentary on Romans*, trans. and ed. Geoffrey W. Bromily (Grand Rapids: Eerdmans, 1980), 258. For some form of "union," see Abasciano, *Paul's Use of the Old Testament in Romans 9:1-9: An Intertextual and Theological Exegesis* (London: T & T Clark, 2005), 92; Dunn, *Romans*, 523; and Murray, *Romans*, 2:3.

5. For the varied uses of ἐν, see BAGD, s.v., "ἐν." Concerning the preposition "ἐν" with the dative to connote "agency," very few clear examples occur in the New Testament, and when they do, they involve a perfect passive verb; Daniel B. Wallace, *Greek Grammar Beyond the Basics: An Exegetical Syntax of the New Testament* (Grand Rapids: Zondervan, 1996), 373. If Paul has been brought "into" Christ for the purpose of revelation, then the preposition with the dative could refer to a spatial connotation. This does not mean that other grammatical possibilities are eliminated, such as association or instrumental emphases. The "in Christ" phrases in Paul are theologically difficult to explain; Murray Harris, "Prepositions and Theology in the Greek

outside of Christ, observing a vision in front of him, but speaks as one who has been brought into the perspective of Christ, a compassionate, sacrificial love for Israel that has its source in God.

Paul, then, is either brought into the perspective of Christ in the moment as he writes, or he presently feels deep emotions based on past revelation. It seems that Paul expresses an immediate emotive response that comes from a previous experience, such as his conversion. But Luke's record of Paul's Damascus event (Acts 9:1-9; 22:6-11; 26:13-19) describes him as standing outside of the person of Christ, seeing light and hearing the voice of the Lord. And on other revelatory occasions, Paul sees visions (Acts 9:12; 16:9-10; 18:9-10; 22:17-21; 23:11; or an angel, 27:23), and in each instance he looks "at" something. But in Romans 9:1-5, he writes as one "in" Christ, feeling deep compassion, and his mind is "in" the Holy Spirit. A closer look at Paul's use of the "in" phrases in his other letters gives helpful insight.

"In Christ"

Paul's "in Christ" phrase (Rom. 9:1) corresponds to what he describes to Corinthian believers where a man is taken to the third heaven and sees "surpassingly great revelations" (2 Cor. 12:7).[6] But the man was

New Testament," in *New International Dictionary of New Testament Theology*, ed. Colin Brown (Carlisle: Paternoster, 1976), 3:1192–93. A locative understanding does not violate grammatical rules, and since Paul's oath formula stresses the veracity of what he says, this sense fits well his supernatural experience. In contrast, Constantine Campbell finds the instrumental and locative rendering insufficient for the "in Christ" and the "in the Holy Spirit" phrases, arguing for a nuance of cause as expressed in "under the control" of Christ and the Spirit; Campbell, *Paul and Union with Christ: An Exegetical and Theological Study* (Grand Rapids: Zondervan, 2012), 95–96. He places this use in a subcategory referring to people's actions "in Christ" (Rom. 9:1, 5:17; 1 Cor. 4:17; 2 Cor. 2:17, 12:19; and Phil. 3:3), but this subcategory can also mean kind and manner and close association. His final definition of "union" involves a spectrum of possibilities: union, participation, identification, and incorporation—each with its own semantic issues; ibid., 101 and 412–14.

6. Such an experience would be a constant memory within his heart and mind. Paul's conversion experience on the way to Damascus and his heavenly experience (2 Cor. 12:1-4) are likely not the same event. The time frame and Paul's purposes are different. It is also interesting

not sure where he was located—whether inside his body or outside his body (2 Cor. 12:1-4):

> I will go on to visions and revelations from the Lord. I know a man in Christ who fourteen years ago was caught up to the third heaven . . . and I know that this man—whether in the body or apart from the body I do not know, but God knows—was caught up to paradise. He heard inexpressible things, things that man is not permitted to tell.

The "in Christ" phrases in Romans 9 and 2 Corinthians 12 complement each other as they express the nature of God's revelation within Paul. In the Letter to the Corinthians, Paul's revelation "in Christ" gives meaning to what follows (12:19): "Do you think that we are defending ourselves to you? We speak before God *in Christ* for the purpose of building you up in all things, beloved." Paul does not speak defensively or persuasively but genuinely as one who has

---

that Paul only uses the word "visions" (ὀπτασία) here in 2 Corinthians, but elsewhere he uses "revelation" (ἀποκάλυψις) in reference to Christ as the source of his gospel, not men (Gal. 1:1; Eph. 3:3). Luke uses ὀπτασία in reference to Paul's visions of angels and Paul's Damascus experience (Luke 1:22, Acts 24:23, and 26:19), but Paul only uses ὀπτασία in 2 Corinthians 12:1.

For the doxological view of Paul's experience on the road to Damascus see S. Kim's work, *The Origin of Paul's Gospel* (Tübingen: Mohr, 1981). Alan Segal makes the case for a mystical theophany in 2 Corinthians 12:1f—as Paul's "spiritual body that is received by and finds residence in Christ . . . [an] ecstatic or paranormal experience rather than a physical transport"; Segal, *Paul the Convert: The Apostolate and Apostasy of Saul the Pharisee* (New Haven, CT: Yale University Press, 1990), 39. Segal's emphasis gives appropriate respect to Paul's experience, that Paul sees the face of Jesus and experiences heaven in Christ, revealing to him a "universal and hidden meaning to history"; *Rebecca's Children: Judaism and Christianity in the Roman World* (Cambridge, MA: Harvard University Press, 1986), 164–68, 172. Segal understands Paul's transformation language of glorification and suffering to include a participatory element, though Paul does not suggest that his ecstatic experience is typical of all believers; ibid.

For the view that Paul's experience is related to Merkabah mysticism (e.g., Ezekiel's vision of God's throne room and the Enoch tradition and Paul's expressions, "caught up," "third heaven," and "paradise") see John Bowker, "Merkabah Visions and the Visions of Paul," *Journal of Semitic Studies* 16, no. 2 (1971): 157–73; and B. Young, "The Ascension Motif of 2 Corinthians 12,"*Grace Theological Journal* 9 (1988): 73–103. Two other works are worth noting: Gershom Scholem, *Major Trends in Jewish Mysticism* (New York: Schocken Books, 1954), and James Tabor, *Things Unutterable: Paul's Ascent to Paradise in Its Greco-Roman, Judaic, and Early Christian Contexts* (Lanham, MD: University Press of America, 1986).

been given the perspective of Christ.[7] He speaks unselfishly with confidence, for "the truth of Christ is in him" (cf. 2 Cor. 11:10).

The use of "in Christ" phrases—and similar phrases such as "in the Lord" and "in him"—are, for the most part, distinctively Pauline.[8] His revelatory experience gives him a bold confidence in writing about mysterious heavenly realities.[9] This means that Paul not only has an understanding of the effective work of God *through* Christ but Paul also sees this work as taking place *in* the sphere of the person of Christ. Thus in Romans 9:1-2, Paul describes a spiritual "sphere," a union with Christ causing an overwhelming compassion, a desire he intensely expresses to the reader concerning Israel.

"In" the Holy Spirit

Paul speaks the truth in Christ with his conscience "bearing witness" to him "in the Holy Spirit."[10] Amidst great emotion, Paul's intellect

---

7. When Paul speaks "in Christ" along with those with him, it is God who has established them in Christ (2 Cor. 12:21). Campbell understands Christ as the cause and reason for Paul's speaking, not self-defense; *Paul and Union*, 99. For a more rhetorical stance that Paul defends himself against questioning in the 2 Corinthians 12:21 context, see Henrich Schlier, *Der Römerbrief: Kommentar* (Freiburg im Breisgau: Herder), 284.

8. Of Paul's 153 "in" phrases, 73 are "in Christ," 6 include the article ("ἐν τῷ Χριστῷ), 24 are "in him," and 50 "in Lord" phrases. One phrase refers to "in the Lord" (Eph. 1:15) and one "in Jesus" phrase (Eph. 4:21). Paul uses the "in Christ" phrase in all of his letters except Titus and 2 Thessalonians. There are only a few other "in Christ" references in the New Testament; see 1 Peter 3:15, 5:10, and 5:14. Most of the uses of "in Christ" phrases emphasize what God has done through Christ or some participation or action of the believer(s) through Christ. But even so the use of the preposition "in" (ἐν) involves a spatial element. For example, Paul boasts "in Christ" and not himself (16:7; 1 Cor. 15:31; and Phil 1:26) and his proclamation is in Christ, before God (1 Cor. 3:1 and 2 Cor. 12:17, 19).

9. Paul's apocalyptic view in this midrashic narrative is the Christ event; Munck, *Paul*, 192. Paul's uses of the "in Christ" and "in him" phrases beg for an explanation of the source of his insight, such as, "For *in him* all the fullness of the Deity in bodily form dwells" (Col. 2:9); "For he chose us *in him* before the foundation of the world to be holy and blameless before him in love" (Eph. 1:4); "God raised us and seated us in the heavenly realms *in Christ Jesus*" (Eph. 2:6); "God the Father has blessed us with all spiritual blessings in the heavenlies *in Christ Jesus* (Eph 1:3); or "The peace of God . . . will guard your hearts and minds *in Christ Jesus*" (Phil. 4:7).

10. Paul's use of the word "conscience" (συνειδήσεώς) refers to an internal guide in choosing right and wrong, much like its use today (see 2:15, 13:5; Acts 23:1, 24:16; 1 Cor. 8:7-12, 10:25-29; 2 Cor 1:12, 4:2, 5:11; 1 Tim. 1:5, 1:19, 3:9, 4:2; 2 Tim. 4:2; and Tit. 1:15). It is interesting

witnesses his heart's anguish. The unique combination in verse 1 of "bearing witness *with*" (the prefix συν) and the pronoun "to me" (μοι) and the pronoun "of me" (μου) seems redundant, but this repetition accurately reflects the intensity of what has happened within Paul.[11] More importantly, Paul's syntax and word choice show that his intellect is functioning well as the Spirit moves within him and his mind is brought into the Spirit.[12] Just as Paul's heart grieves because he has been given Christ's perspective, so also what follows in the discourse in Romans 9–11 comes from the revealed wisdom of God *by* the Holy Spirit.[13] Thus, in Romans 9:1-2, Paul employs a rhetorical

that within the New Testament "bearing witness" (συμμαρτυρέω) and "conscience" only occur together in Romans 9:1 and 2:15, and the difference between these two verses is that in 9:1 another witness than his "conscience" is present with Paul as he speaks of his grief for Israel.

Or the meaning could be that Paul's conscience bears witness "with" him in the Holy Spirit. Paul's use of συμμαρτυρέω in 2:15 and 8:16 may also signify the meaning "to testify." Some representative interpretations are as follows: "as my conscience bears witness to me in the Holy Spirit"—Fitzmyer, *Romans*, 543; "the testimony of Paul's conscience bears witness in the Holy Spirit"—Cranfield, *Critical and Exegetical Commentary*, 453; "My conscience bearing me witness in the Holy Spirit"—Dunn, *Romans*, 523; "by the Holy Spirit"—Gordon Fee, *God's Empowering Presence: The Holy Spirit in the Letters of Paul* (Peabody, MA: Hendrickson, 1994), 592. The text does not suggest that Paul is brought into Christ by the Spirit, though this is consistent with Pauline theology.

11. Although Paul appeals to his conscience as an independent witness (see William Sanday and Arthur Headlam, *A Critical and Exegetical Commentary on the Epistle to the Romans* [Edinburgh: T & T Clark, 1898], 227; Dunn, *Romans*, 523; conforming to the biblical rule of two or three witnesses—Robert Jewett, *Romans: A Commentary*, ed. Eldon Jay Epp [Minneapolis: Fortress Press, 2007], 558), it does not exclude the intensive force of the prefix συμ-.

12. The word "conscience" (συνειδήσεώς) has no Hebrew counterpart. It is always used in relation to the intellect; Fitzmyer, *Romans*, 128. In addition, "Holy Spirit" cannot be linked adjectively with "conscience" without a repetition of the article after the noun; see Bosman, *Conscience in Philo and Paul: A Conceptual History of the Synoida Word Group* (Tübingen: Mohr Siebeck, 2003), 255.

13. Although most of the time an author intends a single meaning for a preposition, semantically speaking there is a little more flexibility in language. It seems more likely that an author emphasizes a primary meaning, such as a "locative," "agency," or "instrumental" sense, but this is not as clear cut and discernable with expressing abstract reality. The Greek case system for nouns allows for subtle imprecision that is held accountable by context. For explanation purposes, a *retired* professor made the statement that according to his wife there is a difference between him being "in" the house and "around" the house. Such subtleties are not so clear in the Greek case system. If indeed, Paul is brought into Christ's perspective, how much more would the preposition ἐν be interpreted as present "in" the Holy Spirit, and also what his mind experiences as "by" the Holy Spirit. The anarthrous expression ἐν πνεύματι ἁγίῳ has various

device, an oath formula, to affirm the genuine, continual sadness that he feels in behalf of Israel, and his use of the "in Christ" and "in the Holy Spirit" phrases describe the nature of God's revelation "in" Paul.

Paul's Prayer

After expressing his grief, Paul writes, *"For I pray to be cursed from Christ on behalf of my brothers according to the flesh,"* 9:3. Trying to make sense of Paul's use of the imperfect tense of the verb "to pray" in verse 3 has resulted in two general possibilities: either Paul prays a prayer that has an impossible outcome—more of a wish—or he prays a prayer that God would not honor, similar to the prayer of Moses (Exod. 32:32).[14]

---

interpretations: Cranfield describes this as Paul's mind being "renewed and illumined by the Holy Spirit" (cf. 8:1-16); *Critical and Exegetical Commentary*, 453; instrumental force—Dunn, Romans, 523; "within" the realm of the Spirit—Kuss, *Der Römerbrief* (Regensburg: Pustet, 1957), 3:670; "by means of"—Moo, *Epistle to the Romans*, 556; and "under the control of the Holy Spirit"—Thomas Schreiner, *Romans* (Grand Rapids: Baker Books, 1998), 479.

14. The infinitive of εὔχομαι in the New Testament makes more sense as translated "to pray" rather than "to wish" (Acts 26:29; 2 Cor. 13:7 and 13:9; and James 5:16). For the argument that the verb εὔχομαι means "to wish," see Barrett, *Epistle to the Romans*, 417; Schreiner, *Romans*, 476. For a reference to prayer, see Cranfield, *Critical and Exegetical Commentary*, 454; Dunn, Romans, 524; Moo, *Epistle to the Romans*, 558.

What seems to be just as much of a concern as the meaning of the verb is its imperfect tense with respect to reconciling the emphasis of the "past" and the "type of action" that unfolds. This is theologically difficult to make sense of in light of an actual prayer to be cursed from Christ. The classical imperfect is sometimes argued in the sense of "unattainable"; see Cranfield, *Critical and Exegetical Commentary*, 455f.

In addition, the Old Testament parallel to Moses is used to make sense of this imperfect tense. Paul's content in Romans 9:3 is similar to Moses' prayer in Exodus 32:32, but there are no verbal similarities. Stuhlmacher draws a direct parallel between the old covenant when Moses intercedes for the people of God and offers himself as an atonement for their apostasy (cf. Exod. 32:32) and the gospel when Paul intercedes for Israel; *Paul's Letter to the Romans: A Commentary*, trans. Scott J. Hafemann (Louisville: Westminster John Knox, 1994), 145. Abasciano argues in detail for the shared intercessory nature of prayer of Moses and Paul based on intertexuality (see also 1 Cor. 10:7; 2 Cor. 3; Phil. 4:3); *Paul's Use*, 65–146. What seems to be different in Paul's situation is that unlike the Old Testament prophets who stood away from God's throne and beheld his glory or heard his council (1 Kgs. 22; Isa. 6; Ezek. 3:12, 23; 8:4; 9:3; 10:4, 18–22; 11:22-25; 43:2-5; 44:4; Jer. 4:19-21; 14:17-22, and Dan. 9), Paul is brought into Christ's perspective.

In the context of Exodus 32, Israel rejects God and makes offerings before the golden calf. Moses intercedes before the Lord on behalf of Israel and then speaks directly to the Israelites concerning their egregious sin, seeking to make atonement on their behalf. He prays to God and asks for his forgiveness for them. If God does not show mercy, Moses would rather die than live ("remove me from your book that you have written").[15] God shows his mercy and reveals his glory to Moses—a theophany—a visual and audible experience (30:12-23). It is likely that Paul relates to Moses's experience in some degree.

The imperfect tense often emphasizes a past event *and* its unfolding action. But the idea that Paul prays in the context of a "continuous" grieving in the past does not make sense in the present context of his letter. To further complicate the understanding of his prayer is that he refers to eternal damnation when he prays to be "cursed" from Christ on behalf of Israel.[16] While this reveals the serious consequence for his fellow Jews who do not believe in Christ, it raises the question concerning his sincerity—how can Paul be "in Christ" yet be cursed "from Christ"? However, since Paul is brought into union with God through Christ, he sees from Christ's perspective, causing his heart to grieve for the chosen people who reject the Messiah. In other words, God's selfless love through Christ moves Paul, for only God's love acts in a manner that finds solution in the curse of his Son on the

---

15. Driver, *Exodus,* 356. It is interesting that Scott Hafemann's analysis of 2 Corinthians 3 and the Exodus 32 background suggests that after God judges Israel, Moses can appeal for God's mercy based on a faithful "remnant" embodied in himself; *Paul, Moses, and the History of Israel: The Letter/Spirit Contrast and the Argument from Scripture in 2 Corinthians 3* (Tübingen: Mohr Siebeck, 1995), 102.

16. The term "curse" (ἀνάθεμα) in the LXX translates in the Hebrew as חרם and refers to devoted things set apart for destruction—see Josh. 6:17-18; 7:1, 11-13; 22:20; 1 Chron. 2:7. The argument can be made for ἀνάθεμα to signify excommunication. For discussion, see Dunn, *Romans,* 524, and Jewett, *Romans,* 561, but the stronger reference to eternal damnation makes better contextual sense. For different views, see Cranfield, *Critical and Exegetical Commentary,* 458; and Moo, *Epistle to the Romans,* 557.

cross. This, then, makes sense of the imperfect tense in Paul's prayer "on behalf" of Israel—God's heart is expressed, a past-continuous aspect, as Paul offers a sincere substitutionary petition[17]—and it makes clear the paradox of Paul speaking "*in Christ*" and desiring "*to be cursed from Christ*"—for only the Father is capable of such love.[18]

Interestingly, when Paul laments for his "brothers according to the flesh," 9:3, he moves the focus of his letter to his "nonbelieving" Jewish brothers. The other times Paul uses the term "brothers" he refers to believers, but here he does not identify himself with "spiritual" brothers but with his brothers according to "physical" descent.[19] Having just explained how God sent his Son in the likeness of human nature "according to the flesh" (in contrast to life by the Spirit in faith, 8:3-13), Paul now communicates what will happen to "Israel according to the flesh." Paul does not use "according to the flesh" in a negative connotation here; rather, his intercessory prayer shows reverence for God's elective purposes in choosing Israel (see 1:3 and 4:2).[20] Furthermore, Paul's use of the personal pronouns

17. For the view of ὑπὲρ ("on behalf of") as substitution; see Käsemann, *Commentary on Romans*, 258; Moo, *Epistle to the Romans*, 559; Morris, *Epistle to the Romans*, 347. Paul's perspective has been brought into God's heart for Israel. The other possible nuance is the more general sense of "for the sake of" or "benefit"; BADG, s.v., ὑπὲρ. In this manner, Paul believes his people stand in a position of eternal judgment to which Paul himself is willing to enter; see Abasciano, *Paul's Use*, 101; Schreiner, *Romans*, 481; and Wagner, *Harolds*, 106. Paul "appears to have developed his stance mainly from a fresh encounter with Scripture in light of his experience with Christ." Abasciano, *Paul's Use*, 215.

18. The Father is capable of being one with his Son yet desires to offer his Son as a curse for many (see Rom. 5:8 and 15).

19. Of the twelve uses of the plural noun for ἀδελφός in Romans, three occur in chapters 9–11 (see 9:3; 10:11 and 25).

20. The uniqueness of Paul's use of "according to the flesh" along with the context in which he uses the phrase in Romans and his other letters suggests that the phrase is part of a logical sequence with theological significance. This means the phrase "according to the flesh," 9:3, is thematic within the letter. Paul contrasts "brothers according to the flesh" with the "Messiah according to the flesh" to make a distinction between physical Israel and Israel by faith. In the New Testament, only Paul uses the phrase "according to the flesh" (κατὰ σάρκα in Rom. 1:3; 4:1; 8:4f, 12f; 9:3, 5; 1 Cor. 1:26; 10:18; 2 Cor. 1:17; 5:16; 10:2f; 11:18; Gal. 4:23, 29; Eph. 6:5; Col. 3:22. There is one exception, John 8:15 where the evangelist records Jesus' words when speaking to the Pharisees concerning not judging "according to the flesh"—κατὰ τὴν

and relational terms—"I," "my" brothers, and "my" race—combine to intensify anticipation for Israel's outcome.

Thus, Paul's experience—the revelation of God's person and character—carries the force of his argument. Paul identifies with Moses as he prays to God concerning rebellious Israel, not because of a need for typological support or rhetorical skill[21] but because his experience brings him to an understanding in which he relates to others to whom God has revealed himself. In this prophetic sense, Paul identifies with his race.

Israel's Messiah, 9:4-5

As an Israelite, Paul recounts in a serious tone the blessings of Israel—God's covenantal gifts:

σάρκα—but the noun is articular). Paul emphasizes the physical descent at the beginning of his letter—Christ descending from David "according to the flesh" (Rom. 1:3)—and physical descent when referring to Abraham the forefather "according to the flesh" (Rom. 4:2). In both of these instances "according to the flesh" shows reverence for God's decision in election and for his promise fulfilled. And these instances are followed by an emphasis of "faith" through spiritual means. In 9:5, Paul will make the distinction of the Messiah "according to the flesh," which similarly brings to light the paradox between the mutually exclusive nature of the Messiah from Israel and Israel not accepting him.

Interestingly, in Galatians, Paul writes allegorically to refer to the son of the bondwoman "according to the flesh" in contrast to the son of the free woman "according to the promise" and the "Spirit" (Gal. 4:23, 29). Paul uses a similar comparison just before Romans 9 between walking "according to the flesh" and "walking according to the Spirit" (8:4-5, 12-13).

Elsewhere Paul uses the term "according to the flesh" generally to mean "earthly" or in a physical sense (1 Cor. 1:26; 2 Cor. 1:17; 10:2-3; 11:18; Eph. 6:5; and Col. 3:22) particularly with reference to Israel "according to the flesh" (1 Cor. 10:18). Furthermore, Paul speaks about the expectation of the Messiah in terms of reconciliation—that we "no longer consider anyone *according to the flesh*, even though we have known the Messiah *according to the flesh*; yet we know him in this way no longer; therefore if anyone is in Christ he is a new creation . . ." (2 Cor. 5:16f).

21. Abasciano suggests that "the totality of his [Paul's] response was typologically oriented and typologically presented" and that Paul who is distraught turns to Scriptures and "from here fashions his understanding" —a view that minimizes Paul's experience; *Paul's Use*, 105.

4   They are Israelites having

the sonship, the glory, the covenants,

the law, spiritual service, and the promises.

Paul creates suspense by calling them by the name Yahweh gave to them: "Israelites."[22] The six blessings that Paul lists represent God's covenant relationship offered to Israel.[23] The narratives of the Torah give the essential background for the meaning of these gifts, but it seems that Paul intends a broader context beyond a specific period in Israel's history—underscoring God faithfulness in his relationship with his people and also (based on Paul's level of grief) foreshadowing Israel's failure in their relationship to God.[24]

22. Paul's use of "Israelites" pulls upon the connotation of God's covenant relationship with Israel. Cranfield notes the salvation historical significance of the names "Israel" and "Israelite" in the New Testament (particularly John 1:31; 47-49; 3:10, and 12:13), and recognizes the use of these names in Romans 9–11 in contrast to "Jews" in the other portions of his letter; Cranfield, *Critical and Exegetical Commentary*,461 and 526. Outside the New Testament, Josephus in the *Antiquities* uses "Jews" as a contemporary term and "Israelite" as an identification during the Maccabean era and before; see Horst Kuhli, "Ἰσραηλῖται," *EDNT*, 2:205.

23. Paul may have paired these six nouns based on assonance (in Greek, sonship and law end in "-θεσια", glory and service end in "-α," and covenant and promise end in "-αι"). The fact that two of these words, sonship (υἱοθεσία) and law (νομοθεσία), are mentioned only here in the NT and not at all in the Greek Old Testament gives added support for the parallel. The only exceptions in the LXX are in the noncanonical books: 2 Macc. 6:23, 4 Macc. 5:35 and 17:16. It could also be that Paul intended a thematic parallel, too. As God's *adopted children* they received God's *law*; in the Tabernacle, they experienced his presence, his *glory* (e.g., Exod. 16:10; 24:15; 40:34; Lev. 9:23) and with this came the privilege of *priestly service*; and Yahweh initiated *covenants* with them based on his *promises* to their fathers. These early themes of covenant and promise are important to the development of Paul's letter and Romans 9–11 (see Rom. 11:27; Isa. 59:20-21, Isa 27:9), revealing God's forgiveness for Israel and Paul's explanation of the promise given to Abraham concerning multiplying and land (4:13, 20; 9:8; 15:8). For promises made to the patriarchs elsewhere in Paul's letters, see Gal. 3:14-29; 4:23, 28; and Eph. 2:12, 3:6. For a synoptic view of the rhyming pairs, see Schreiner, *Romans*, 483. Though "sonship" is not explicitly mentioned, this status was conferred upon Israel at the Exodus (Exod. 4:22); Gary Burnett, *Paul and the Salvation of the Individual* (Leiden: Brill, 2001),177.

24. These are rooted in the story of Israel (Gen. 15 and 17; Exod. 2:24, 19:5, 24:1-8; Deut. 29; 2 Kgs. 23:5); Christopher Bryan, *Preface to Romans: Notes on the Epistle in Its Literary and Cultural Setting* (Oxford: Oxford University Press, 2000), 169–70.

All six blessings demonstrate God's divine action and refer to God's unique relationship with his covenant people (and in some ways they may have been selected for their significance with regard to the Messiah[25]). Each of the nouns are articular, giving them a formal and particular significance, referring to the covenant relationship.[26] "Adoption" is rooted in the concept of God's personal relationship with Israel as his son (e.g, Exod. 4:22-23; Deut. 1:31; 14:1; 32:6; Isa. 63:16; Jer. 3:19f; and 2 Sam. 7:14).[27] "Glory" brings to mind God's manifested presence among his people (e.g., in the cloud, Exod. 13:21; at Mount Sinai, Exod. 19:9f and 24:12f; at the Tabernacle and Temple, Exod. 29:43; 33:7f; 40:34; 1 Kgs. 8:11). "The covenants" refer specifically to God's covenants made with Abraham and his sons but could have a more general referent.[28] The term "law-giving"

---

25. This is not to say that Romans 9:1-5 concerns the believer. Paul in his other letters references the Messiah in light of these topics (e.g., Jesus is the fulfillment of "sonship," Rom. 1:4; "glory," 2 Cor. 4:4-6; the covenants, Eph. 2:12; "law-giving," Rom. 10:5f; "service" with respect to the Passover, 1 Cor. 5:7; and the promises, Gal. 3:16).

26. The article before each of the nouns gives either a unique sense (a monadic emphasis) or an individualizing meaning as in "a class by itself" (par excellence); for categories, see Wallace, *Greek Grammar*, 222-23. But since the gifts refer to God's covenant relationship with Israel, the antecedents for these articular nouns likely refer to the Old Testament concepts. It is also possible, that the article before each gift expresses a certain formality and tone, similar to the Greeks' personification of a virtue. For example, the use of the article before glory, ἡ δόξα, is not found in Jewish sources; *TDNT*, s.v., δοξάζω; and Otto Michel, *Der Brief an die Römer*, 295. These qualities are God's offering of a deeply personal relationship involving commitment and his presence.

27. Adoption (ἡ υἱοθεσία) is only used by Paul in the New Testament and is not found at all in the LXX. For further explanation of Paul's use of "adoption," see James Scott, *Adoption as Sons of God: An Exegetical Investigation into the Background of Yiothesia in the Pauline Corpus* (Tubingen: Mohr Siebeck, 1992), 13-57. For emphasis on 2 Samuel 7:14 as a backdrop for the meaning, see *DPL*, s.v., "adoption." It is also relevant to point out that the argument that follows concerning "sonship" in 9:8 and 11:30-32 depends on a proper respect for Israel's sonship in 9:4; see Jewett, *Romans*, 563.

28. The plural use of the term, along with Paul's emphasis concerning David and Moses elsewhere in his letter, gives reason for a more general sense for the term. Romans 9–11 is foreshadowed in the salutation of the letter in describing God's son, a descendant of David (1:3); and when discussing the promise to Abraham, Paul quotes David (4:6; see also 11:9). Paul writes in terms of Israel's history with Moses in mind (5:14) and utilizes Moses' words for support in the argument following 9:1-5 (see 9:15; 10:5, 19). It is also suggested that the use of the plural is meant to include the New Covenant, but Paul is not celebrating the life of the believer here in 9:1-5 as he did in chapter 8; rather, he grieves for his ethnic people. For a good summary of the

emphasizes God's divine action in giving the law. This would also naturally infer the meaning—the law itself.[29] But Paul's particular use of the term "law-giving" seems to stress the blessing bestowed to Israel and distinguish this use from his other uses of the "law" in relationship to "works," "sin," or "righteousness."[30] "Service" can specifically refer to the celebration of the Passover.[31] The general meaning refers to the priestly and Levitical sacrificial worship as directed by Yahweh, giving Israel a unique opportunity among nations to participate in relationship with God.[32]

The placement of the sixth blessing on Paul's list—the "promises"—is in the plural (similar to "covenants" above) and refers to the promises of Abraham and the patriarchs but is not limited to these. Earlier Paul discusses God's promise to Abraham using the singular "promise" (4:13, 14, 16, 20),[33] but here in 9:4 he uses the

arguments for "covenants," see Moo, *Epistle to the Romans*, 563f and C. J. Roetzel, "Διαθῆκαι in Romans 9,4," *Bib* 51 (1970): 377–90.

29. Either Paul stresses the active meaning "lawgiving" or the passive "the law given"; Dunn, 527; see also Cranfield, *Critical and Exegetical Commentary*, 462 and Moo, *Epistle to the Romans*, 563.

30. The term "lawgiving" (ἡνομοθεσία) occurs only here in the New Testament. For nonbiblical references, see 2 Macc. 6:23; 4 Macc. 5:45 and 17:16; Philo, *Abr.* 5; Plutarch, *Moralia* 240B. This use stands in contrast to Paul's discussion of "law" (νόμος) that permeates each major section of his letter.

31. The noun is only used three times in the Torah (Exod. 12:25-26 and 13:5) and refers to the Passover ceremony. It is interesting that this is an eternal service for Israel, defined again and again for her descendants. Two other uses occur in the LXX—one with the article (ἡ λατρεία) referring to the priestly and Levitical service in the Temple (1 Chron. 28:13) and the other without the article referring to offerings made as a sign of devotion to Yahweh (Josh. 22:27).

Paul uses the term "service" (λατρεία) without the article in his practical admonitions to believers (12:1) and adds the description "spiritual" service, which brings together meaning from 3:21-26 and chapters 6–8 with respect to the conformity of believers as the body of Christ and their lifestyle. Of the other relevant uses in the New Testament (John 16:2; Heb. 9:1 and 6), only the author of Hebrews uses "service" with the article (ἡ λατρεία) to refer to the priestly services of worship (9:6).

32. In a broad religious context, the noun "service" (ἡ λατρεία) can generally be defined as "the worship of a deity by performing cultic acts in a religious vocation"; see Jobes, "Distinguishing the Meaning," 190.

33. Only Paul uses the plural form (ἁι ἐπαγγελίαι) in the New Testament. Of the two other instances—2 Cor. 1:20 and Gal. 3:15—Paul directly references "many promises" in relation to the Messiah (2 Cor. 1:20), but he uses the article with "promises" (ἁι ἐπαγγελίαι) to refer to the promise made to Abraham and to his seed, the Messiah (Gal. 3:15).

plural "promises" which could also be taken in its broader sense, referring to a range of promises in the Old Testament made by God to his people.[34] It is also interesting that Paul lists "promises" as the last privilege on the list of six before mentioning "the fathers," a stylistic and intentional order.

A block diagram with a literal translation shows the connection between these verses and the relative pronoun "who" (ὧν):[35]

3　For I pray to be cursed from Christ

　on behalf of my <u>brothers</u> according to the flesh.

4　They are <u>Israelites</u> **who** [have] the sonship, the glory ... promises

　[from] **whom** [are] the fathers

　and from **whom** [comes] the Messiah according to the flesh,

5　who is above all God blessed into the ages, Amen.

Based on repetition, the antecedent for the relative pronoun "whom" (ὧν) may refer to the "Israelites" in verse 4, the Jewish people. But more likely, Paul intends a "stair-step" parallel in which "fathers"

---

34. For the view that "promises" include David, see Fitzmyer, *Romans*, 547; for messianic promises, see Barrett, *Epistle to the Romans*, 178; Cranfield, *Critical and Exegetical Commentary*, 464; and for Israel, see Morris, *Epistle to the Romans*, 349.

35. The antecedent for the relative clause ὧν in the first two clauses refers to the Israelites, but the additional phrase "and from whom" (καὶ ἐξ ὧν) that follows "the fathers" but precedes "the Messiah" gives a subtle connection between the patriarchs and the Messiah as well as referring to the Israelites. In other words, the content which follows will involve the nature of Israel's relationship to the Messiah and God's covenant with the patriarchs. It may be that the clause—"and from them comes the Messiah according to the flesh"—along with the doxology (v. 5b) forms a parallel making "the Messiah" a distinct stanza from the blessings of the covenant and the fathers (9:4).

Schreiner makes a connection based on order but does not emphasize a grammatical connection; *Romans*, 486. Piper understands the intervening καὶ to the last ὧν as referring to Israelites rather than "fathers"; Piper, *The Justification of God: An Exegetical and Theological Study of Romans 9:1-23* (Grand Rapids: Baker Books, 1993), 21. Cranfield sees the three relative clauses as dependent on "my fellow countrymen according to the flesh," *Critical and Exegetical Commentary*, 460f; but the meaning is not much different since these are the Israelites.

becomes the antecedent for the third relative clause (see above), and by following "the fathers" with the third relative clause—"and from whom [comes] the Messiah"—Paul scores a subtle crescendo. This intention is confirmed by the conjunction "and" with the preposition "out of," showing distinction and significance.[36] "Fathers" specifically refers to Abraham, Isaac, and Jacob,[37] but could include David as well,[38] and less probably, the general reference to significant ancestors in Israel's redemptive history.[39]

It is important to note a subtle connection with this lament and Paul's foreshadowing words at the beginning of his letter in the salutation, 1:1-7. The phrase "concerning his son, *the one born of David according to the flesh*" (. . . ἐκ σπέρματος δαυὶδ κατὰ σάρκα; 1:3) prepares the listener for a discussion on the topic of the Davidic Messiah.[40] Only in 9:5 does Paul mention again a direct reference to

36. The conjunction "and" (καί) with the preposition "from" (ἐξ) distinguishes the third relative pronoun from the first two, and this distinction fits consistently with Paul's parallel thought. The "from whom Christ" phrase (v. 4) signifies ethnicity and the "out of Israel" phrase (v. 6) suggests that Israel has not acted "out of faith" and has rejected their own Messiah (Moo, *Epistle to the Romans*, 565; Schreiner, *Romans*, 486; Piper, *Justification of God*, 42; and Abasciano, *Paul's Use*, 138). "Messiah" as the third term on the list follows "fathers," which may show that the Messiah represents the fulfillment of the promises made to the fathers; see Schreiner, *Romans*, 486; Piper, *Justification of God*, 21. This also means that the covenant and the benefits of this relationship offered by Yahweh culminate in the Messiah—if there is a progression intended. Due to the fact that the "fathers" were the chief recipients of the promises, a close connection exists; see Ernst Kühl, *Der Brief des Paulus an die Römer* (Leipzig: Quelle & Meyer, 1913), 315.

Romans 9–11 fits into the Deuteronomic view of Israel's history (Scott, "Restoration," 802f), in which a sin-judgment-restoration pattern can be detected. It seems, however, that Paul identifies with the Old Testament prophets, such as Moses, Isaiah, and Elijah, not because of a "mediator" role but as one who is brought into Christ's perspective. This has interesting parallels to the intercession and story of Exodus 32–34—Abasciano, *Paul's Use*, 45–146. Abasciano writes, "Paul has taken upon himself the mediatorial, intercessory, and prophetic aura of Moses in a typologically conditional response that conceives of his own ministry as the vehicle through which the election-bestowing 'glory of God in the face of Christ' is brought back to Israel in 'the gospel of the glory of Christ, who is the image of God' (2 Cor 4:4, 6)"; ibid., 143.

37. Abasciano, *Paul's Use*, 137; Schreiner, *Romans*, 486.

38. Stuhlmacher, *Paul's Letter to the Romans*, 145–46.

39. Murray, *Epistle to the Romans*, 2:6.

40. Interestingly, the topic of "seed" in Romans only occurs in the discussion of Abraham's descendants in 4:13-18 concerning the promise and righteousness, and in the discussion of

the Messiah who descends from the patriarchs (ἐξ ὧν ὁ Χριστὸς κατὰ σάρκα), which he elaborates on in more detail (9:6f). Paul, in essence, underscores the incarnation—he lists six privileges that God gives to Israel (9:4-5a) and then mentions that the "Messiah according to the flesh" is a descendant of the "fathers."[41]

Christ's Divinity

5   *who is above all God blessed into the ages, Amen.*

Paul's grammatical arrangement of phrases becomes important in understanding the brief but well-debated doxology in verse 5, "*who is above all God blessed into the ages, Amen.*"[42] Some scholars place a punctuation mark after "above all" to make a theological distinction between the Father and the Son: "who is above all, God blessed into the ages. Amen."[43] However, grammatically and contextually, it seems that Paul did not intend a comma: "who is above all God blessed into the ages, Amen."[44] With or without punctuation, an

---

Abraham concerning the children of promise, 9:7-8, 29 (the occurrence in 11:1 refers to Paul as a natural "descendent" of Abraham).

41. The phrase "according to the flesh" makes the distinction that Israel's connection with the messiah is from natural descent in contrast to a spiritual faith; see BADG, s.v. "σάρξ."

42. This information will make more sense at the end of Paul's argument when he mentions the patriarchs and God's plan for Israel, 11:1-32. The ὁ ὧν phrase refers to Christ rather than God, which is better Greek; see Bryan, *A Preface to Romans*, 170–71. Witherington understands the equivalent in Philippians 2:5-11 in naming Christ as "Lord," which is also equivalent to the confession of the divine name in the LXX (see Rom. 10:9 and 10:13; Joel 3:5 LXX); Witherington, *Romans*, 251–52.

43. For representative views, see Cranfield, *Critical and Exegetical Commentary*, 456-70; Sanday and Headlam, *Critical and Exegetical Commentary*, 233–38; and Metzger, *Textual Commentary*, 520. Primary support includes the parallel of Ephesians 4:6; the lack of a parallel of "blessed" with respect to Christ (2 Cor. 1:3; 11:31; and Eph. 1:3); no reference of θεός as ὁ Χριστός, and Paul ends this lament with praise to God, 11:33-36, not to Christ. For a summary of the different views, see Fitzmyer, *Romans*, 548–49.

44. The primary reason includes that doxologies begin with the word "blessed" and are not found in the middle of the sentence. The clause, "the one who is above all . . . ," parallels the preceding clause, "the one who according to the flesh . . .", and the phrase "the one who is . . ." always refers to the preceding noun (for use in Romans, see 1:25 and 11:36; for use in other Pauline letters, see 2 Cor. 11:31; Gal. 1:5; Eph. 3:21; Phil. 4:20; 1 Tim. 1:17; and 2 Tim. 4:18; also see, Heb. 13:21; 1 Pet. 4:11; 2 Pet. 3:18).

emphasis of the divinity of Christ is intended.[45] But what is also difficult to comprehend is how Paul writes with confidence and authority as one who is "in" Christ concerning God's plan for Israel and humankind.

In summary, in Romans 9:1-5, Israel has received the benefits of election, yet Israel stands in judgment, giving Paul reason to grieve. The present tense of the verb "to be," 9:4, shows that Paul sees these blessings as present,[46] and he refers to his ethnic brothers who have not believed in Jesus the Messiah—evidenced by his choice of the term "Israelites" and his mentioning of "the fathers." The contrast between Paul's grief in responding to the separation of nonbelieving Israel, 9:1-5, and the intimacy of the believer in Christ, 5:12-8:39, creates suspense—"How will this tension be resolved *in relation to God's character?*

What follows in the body of the lament, 9:6—11:32, is Paul's defense of the character of God in response to a topic he introduced

---

45. The implication is that Christ shares the divine nature of the Father but the passage does not say Christ is God in "an exhaustive sense"; Schreiner, *Romans*, 486–89. The neuter article in this sentence instead of the masculine greatly emphasizes the limitation, Cranfield 2:464; also, Dunn, *Romans*, 2:538.

46. See Cranfield, *Critical and Exegetical Commentary*, 460; Dunn, *Romans*, 526, Fitzmyer. *Romans*, 545; Moo, *Epistle to the Romans*, 561; Schreiner, *Romans*, 485.

Paul's list of privileges does not necessarily accent Israel's participation but that which God offered to them. Just like the faith of the patriarchs does not save current unbelieving Israel, neither do the benefits offered. Israel, both present and past, have rejected the Messiah, the faith of their fathers, and relationship offered to them. In this sense, these privileges are covenantal—to be accepted or rejected. It seems that the Israel that rejected God in the wilderness before Moses, the Israel that rejected the words of the prophets are still at a place of non-belief. Paul later identifies himself as an Israelite (11:1f) with Elijah—he is not saying that all Israelites are under eternal judgment but he is generally responding to the theological issue of God's faithfulness and how God's selected people could fail. The initial discussion begins with deep compassion.

Paul will also argue later that the "word" that was near the Israelites is the "word" that Paul preaches, 11:5-17. In this sense the "faith" aspect in God's promises, particularly as it points to the Messiah, is what makes the privileges relevant. So Paul's list applies to ethnic Israel in the sense that God has not withdrawn his covenant, but the covenant has always involved faith. In this way, these privileges are part of historical Israel, Israel in Paul's day, and Israel in the present.

earlier in his letter. In 3:1-8, after defining a "Jew" as one who is circumcised of the heart by the Spirit, Paul asks, "What advantage is there in being Jewish?" (3:1).[47] Paul emphasizes that in every way there is an advantage to being a Jew, for the Jews were entrusted with the words of God. Logically, this raises two issues concerning God's character—his faithfulness and his righteousness, 3:3-5 (For why did God's choice fail?). In Romans 9:6-11:32, Paul responds (1) by explaining that God is faithful in his promise to the patriarchs and (2) by demonstrating that God is righteous, though Israel remains unfaithful. But before analyzing Paul's in-depth answer in the chapters that follow, it is appropriate to show first that "intercession" is a consistent theme in Romans 9–11, and in the rest of the letter.

Letter Continuity, Romans 9–11

Paul explicitly and implicitly identifies with Old Testament prophets—Moses, Isaiah, and Elijah—who grieve for Israel.[48] In the first section of the body of his argument, Paul quotes Exodus 33:19 (Rom. 9:15), a context that is similar to his own. Here, Israel has sinned against God, Moses intercedes for them, and God reveals his Person to Moses. By quoting Exodus, Paul brings to light Moses's personal experience concerning God's compassion and goodness—and not for literary purposes only. Paul also quotes Isaiah (10:22-23; Rom. 9:27) in his argument concerning gentile inclusion and prefixes the quotation with the citation formula: "But Isaiah is crying out on behalf of Israel . . .". The words "crying out on behalf

---

47. The word "Jewish" is a paraphrase of the word "Jew" so as not to confuse Paul's definition with the ethnic referent.

48. Abasciano explains that Paul acts in the mediatorial, prophetic, and intercessory "aura of Moses" in a typologically conditioned response so that Paul's ministry is seen as a vehicle through which the election—a bestowal of God's glory in the face of Christ—is brought back to Israel in "the gospel of the glory of Christ, the image of God"; *Paul's Use*, 43.

of" (κράζει ὑπέρ) indicate hope and promise as well as judgment.[49] The Spirit that moves Isaiah also moves Paul.[50]

A few verses following the above Isaiah quotation, 9:27, Paul concludes that Christ Jesus is the "stone" that causes Israel to stumble, 9:33. This is the first mention of Christ, 10:1, since his expression of grief, 9:2-3, and Paul's heart lightens:

Brothers, it pleases my heart to petition God on your behalf for salvation (10:1)

For great is my grief and unceasing is the anguish of my heart

for I could wish to be an anathema from Christ on behalf of my brothers (9:2-3)

Notice the repeated references to "heart," "on behalf of," and "brothers." It seems that the humbling of Israel brings hope for their repentance. In a more direct expression of God's heart toward Israel, Paul quotes Isaiah 65:2 (Rom. 10:21) where God extends his hands "all day long" to a disobedient and obstinate people—a compassionate God.[51]

Concerning Israel, Paul perceives the merciful nature of God in the Old Testament context and in his present context. In other words, he does not project his subjective feelings on to a text, but

---

49. Although Isaiah's tone may be considered "accusing"—Sanday and Headlam, *Critical and Exegetical Commentary*, 265; "threatening"—Godet, *Commentary on Romans*, 366; "urgent"—Käsemann, *Commentary on Romans*, 371; or as a regular expression for inspired prophetic utterances—Black, Romans, 135; Paul's use of "crying out" with the preposition "on behalf of" (κράζει ὑπέρ) is a prayer and proclamation—Fitzmyer, *Romans*,575; a cry of hope rather than a threat—Richard Hays, *Echoes of Scripture in the Letters of Paul* (New Haven, CT: Yale University Press, 1989), 68; as well as an announcement of love as judgment and promise—Karl Barth, *The Epistle to the Romans*, trans. Edwyn C. Hoskyns (London: Oxford University Press, 1968), 361. Outside of the common use of κράζω in Hellenistic and Attic Greek, this phrase is distinctively Pauline; Blass and Debrunner, *Greek Grammar*, 231.

50. Paul uses κράζω only two other times in his letters: when the sons of God who are led by the Spirit cry out (κράζομεν) to the Father (Rom. 8:15), and when God sends the Spirit of his Son into the hearts of believers to cry out (κρᾶζον) to the Father (Gal. 4:6).

51. The only change in this Old Testament quotation from the LXX is the word order—Paul emphatically moves the phrase "all day long" to the front of the sentence.

simply amplifies the mercy of God in both contexts. In 11:1–5, Paul identifies with Elijah and makes both explicit and implicit statements to reveal God's heart toward the remnant (see chapter 4 for complete argument):

a	v.1	Did God reject his people?
b		No, I am an Israelite.
a	v.2	Did God reject his people?
b		Elijah interceded against Israel:
c	v.3-4	God leaves a remnant then.
c	v.5	God calls a remnant now.

The thought structure serves the purpose of reinforcing Paul's main point that God has called the remnant now, 11:5. The similarities between then and now demonstrate that there is a "remnant." Logically speaking, the more parallel the factors—Paul, Elijah, Israel then, Israel now—the more true the conclusion:

a	Question
b	Paul—a "remnant" Israelite
a	Question
b	Elijah—a "remnant" Israelite

Paul directly states in 11:2: *"Elijah intercedes against Israel . . ."*[52] Elijah, pursued and dejected, grieves for himself as he protests against Israel. Amidst this complaining, God personally reveals Himself to Elijah: *"Go stand on the mountain in the presence of the Lord for the Lord is about*

---

52. This insertion of "intercede" (ἐντυγχάνω) is not found in 1 Kings 19:10 and 14 (LXX or MT).

to pass by . . ." (1 Kings 11:11f). If this parallel is congruous, Paul also speaks the truth against Israel.

In both the context of Romans and 1 Kings, Israel has been judged guilty, God has revealed his Person to the person interceding, and God has reserved a "remnant" by grace. But Paul does not complain as Elijah does. Rather, Paul writes to reveal God's wise and merciful plan on behalf of Israel: God blesses the gentiles so that "hardened" Israel might become jealous and repent. Furthermore, Paul follows an Old Testament lament pattern when he frames this text with a repetitive question meant to be understood as an objection: "*God does not reject His people.*"[53] Thus Paul authenticates his analogy by weaving the two contexts together—then and now—identifying with Elijah as a "remnant" Israelite, as one who speaks against "hardened" Israel, and as one who has experienced God's presence. However, where Elijah focuses on his own circumstances, Paul sees God's compassionate mind at work in both the Old Testament context and his own.

Throughout Romans 9–11, Paul expresses God's mercy toward a rebellious people, which confirms the overwhelming sense of sadness that Paul feels in response to Israel's decisions—9:1-5, 9:15, 9:27, 10:1, 10:21, and 11:1-10. This compassionate and sacrificial mindset fits within the continuity of the rest of his letter as well—3:21-26; 5:6-8; 12:1-3, 14-20; and 15:7-8.

Thematic Unity, Romans 1–16

In the first major section of the letter, 1:1—5:11, God is not depicted as an arrogant judge who brings down his gavel against sinful man with satisfaction; instead, he chooses to bring punishment upon his

---

53. Paul alludes to 1 Samuel 12:22 or to Psalm 94, a personal lamentation for deliverance, in which he frames the question as an objection; Fitzmyer, *Romans*, 603.

own Son, 3:21-24. In the second major section of the letter, at great cost God offers sonship to those who believe in his Son—and his Spirit and his Son intercede on behalf of his children, 5:12—8:39. The tone of the letter shifts dramatically from bright unity, 8:1-39, to feelings of separation, 9:1-5, a contrast that accents the emotional color of both realities. For example, Paul writes about intimacy, love, and security from the Father to His children in 8:17:

> we received the spirit of adoption
>
> by whom we are crying, Abba Father
>
> the same Spirit is bearing witness with our spirit
>
> that we are children of God

In contrast, Paul feels separation, loss, and pain, 9:2-3:

> The truth I am speaking in Christ, I am not lying;
>
> my conscience bears witness to me in the Holy Spirit
>
> that my grief is great
>
> and my anguish is unceasing.
>
> For I pray to be cursed from Christ . . .

Paul refers to the Father, the Spirit, and Christ in these transitional passages. It is Christ and the Spirit who intercede (8:26-27, 34), and likewise, it is Christ and the Spirit moving upon Paul to grieve on behalf of Israel, 9:1-5.

In the final section of the body of his letter, 12:1—15:13, the apostle exhorts the believers in Rome by the *mercies of God* to be humble minded, 12:1.[54] Paul uses the noun and verb forms of "mercy" more in Romans 9–11 than in any other part of the Pauline Corpus,[55] so it makes sense that he transitions with the phrase "by the *mercies of God*" from his third main section, 9:1—11:36, into his final section of the body, 12:1—15:13.[56] Therefore, just as Christ offered himself up as a mercy offering for all men, 1:18—5:11, Christ continues to compassionately intercede for the believer, 5:12—8:39. So also Paul—as one who is brought into the perspective of Christ and willingly grieves on behalf of Israel (9:1—11:36)—commands the church to renew their minds in accordance with the humble, sacrificial mind of Christ on behalf of each other, 12:1—15:13. Now that the theme of "intercession" has been demonstrated as an important aspect in Paul's lament for Israel, the focus turns to *God's character* in his choosing the "younger" son.

54. Paul's use of the phrase "Holy Spirit" in 9:2 and his use of the phrase "mercies of God" in 12:1 serves as a link to the major sections that precede them. The use of "Holy Spirit" in 9:1 reveals a continuous relationship from the end of Paul's second major section of the body of his letter, 5:13—8:39, to the beginning of his third major section, 9:1—11:36. The only time the "Holy Spirit" is mentioned in Romans 9–11 is in 9:1. Therefore, the absence of the word "Spirit" in 9:2—11:36 and its abundant use in the previous section, 5:13—8:39, indicates that the "Holy Spirit" in 9:1 serves as a transition between the two major sections.

55. See Cranfield, *Critical and Exegetical Commentary*, 595.

56. The phrase "mercies of God" (τῶν οἰκτιρμῶν τοῦ θεοῦ), which begins the fourth major section of Paul's letter, 12:1—15:3, serves as a transition phrase from Romans 9–11 (in the New Testament, the noun οἰκτιρμός is used only here in Romans; and the only use of the verb οἰκτίρω is in 9:15). The verb ἐλεέω is not used in 12:1—15:13. The proper noun "Holy Spirit" in a literary sense serves in a similar manner as a transition between 5:12—8:39 and 9:1—11:36.

2

———

God's Faithful Election of Israel, 9:6–29

It is not as though the Word of God has failed? For not all those of Israel are Israel. Neither are the seed of Abraham all children but "In Isaac will be called your seed." That is, the children of the flesh are not children of God, but the children of promise will be reckoned into the seed. For the word of promise is like this, "According to this time I will come and it will be to Sarah a son." Not only that but also from Rebekah's womb they will come having the same father, Isaac. For they were not yet born and had not yet done good or evil, so that the elect plan of God might remain, not on the basis of works but by the One who calls. She was told, "The greater will serve the younger." As it is written, "Jacob He loved, Esau He hated."

What therefore are we saying, "Is unrighteousness from God?" By no means. To Moses He is saying, "I will show mercy to whom I will show mercy." Now therefore, it is not the one desiring, neither the one making effort, but it is God who shows mercy. For scripture is saying to Pharaoh, "For this reason I raised you up in order that I might demonstrate My power and in order that My name might be proclaimed in all the earth." Now therefore, to whom He wills He shows mercy and to whom He wills He hardens.

Therefore you say to me, "Why does he still find fault? For who resists his will?" O man, indeed, who are you the one answering back to God? Does that which is molded say to the one molding, "Why have you made me this way?"

Does not the potter have authority over of the lump of clay to make it into
vessels of honor and also into dishonor? But if God wills to demonstrate his
wrath and to make known his power, bearing with great patience vessels of
wrath to be prepared for destruction and in order that he might make known the
riches of his glory upon vessels of mercy which he prepared into glory? Even
us whom he also called, not only from the Jews but also from the nations.

And as in Hosea he says, "I will call those 'not my people' 'my people' and
those 'not being loved' 'beloved.'" And it will be in that place which was said
to them, "'You are not my people.' They will be called sons of the living God."
But Isaiah cries out on behalf of Israel, "If the number of the sons of Israel
as the sand of the sea, the remnant will be saved. For the Lord will execute
his word swiftly and completely." And even as Isaiah prophesied, "If not the
Lord of the Sabbath left to us a seed we would become as Sodom, we would
be likened to Gomorrah."

Midrashic Form, 9:6-29

Paul's style is unlike contemporary rabbinical forms of his time, as
evidenced by his succinct yet integrated treatment.[1] Although Paul's
sequence, thematic coherence, and use of the Old Testament show
use of midrashic elements,[2] his arguments evidence a mix of forms.[3]
This means that one must (1) think step by step with Paul and the
Old Testament contexts, (2) follow Paul's knitting of logical parts
to the whole argument, and (3) be observant of his form and subtle
use of stylistic devices. With this literary awareness, Paul's intentions

1. E. Earle Ellis, *Paul's Use of the Old Testament* (Edinburgh: Oliver & Boyd, 1957), 46.
2. The term "midrashic argument" is not used in a technical, formal sense, but is used to recognize
   Paul's use of the Old Testament with midrashic elements, such as the use of key words and
   commentary. It is not certain if Paul borrows a particular form or he creates his logical units
   based on the need of the situation. Regardless, the form change from Romans 1–8 to Romans
   9–11 is significant and needs a descriptive title for discussion purposes.

   "Midrash" is not a dependable term; it seems to be a catchword for a linkage of two texts;
   Richard B. Hays, *Echoes of Scripture in the Letters of Paul* (New Haven, CT: Yale University
   Press, 1989), 10–12. Within these texts, readers would know Scripture and recognize certain
   catchwords; William Stegner, "Romans 9:6-29 - A Midrash," *JSNT* 22, no. 1 (1984): 40–41.
3. Paul does not employ rhetoric in the formal sense, but his style and some of his form evidence
   logic and literary technique, common to his culture. For a more favorable view of Paul's use of
   rhetoric in Romans 9–11, see Johann D. Kim, *God, Israel, and the Gentiles: Rhetoric and Situation
   in Romans 9-11* (Atlanta: SBL, 2000), 115–39.

become clear, giving the reader an understanding of God's salvific plan for "Israel."

Although the midrashic argument of Romans 9:6-29 is one complete unit,[4] I will discuss the passage based on the following internal divisions:

Midrashic argument	9:6-18
List of Questions (*diatribe*)	9:19-24
List of Old Testament verses (*testimonia*)	9:25-29

After examining form, I will then explain content. For example, after analyzing the midrashic argument of 9:6-18, a theological discussion follows concerning God's merciful character in his election of Israel, 9:6-13, and his merciful character to the nations, 9:14-18. This same order of analysis—form, then content—is followed for the *diatribe* and *testimonia* sections, 9:19-24; 9:25-29.

---

4. The internal divisions are somewhat artificial in that the whole unit is a cohesive argument using a variety of elements. For example, there are elements of diatribe that are not limited to 9:19-24. But the above divisions are utilized for explanation purposes.

Paul's techniques share some similarities to later midrash forms. Paul's formal training as a Pharisee would prepare him in the contemporary rabbinical traditions. However, Paul does not precisely imitate traditional rabbinical forms. He exhibits a unique style, requiring the interpreter to study his logic and form as they develop. Here in 9:6-29, Paul utilizes midrashic techniques where a theme and an initial text are introduced, 9:6-7, followed with a second supplemental text, 9:9. These themes and texts include key words—"called," "son," and "seed"—which link these texts to Paul's exposition and other Old Testament citations that also contain the key words "called," "son," and "seed."

Verses 19-24 comprise a list of questions, a diatribe, where the teacher speaks to an imaginary interlocutor. In these verses Paul incorporates an interlocutor question, "Therefore are you saying to me?" (v. 19) and the phrase, "Oh man . . ." (v. 20), which are elements characteristic of *diatribe*. For a more in depth discussion, see Stanley Stowers, *A Rereading of Romans: Justice, Jews, and Gentiles* (New Haven, CT: Yale University Press), 1994; and for the organization of Romans 9–11 as *diatribe*, see Changwon Song, *Reading Romans as a Diatribe* (New York: Lang, 2004).

Sovereign Election, 9:6-18

In 9:6-18, Paul defends the merciful nature of God in election. Paul's initial question—"It is not as though the Word of God has fallen?"—in terms of human reasoning, is logical. For if God selected the nation Israel and they failed, is there something wrong with God's selection process—his faithfulness or his words? (Figuratively speaking, if God chose an athlete to run a race, why did God's chosen runner fail?)

In this sense, Paul presents the case in question form, asking whether Israel's unfaithfulness somehow communicates the message (1) that God's word has failed or (2) that God is unrighteous. Paul counters these logical possibilities by selecting sentences from the Genesis story that narrate the actions of God in his relationship with his chosen people. God's *character* is made known in his choice of Jacob over Esau, a decision that necessitated obedience. In the first part of Paul's "narrative" argument, 9:6-18,[5] God remains patient with Israel, despite her disobedience, leaving the listener wondering what will happen to God's chosen people.

---

5. Paul's use of Genesis 21:12 as a primary text for 9:6-29 and a secondary text of Genesis 18:10 and 14 is similar to later rabbinic midrash forms. However, there is no clear parallel to Paul's use of midrash in Romans 9–11, and for the purpose of discussion, the term "midrashic elements" and "midrashic argument" are used generally throughout this work for Romans 9–11. Each major section is also considered a "midrashic form"—9:6-29; 9:30—10:21; and 11:1-32.

For the argument in favor of "midrash," see Stegner, "Romans 9:6-29," 37–52. For a representative discussion against the technical designation, see H. Räisänen, "Römer 9-11: Analyse eines geistigen Ringens." *ANRW* II 25, no. 4 (1987): 2897–98; and Robin Scroggs, "Paul as Rhetorician: Two Homilies in Romans 1-11," in *Jews, Greeks, and Christians; Religious Cultures in Late Antiquity: Essays in Honor of William David Davies*, eds. Robert Hamerton-Kelly and Robin Scroggs (Leiden: Brill, 1976), 278. Furthermore, even though Paul's form is unlike his contemporaries, he shares similar themes and interpretive traditions concerning: God's word to Israel, God's mercy, salvation for gentiles, God's sovereignty and foreknowledge, human free will, and faith; Brian J. Abasciano, *Paul's Use of the Old Testament in Romans 9:1-9: An Intertextual and Theological Exegesis* (London: T & T Clark, 2005), 214–15.

Midrashic Form, 9:6-18

Paul's sequence of argument in Romans 9:6-18 hinges on two themes, in question form, which introduce each subsection: the faithfulness of God's word, 9:6, and the source of unrighteousness, 9:14. Paul's logical progression for each subsection—9:6-13 and 9:14-17—follows an alternating pattern (he makes an assertion followed by an Old Testament proof). His assertions are supported primarily with verses from the Pentateuch, which lead to two conclusions, one for each subsection (see verse 12 and 16):[6]

<u>It is not as though the word of God has fallen?</u>	v.6	Question
Not all the ones from Israel are Israel	v.7	Statement
Gen. 21:12		Support
Not the children of the flesh but those of promise	v.8	Statement
Gen. 18:10,14	v.9	Support
Gen. 25:21 (?)	v.10	Support
Not by works, but by the One who calls	v.12	Conclusion (theme)
Gen. 25:23		Support
Mal. 1:1,2	v.13	Support

---

6. Based on the sequence of support moving from Genesis to Exodus, it seems that Paul retells Israel's history in 9:6—10:21; see Wright, "Letter to the Romans," 622. Wright adopts Hays's narrative approach in interpreting these passages, but emphasizes Jesus as the hermeneutical key to the story of God's relationship to Israel; Wright, *Paul, In Fresh Perspective*, 9. Also in these chapters, Paul intelligently undermines the pretensions of Rome itself by "upstaging" Augustus; Wright, "Letter to the Romans," 623–24. For a more detailed argument concerning the imperial context, see David Wallace, *The Gospel of God: Romans as Paul's Aeneid* (Eugene, OR: Pickwick, 2008), 3–37.

<u>Is unrighteousness from God?</u>	v.14	Question
By no means.		Statement
Exod. 33:19	v.15	Support
Not by man's will or effort, *but by the One who shows mercy*	v.16	Conclusion (theme)
Exod. 9:16	v.17	Support
According to his will, he shows mercy and hardens	v.18	Transition

(Verse 18 concludes verses 14-17 and transitions into 9:19-25)

In the above outline, the Old Testament quotations clarify Paul's statements so that the assertions themselves carry *semantic* momentum into two parallel summary statements (*)—or topic sentences:

Not by works,

    but by the One who calls   v.12

Not by man's will or effort,

    but by the One who shows mercy   v.16

In other words, Paul's parallel thought flow brings the reader to the conclusion that <u>God's</u> *elective decisions* and his *merciful character* function apart from man's doing.

An additional connection must be made before the individual verses of Romans 9:6-18 are explained. The unity and overall development in 9:6-18 is connected to an earlier portion of Paul's letter. In Romans 2:29, Paul's defines a Jew as someone other than an ethnic Jew—or someone other than one who practices the law—which calls into question the logical reason for God's original purpose in calling the Israelites (his righteousness—How could God now accept those who are not righteous, those who do not adhere to the law?). And Paul's definition calls into question whether God's promise to the patriarchs is still true (his faithfulness—People who are not Jewish by birth are considered to be accepted as among the promised people of God?). In Romans 3:1-5, Paul introduces these two themes—God's faithfulness and God's righteousness—but does not elaborate:

> What then is the advantage in being a Jew or what is the benefit of circumcision? Much in every way. First, they were entrusted with the words of God. What then? If some did not believe, will not their unfaithfulness nullify God's faithfulness? By no means. Let God be true and every man a liar . . . But if our unrighteousness makes God's righteousness more glorious, what are we saying? Isn't God who bears wrath *unjust?* (I am speaking using human argument).

Thus in 3:1-8, Paul appropriately introduces the topics he will later defend: God's faithfulness and God's righteous character. Paul's question as to whether the unbelief of the Jews nullifies *God's faithfulness* (3:3) might be phrased in this way, "What does Israel's unfaithfulness say about God's character in choosing a nation that fails?" (Failure associated with God?) Paul is quick to respond that God's words are true, but then he abruptly introduces a second topic concerning God's "unrighteousness." He asks whether God's righteousness is made "more glorious" because of sin, 3:5, which raises a logical concern as to whether God is *unjust* for judging? In other words, does God gain an advantage because of sin and then judge people for that sin? Paul delays his answer to these two questions until here in Romans 9:6-18.[7]

---

7. Consequently, Romans 9–11 is an integral part of the letter and relevant to the theological significance of Christ's sacrifice, 3:21-26.

Merciful Election, 9:6-18

After grieving for his people, 9:3, Paul concentrates his reasoning and support on God's elective and merciful character on behalf of Israel. And as in a traditional lament, God's *faithfulness* receives the focus. Not surprisingly, Paul begins the body of his argument with this theme in the form of a question implying that God's "word" has not failed, 9:6 (picking up on the topic he broached earlier in his letter):[8]

It is not as though the word of God has failed?	6
For not all those of Israel are Israel	7
Neither are the seed of Abraham, all children [of Abraham]	
but, **"In Isaac will be called your seed"**[9]	

The "word of God" refers to God's election of Israel, his faithfulness to his promise.[10] Paul's initial text, from Genesis, introduces the key

---

8. For the full text of 9:6-18 in outline form, see page 78.
9. In this chapter, Paul's Old Testament quotations are placed in bold letters for visual comprehension.
10. Since Romans 9:6-29 continues Paul's earlier discussion in 3:1f, the phrase "word of God" (9:6) probably has a close semantic connection with the Jews being entrusted with the "words of God" (τὰ λόγια τοῦ θεοῦ) in 3:1. The phrase ὁ λόγος τοῦ θεοῦ in 9:6 refers to the gospel message in other Pauline letters—for example, 1 Cor. 14:36; 2 Cor. 2:17; 4:2; Col. 1:25; 1 Thess. 1:8; 2:13; 1 Tim. 4:5; 2 Tim. 2:9; Tit. 2:5. See also R. Kotansky, "Note on Romans 9,6: *Ho logos tou Theou* as the Proclamation of the Gospels," *Studia Biblica* 7 (1977): 24-30. Other possible referents include: "Scripture"—Douglas J. Moo, *The Epistle to the Romans* (Grand Rapids: Eerdmans, 1996), 572–73; "whole of God's address"—Byrne, *Romans*, 293; "purpose"—C. E. B. Cranfield, *A Critical and Exegetical Commentary on the Epistle to the Romans* (Edinburgh: T & T Clark, 1975–79), 472f; "promises"—Dunn, *Romans*, 539, and Westerholm, Paul and the Law in Romans 9-11," in *Paul and the Mosaic Law*, ed. James D. G. Dunn (Tübingen: Mohr, 1996), 215–37. Robert Jewett sees the singular "word of God" in contrast to the plural (3:2, 4) as roughly synonymous with the gospel—relating to the doxology in the previous verse, whether "God in Christ is to be powerful enough over all"; *Romans: A Commentary*, ed. Eldon Jay Epp (Minneapolis: Fortress Press, 2007), 574. In this sense, Romans 9–11 would affirm the thesis of 1:16-17.

Paul is not raising a new question but argues for a neological solution. For example, in the compilation of the rabbinical interpretations of the oral law, a few opinions are referenced concerning the definition of "Israel" concerning "who" belongs to Israel. In the Babylonian

words "called" and "seed," which link these verses to the rest of his midrashic argument.[11] It is important to note that in some of Paul's quotations, his key word or concept is not found in the Old Testament quotation itself but in the Old Testament context. It is probable, then, that Paul expects his audience to recall the key word, *which may be absent from his quotation but is within the Old Testament passage from which he quotes*—a challenging didactic method.

When Paul writes, "not all those of Israel are Israel," he makes the statement that some of the ethnic Jews are not part of the "true" Israel. At this point he says nothing about the gentiles; he simply exposes the division among the Jews—some are "in" and some are not.[12] Yet keep in mind that this initial phrase "all Israel" introduces the current section, 9:6-29, and carries semantic relevance to the larger argument as a whole, 9:6—11:32. Since Paul will make the case for gentile inclusion within this section, 9:6-29 (and since this phrase will contribute to the difficult conclusion in 11:26 where "all Israel" is saved), an indirect reference to gentile believers must not be dismissed.[13] Paul clarifies what he means in the following sentence.

Talmud, *Sanhedrin* 59b, a reference is made to the children of Esau and a delineation as to who is in Isaac and who is not in Isaac. In the Jerusalem Talmud, *Nedarim* 2:10, Genesis 21:12 is cited to support the view of two worlds, which may suggest a Palestinian tradition and method of interpretation.

11. For a chiastic arrangement of 9:6-29 based on repetition of key words, see Dunn, *Romans*, 537. However, the Old Testament verse list is awkwardly divided with this pattern.

12. Moo rejects the interpretation of "gentile Christians" as included in Paul's meaning of the second "Israel" in verse 6 based on the following reasons: (1) 9:1-5 establishes the parameters for Paul's language for "Israel"; (2) Paul's explanation for v. 6b-13 concerns people *within* ethnic Israel; and (3) the Old Testament quotations in verses 27-29 signify a "remnant" within ethnic Israel; Moo, *Epistle to the Romans*, 574. In contrast, Günther Juncker considers the context of Galatians 3–4 and Romans 4 and 9:7-13 to conclude that "Israel" in 9:6b refers to spiritual Israel, the church; see Juncker, "'Children of Promise': Spiritual Paternity and Patriarch Typology in Galatians and Romans," *Bulletin for Biblical Research* 17 (2007): 145f.

Twenty-eight times in the LXX the phrase ἐξ Ἰσραήλ refers to the commonwealth—six of these instances in 1 Maccabees. It seems obvious that Paul means that not all Jews are "Israel," but based on the context of this section, 9:6-29, Paul initiates in 9:6 the possibility that some gentiles are included in "Israel."

The clause "Neither are the seed of Abraham, all children [of Abraham]" (v. 7b) restates Paul's bold claim that some of the descendants of Abraham are not "children" of Abraham.[14] The "seed of Abraham" is used synonymously for the "descendants of Israel."[15] By transitioning his topic from "Israel" to the "seed of Abraham," he (1) focuses the discussion on the patriarchs,[16] and (2) stresses that there are other children born to Abraham—referring to Ishmael and Esau[17]—but rhetorically, he leaves room for the general interpretation of "gentiles." Just as Paul radically redefines the meaning of a "Jew" as one circumcised by the heart by the Spirit, 2:29, here he explains "Israel" not in terms of ethnicity but in relation to faith. Simply stated: "Not all of ethnic Israel have believed God's word."

13. Scholars use various terms for "believing Israel." For example, "spiritual" Israel—Moo, *Epistle to the Romans*, 572; "those of faith"—Dunn, 539; Israel in a "selective" sense—Cranfield, *Critical and Exegetical Commentary*, 473.

14. "Those of Israel" parallels "the seed of Abraham" and "Israel" with "not children."

15. Grammatically, the "seed of Abraham" is the subject, see Byrne, *Sons*, 131; Dunn, *Romans*, 2:540. (Also see John 8:37 and 2 Cor. 11:22.) "Seed of Abraham" (σπέρμα Αβρααμ) in the LXX refers to Jacob and his descendants (e.g. Ps. 104:6; Pss. 9:9, 18:3; and Isa. 41:8). For the phrase "children of Abraham" to include Ishmael, Esau and others, see Joseph Fitzmyer, *Romans* (New York: Doubleday, 1993), 560; this in contrast to the "seed of Abraham," which would refer only to Isaac, Jacob, and Jacob's descendants. If true, Paul desires to show that not all physical "seed" of Abraham are included as "elected children" of Abraham. But this conflicts with the meaning of "seed" in verse 7b, and this first midrashic section as a whole (9:6-29) is concerned about the remnant and gentile inclusion. "Children" refers to "spiritual" children and "seed of Abraham" refers to those of physical descent. In this case, by distinguishing Isaac and Jacob in the following verses it causes grief to know that the physical children of Abraham—the sons of Jacob—may be in a similar state as Ishmael and Esau.

But "Abraham's seed" can be taken in a spiritual sense (Gal. 3:29) as Paul does in the quotation in Romans 4:18 (Gen. 15:5-6, "So shall your seed be"). Although "Abraham's seed" can have a physical connotation and a spiritual one, the context in Romans 9:7 refers to physical descent. For "Abraham" in Romans 9–11, see K. Berger, "Abraham in den . . .," 77–83; and for a survey of the Jewish view of Abraham, see Jeffrey Siker, *Disinheriting the Jews: Abraham in Early Christian Controversy* (Louisville: Westminster John Knox, 1991), 17–27.

16. This sequence is reversed in chapter 11, where Paul will move the discussion from the patriarchs, 11:12, to "all Israel," 11:26.

17. God's election of Isaac in fulfilling God's special purpose does not negate God's merciful character toward Ishmael (Gen. 21:13, 17-21; 16:10-14; 17:20); see Cranfield, *Critical and Exegetical Commentary*, 475. What Paul emphasizes here is sonship and election; Wagner, Heralds, 48.

For his initial supporting text, Paul quotes Genesis 21:12 (Rom. 9:7b) "in Isaac shall be your seed." In the Genesis context, Sarah gives birth to Isaac and does not want Abraham's son through her maidservant, Hagar, to share in Isaac's inheritance. God confirms to Abraham that it would be through Isaac that his seed would be named (καλέω), and that his son Ishmael would not share in the inheritance but would become a great nation (Gen. 21:18).[18] By quoting the Genesis sentence—"In Isaac will be called your seed" (9:7)— Paul makes plain God's *distinctive* election (καλέω) of Isaac and his descendants. But it is not clear at this point what Paul means when he writes that not all of the "seed of Abraham [are] all children [of Abraham]" (9:7b).

Paul's expounds on his meaning of "seed" with a second assertion and secondary text stressing God's faithfulness to his promise. The previous proof text (9:7b; Gen. 21:18) referred to God's commitment to his promise in selecting Isaac over Ishmael, but the second proof text and its context gives some insight as to what Paul means by "not all those of Israel are Israel":

That is, the children of the flesh are not children of God,   8

but the children of promise will be reckoned into the seed

For the word of promise is like this,   9

"According to this time I will come and it will be to Sarah a son"

---

18. In Jewish tradition, "Ishmael" represented all who were not included in the Abrahamic covenant, those who were not elected; for example, see *Jub.* 12:22-24 and 15:8. "Ishmael" serves as the first gentile representative; Timothy Berkley, *From a Broken Covenant to Circumcision of the Heart: Pauline Intertextual Exegesis in Romans 2:17-29* (Atlanta: Society of Biblical Literature, 2000), 169. He was included as a son of Abraham but not included in the covenant; ibid., 170. See also Gen. 37, Ps. 83:7; *Jub.* 15:30-32 and 16:16-18. They were enemies of Israel—Amos 1:1; Obad.; and Ps. 137:7. See also, S. Lyonnet, "Le role d'Israel dans l'histoire du salut selon Rom. 9-11," in *Etudes sur l'epître aux Romains* (Rome: Gregorian University Press, 1989), 264-73.

The phrase "children of the flesh," 9:8, has a double meaning. Based on the Genesis context, "children of flesh" refers to the descendants of Ishmael.[19] But in the present context of the letter, Paul's own people, the ethnic Jews, are now "children of the flesh" and not part of Israel[20]—a reversal that brings him great sorrow. Paul's use of the term "flesh" in his lament (9:3, 5, 8) stresses the "natural" or "physical," and here "flesh" stands in an antithetical relationship to "promise." Thus verses 9:7-9 can be summarized as "some of the descendants of Israel—the descendants (σπέρμα) of Abraham—are children of the flesh and are not children of God." Paul does not define Israel based on race but based on promise. The "children of God" are "children of promise," according to the "seed."[21]

This reasoning fits with Paul's earlier argument in the letter concerning God's promise to Abraham concerning his "seed"—a promise that came before the act of circumcision was required and before the law was given (Rom. 4:10-16; Gen. 15:5-6). Paul had argued that Abraham is the father of "all" who believe. In the section of 9:6-18, Paul uses similar content but his purpose is different—to show the role of *God's character* in his election of Abraham and his descendants.

To do this, Paul in his secondary text explains what he means by "promise": "According to this time I will come and it will be to Sarah a son" (Rom. 9:9; Gen. 18:10, 14). In the Genesis context, Isaac is not born yet. The Lord promises Abraham that Sarah would have a son in a year. Sarah laughs because she is old, and God repeats his promise, "According to this time I will come and it will be to Sarah a son." The Lord then declares to Abraham that he will become a great and mighty nation, and all nations (gentiles) on earth

---

19. See also Gal. 4:23.
20. The creative freedom of God reckons or creates righteousness by counting it; Black, *Romans*, 131.
21. In Genesis 18, it may be worth noting that Abraham *intercedes* for the righteous.

will be blessed through him. In the initial Genesis proof text (Rom. 9:7; Gen. 21:12), God spoke to Abraham *after* Isaac had been born, but here in this second proof text (Rom. 9:9; Gen. 18:10), Isaac has not been born, which means that Paul emphasizes how God's "promise" expresses God's *faithfulness* concerning his promised son, Isaac, 9:9. Significantly, the key words "seed" and "son," 9:7-9, are introduced in the setting of "promise" and blessing, to Abraham and his descendants, as well as to all nations.[22] In this way, Paul selects excerpts from the Genesis story—not based on their original time sequence but to explain a truth—God's faithfulness in his calling of the son, Isaac, was not according to natural descent but according to the "promise," a spiritual emphasis.

Paul further expounds on God's character in his election of Israel. Before Isaac's twins were born through Rebekah, God communicated his plan:

---

22. Concerning the individual and collective nature of the individual in Judaism, the individual is important but there is no apparent shift from the corporate to the individual until the exile. After the exile, everlasting life (e.g., Dan. 12:2) becomes the focus of an individual's decision; see Gary Burnett, *Paul and the Salvation of the Individual* (Leiden: Brill, 2001), 77. Personal piety becomes of greater importance in Judaism. The separation of corporate identity and the individual is not easily distinguished in these texts—Abraham's decisions and the decisions of his "seed" affect the community, yet each is responsible for his own actions (Rom. 2:6f). For the continued debate, see Thomas Schreiner, "Corporate and Individual Election in Romans 9: A Response to Brian Abasciano." *JETS* 49, no. 2 (2006): 373–86; and Abasciano, "Corporate Election in Romans 9: A Reply to Thomas Schreiner." *JETS* 49, no. 2 (2006): 351–71.

> Not only but also from Rebekah's womb they will come   10
>
> having the same father, Isaac.
>
> For they were not yet born and had not yet done good or evil,   11
>
> so that the elect plan of God might remain,
>
> *not on the basis of works but by the One who calls*   12
>
> She was told, **"The greater will serve the younger"**
>
> As it is written, **"Jacob He loved, Esau He hated"**   13

Since neither son—Jacob or Esau—had been born or had done good or evil, the only "variable"[23] is God's choice, revealing his character. Paul's assertions and support in 9:6-12 lead to his main topic that God's election is not based on works but is based on his faithfulness, 9:12a.

Paul quotes Genesis 25:23 (Rom. 9:11b) to explain what he means by the character of "the One who calls," and in so doing he implies that God chooses the son in the *lesser* position:

> She [Rebekah] was told that:
>
> "The greater [μειζων] will serve the younger [ελασσονι]."

The recipients of this letter who knew Torah, particularly Genesis, would make sense of Paul's simple point: God's character is evidenced in his choice of the *younger* (ἐλάσσονι; Gen. 25:23):

---

23. "Variable" is used adjectively here (in a mathematical sense of "equation") and does not suggest in any way that God's decision varies.

     Dunn notes the choice of φαῦλος as the contrast to ἀγαθός instead of καλός. He interprets this as an emphasis on the twins' behavior (see Rom. 2:9-10; 3:8; 12:21; and 16:19); Dunn, *Romans*, 542. Paul's subtle but meticulous attention to detail in his parallel can also be seen in verse 13 where he reverses the order of "Jacob" and "loved" in the LXX to form a better parallel; Christopher D. Stanley, *Paul and the Language of Scripture: Citation Technique in the Pauline Epistles and Contemporary Literature* (Cambridge: Cambridge University Press, 1992), 105.

Two nations are in your womb

two people from within you will be set apart

One people will be stronger than the other,

the greater will serve the younger.

The Old Testament text implies that the "younger" is the son in the "weak" position, though it is not explicitly stated. The older son, Esau and his descendants, is "stronger" (אמץ[24], which means Jacob and his descendants are younger—or weaker).[25] This makes sense when taking into account the priority of the "firstborn" in the Jewish family, receiving the birthright and a double portion of the inheritance. The LXX also reads ἐλάσσονι, which is best rendered to mean "younger." However, regardless of which rendering —"weaker," "lesser," or "younger"— it seems that Paul wants his Jewish and gentile readers to know that *God's character is evidenced in his election of the son in the humble position.*[26]

Paul immediately follows the quotation about Rebekah's two sons with a quotation from Malachi (Rom. 9:12b; Mal. 1:1-2) for the purpose of illustrating and elaborating upon God's character (v. 9:12b; Gen. 25:23). It is important to note that in the flow of Paul's argument, the Malachi quotation supports his main assertion in verse 11 ("by the one calling"):

---

24. The LXX translates ὑπερέχω in terms of authority.

25. The MT (צעיר) can be translated "little in significance."

26. The idea of "weaker" gives semantic weight to the meaning of the terms "weak" and "strong" in chapters 14–15. Significantly, Paul's reasoning and support in Romans 9–11 are part of the theological foundation for the practical issue of the "strong" choosing humility in their attitude to those "weak" in faith.

For the idea that Paul shares the doctrine of Jacob's divine election with his contemporaries, see Dunn, 544. Yet for uses of "greater" (μέγας) for older, see Gen. 10:21 and 29:16; and for "younger" (ἐλάσσων), see Gen. 27:6 and Josh. 6:29. For support of LXX as more clear than the Hebrew text in verse 12, see Fitzmyer, *Romans*, 563.

So that the elect plan of God might remain,

not on the basis of works but by the one calling

She [Rebecca] was told:

"The greater will serve the younger"   Gen. 25.23

As it is written:

"Jacob he loved, Esau he hated."   Mal. 1:1-2

Paul's quotation from Malachi—"Jacob he loved, Esau he hated"—stands out among the series of quotations from Genesis. In this way, Paul gives historical proof of the disobedience of the nations: Esau's descendants, the Edomites, rebelled and so did Jacob's descendants, the Israelites.

Paul creates a powerful message with the Malachi quotation and its context. In the Old Testament passage, the prophet juxtaposes God's wrath to Edom in his prologue (Mal. 1:2-5) pronouncing an impending and lengthy judgment of God against Israel (Mal. 1:6f).[27]

27. The meaning of "to hate," μισέω, should be understood in light of its antithesis, ἀγαπάω, and the contrast is a common biblical expression carrying the meaning of "turn away," "reject" or "strongly dislike" (for "loved less" see Fitzmyer, *Romans*, 563; contra Cranfield, *Critical and Exegetical Commentary*,480). A good example is God's command concerning two wives (Deut. 21:15): a man is to show honor to his firstborn son whether it is the wife he "hates" or the wife he "loves." The nature of God in choosing the younger son stands out in relation to a law abiding Jew. For similar "love-hate" texts, see Deut. 22:13; 24:3; Judg. 14:16; Prov. 13:24 and 15:32. The contrast between "love" and "hate" is not an emotional one but concerns the will and action (*TDNT* 4:687; see also Matt. 5:43f; 6:24f; and 1 John 4:20). The Malachi quotation expresses God's wrath against the Edomites, who rebelled. This does not necessarily mean that God's attitude in electing Jacob *at birth* was "against" Esau and his descendants.

Paul intends to separate "Israel" from her relatives—the descendants of Ishmael and Esau. Rather than identifying these foreign nations as part of ethnic Israel (see H. Räisänen, "Romans 9-11 and the 'History of Early Christian Religion,'" in *Text and Contexts: Biblical Texts in Their Textual and Situational Contexts: Essays in Honor of Lars Hartman*, eds. Tord Fornberg and David Hellholm [Oslo: Scandinavian University Press, 1995], 182), it seems that he is making a distinction to highlight God's character. He also opens the argument to the possibility of God's plan to include them as a gentile nation.

For the argument for Esau's salvation, see Blomberg, "Elijah, Election, and the Use of

Those familiar with the oracle of Malachi would recall the stubborn nature of the gentile nation (Mal. 1:4):

> Edom says,
>
> "Though we have been crushed, we will return to build the ruins."
>
> Now the Lord almighty says,
>
> "They may build, but I will demolish."

Yet, the rest of the oracle in Malachi speaks against Israel and her rebellious priests. Rhetorically, this introduction in Malachi acts as a springboard to more wrath, intensifying the deserved judgment of God against rebellious Israel. In both the Malachi context and in the present argument in Romans, it seems appropriate that since Israel was blessed with the benefits of election (cf. 9:4), blessings Esau and his descendants were not given, Israel would incur severe punishment for her disobedience.

What needs to be pointed out in light of Paul's midrashic style is that the emphasis of the Malachi quotation introduces God's faithful character in *showing mercy* as well as wrath. A careful look at Paul's use of Old Testament support in light of his "narrative" purpose shows that Paul underscores God's divine action and character. When Paul quotes Malachi—"Jacob he loved, Esau he hated"—he (1) draws upon the context of God expressing wrath to Esau's descendants, the Edomites, and at the same time he (2) draws upon the context of God sending an indirect warning to unrepentant Israel. In other words, God first punishes the "older" son (the descendants of Esau, Mal. 1:3-4), which is an act that also proves his patience and mercy toward

Malachi," 109–16, and Cranfield, *Critical and Exegetical Commentary*, 480. For eternal wrath, see Schreiner, *Romans*, 503—who bases his argument on Mal. 1:4; Isa. 34; 63:1-6; Jer. 49:7-22; Ezek. 25:12-14; Amos 1:11-12; Obad.; also *1 En.* 89:11-12; *Jub.* 29:14-20; 35:9, 13-17; 37:1-38:24; and 2 Esdr. 3:16.

the "younger" son—the descendants of Israel. In this sense, Israel is given a visual demonstration of the consequences of disobedience, an opportunity for repentance. The emphasis here is upon God's desire for change in the heart of the younger son, the nation of Israel. Thus, the quotation of "Esau I hated, Jacob I loved" in Malachi accents Israel's failure and stresses God's love for them.[28]

In the context of Paul's letter, 9:12, the quotation "Esau I hated, Jacob I loved" does not intend that Jacob was more pleasing to God than Esau, nor that God held animosity;[29] rather, it implicitly accents God's covenant faithfulness amidst Israel's disobedience.[30] Keep in mind that Paul has just highlighted a single variable in God's election of Jacob—that God elected the "younger" son (Rom. 9:12; Gen. 25:23). The emphasis of the Malachi quotation and its context gives insight into God's consistent character in showing both mercy and wrath to Israel, and impartiality to Esau in relation to election ("Is not Esau Jacob's brother?"; Mal 1:2).

From a theological perspective, God desires the repentance of Israel in the oracles of Malachi. God's choice of Jacob reveals his desire for humble service from both the son in a "weaker" position and service from the "older" son. On the one hand, Esau and his descendants were to serve Yahweh by honoring God's choice of Jacob,[31] but

---

28. The quotation from the LXX is exact, except the object "Jacob" is moved before the verb, stressing God's blessing of Israel. This makes sense in light of Paul's current grief, 9:1-5, and in light of the context of wrath from the Malachi quotation. John Calvin writes, ". . . Ye [Israel] are then so much the worse, in as much as the remembrance of so great a favor cannot stimulate you to adore my majesty"; *The Epistles of Paul the Apostle to the Romans and the Thessalonians*, eds. Ross Mackenzie, David W. Torrance, and Thomas F. Torrance (London: Oliver & Boyd, 1961), 352. For a summary of Calvin's views on 9:13-14, see David Demson, "John Calvin," in *Reading Romans through the Centuries: From the Early Church to Karl Barth*, eds. Jeffrey Greenman and Timothy Larsen (Grand Rapids: Brazos, 2005), 137–48.
29. Baldwin, *Malachi*, 222. For blessing to Esau, see Deut. 2:22 and 11:20.
30. God loved Israel and wanted Israel's love in return: Deut. 4:37, 5:10, 6:5, 7:7, 10:15, and 11:1f.
31. See Genesis 27:37-40 and 2 Samuel 8:14. Edom is included in the nations surrounding Israel from whom God desired to see repentance. If they repented and followed the religious practices of Israel, God would call them his own; Jer. 12:14f.

they did not. For God judges Esau's descendants because of their decision to act with resentment and hostility to Israel.[32] On the other hand, Jacob's descendants were chosen to serve Yahweh, but they rebelled. Ironically, however, the Israelites were graced with all of the goodness and allotted riches that come with election. In this sense, the volume of their disobedience speaks louder than the disobedience of those who were not chosen. Therefore, Paul implies that both nations failed,[33] and much more so did Israel—revealing the *merciful*, patient character of the One who calls.[34] It is this contrast of human disobedience against God's steadfast character that raises the logical question concerning the source of Israel's failure and whether God benefits from Israel's unrighteousness.

Merciful Character, 9:14-18

Paul began the body of the argument—"It is not as though God's word has failed?" (v. 6)—as a thematic introduction to a discussion concerning God's *faithfulness* in his relationship with Israel. Here in the second part of this section the topic changes to *righteousness*, 9:14-18, and Paul asks another question in defense of God's character: "What therefore are we saying, 'Is unrighteousness from God?'" (As previously mentioned, Paul addresses here, in greater length, one of two topics that he first introduced in Rom. 3:1-8.) Paul's scriptural support for his assertions comes from Exodus, leading to a conclusion concerning God's compassionate character:

---

32. See Gen. 27:41; 2 Kgs. 8:22; Ps. 83:6; Ezek. 25:12; Amos 1:6f; Obad. 10-11.
33. Ishmael and Esau are grouped as gentiles; Dodd, *Romans*, 187.
34. Paul's arguments begin and end with the disobedience of the gentiles and the Jews—see 9:13f and 11:30-32. God acts not only based on his covenant but also because of disobedience—see Deut. 9:4.

What therefore are we saying, "Is unrighteousness from God?" 14

By no means.

To Moses He is saying,

"I will show mercy to whom I will show mercy 15

and I will show compassion to whom I show compassion."

Now therefore, it is not the one desiring neither the one 16

making effort, but God who is showing mercy.

For scripture is saying to Pharaoh, 17

"For this reason I raised you up

in order that I might demonstrate My power and

in order that My name might be proclaimed in all the earth."

Now therefore, to whom He wills He shows mercy 18

and to whom He wills He hardens.

Below is an outline of the above passage showing more clearly Paul's line of reasoning with the source of his textual proofs:

Is unrighteousness from God? 14

By no means.

Exod. 33:19 15

Not by man's will or effort, but by the One showing mercy 16

Exod. 9:16 17

Transition 18

Based on Paul's reasoning up to this point, 9:6-13, a paraphrase of his question in verse 14 ("Is unrighteousness from God?") might help make sense of the issue—"Does God's choice of the son in the lesser position make God responsible for the son's actions?"[35] Paul's question and emphatic negative answer—"By no means"—places the responsibility of Israel's failure upon Israel.[36] In response, Paul gives evidence supporting God's goodness in his decision.

Paul reiterates his main topic in this section but he does so in relation to God's righteousness—that it is "not by man's will or effort" (v. 16)[37]—and quotes God's words to Moses: "I will show mercy to whom I will show mercy, and I will show compassion to whom I will show compassion" (Rom. 9:15; Exod. 33:19).[38] In the Old Testament context, Israel worships the golden calf, incurs judgment, and now God speaks to Moses within a context of goodness (Exod. 33:19):

And the Lord said,

I will make my <u>goodness</u> to pass before you

and will <u>proclaim the name</u> of the Lord before you.

I will have mercy on whom I will have mercy

and compassion on whom I will have compassion.

---

35. This question can also be asked concerning the actions of the stronger son, Esau (and his descendants), who was not chosen.
36. Leon Morris's translation communicates this question well: "Is there injustice with God?"; *The Epistle to the Romans* (Grand Rapids: Eerdmans, 1988), 359.
37. Based on the context of this whole section (Rom. 9–11), the verb for "effort" (τρέχω) might better be translated as "run" or "strive." While "running" may have some relevance in light of Hellenistic Judaism (see Ps. 119:32 and *Ps. Sol.* 9:2-5), it certainly has a Greco-Roman connotation; Stowers, *Rereading of Romans*, 92; and Wallace, *Gospel of God*, 133f. Devout Jews may naturally associate this metaphor with Psalm 119:32; Jewett, *Romans*, 583.
38. The verb οἰκτίρω is used only here in the NT. The verb ἐλεέω is used in 9:15, 18; 11:30-32; and 12:1. The focus is on God's purpose; Cranfield, *Critical and Exegetical Commentary*, 480; and on the benefits of those whom God calls; Jewett, *Romans*, 582.

Two apparent aspects of the above Exodus situation carry over into the meaning of Paul's argument in Romans: first, notice that "proclaim the name of the Lord" is synonymous with "goodness" passing before Moses." In this sense, God's presence and the proclamation of God's name is goodness. Second, God sovereignly chooses those to whom he shows mercy.

Paul's assertion that follows affirms this conclusion (9:16):

> Neither by the ones willing nor the ones making effort,
>
> but by the One showing mercy.

This "topic sentence" for this section, 9:14-18, parallels Paul's other main assertion in his previous section, 9:12:

> Not by works,
>
> but by the One calling.

The phrase, "the ones making effort" (v. 16) is synonymous with "works" (v. 12), which means that Paul implies that "the One calling" is "the One showing mercy." Thus Paul's intended parallel answers for the reader the previous question concerning God and unrighteousness—unrighteousness does not come from God; rather, *his call is merciful.*

Evidently the semantic weight of Paul's assertions accumulates. In addition to using a step-by-step argument with Old Testament proofs in this section of his letter, 9:6-16, he arranges his argument so that each part becomes important in discerning the whole midrashic narrative. In this way, Paul's approach evokes suspense and anticipation as the story unfolds.

In support of his claim that God's mercy is not based on man's effort, Paul quotes Exodus a second time. God's mercy extends to the Jewish people and the gentile nations (Rom. 9:17; Exod. 9:16):[39]

> For Scripture says to Pharaoh **for this reason** *I raised you up*
>
> **in order that I might demonstrate in you my power and**
>
> **in order that I might proclaim my Name in all the earth.**

In the Exodus account, God tells Moses to inform Pharaoh that God will send plagues on the Egyptians so that Pharaoh will know there is no one like God in all of the earth.[40] Interestingly, the verb "raised you up" (ἐξήγειρά) is not in the LXX (nor the MT). Paul seeks to point out God's powerful action of wrath against Pharaoh, which results in the proclamation of God's name to all peoples.

Significantly, Paul's meaning builds in relation to the previous quotation from Exodus: God proclaims his name to Moses, which demonstrates *his mercy* (Rom. 9:15; Exod. 33:19). In the second Exodus quotation—God proclaims his name to the whole earth,

39. The differences in Paul's quotation against the LXX likely reveal his theological emphasis: "For this reason I have raised you up so that . . ." (εἰς αὐτὸ τοῦτο ἐξήγειρά σε ὅπως . . .; Rom. 9:17) stresses God's purpose in raising Pharaoh up—compared to the LXX "For this reason I preserved you in order that" (ἕνεκεν τούτου διετηρήθης ἵνα . . .; Exod. 9:16). Paul's use of the term "power" (δύναμις) instead of "strength" (ἰσχύς) shows Paul's attentiveness to his theme: see Cranfield, *Critical and Exegetical Commentary*, 487; Käsemann, *A Commentary on Romans*, trans. and ed. Geoffrey W. Bromily (Grand Rapids: Eerdmanns, 1980), 268; Ernst Kühl, *Der Brief des Paulus an die Römer* (Leipzig: Quelle & Meyer, 1913), 326. More importantly, God's "power" and "name" (ὄνομα) are synonymous (e.g. Ps. 53:3; 54:1; Jer. 16:24; Acts 4:7; 1 Cor. 5:4).

    Cranfield stresses the importance of these two actions—ἐλεέω and σκληρύνω originating from the same merciful will; Cranfield, *Critical and Exegetical Commentary*, 472. This continuous, simultaneous, and active nature shares similarities with the nature of God's righteousness and wrath revealed; see 1:17-18.

40. Watson points out that a prophetic sequence occurs in addition to the narrative sequence. In each case—Isaac and Ishmael, Jacob and Esau, Moses and Pharaoh—God speaks and his divine utterance exacts a division; Francis Watson, *Paul, Judaism, and the Gentiles: A Sociological Approach* (Cambridge: Cambridge University Press, 1998), 309–10.

which demonstrates *his power* (Rom. 9:16; Exod. 9:16). This is neatly summarized—*God's name is merciful and the demonstration of his power is proclaimed to the nations* (gentiles). Notice that both Exodus citations support Paul's previous assertion that God's mercy is not based on man's effort, 9:16.

Main point: Not by man's will or effort, but by the One who shows mercy

Support 1:   God's name, his mercy, is revealed to Moses (Exod. 33:19)

Support 2:   God's name, his power, is revealed to the gentiles (Exod. 9:16)

The two supporting citations affirm that (a) God's decisions are separate from human decision or action, and they also evidence that (b) God's decisions reveal his mercy. Therefore, God's wrath to Pharaoh brings about the knowledge of God's name to the gentiles—a merciful act of revelation.[41] What is indirectly stated here—God's mercy to the gentiles—is stated more explicitly in the verses that follow.

Paul summarizes this first section, 9:14-17, and also transitions into the next section, 9:18-23, by stating:

Now therefore, to whom he wills he shows mercy   18a

and to whom he wills he hardens.   18b

---

41. "'My name' is a gospel term; the revelation of who and what God really is in his love, mercy, and saving power"; R. C. H. Lenski, *The Interpretation of St. Paul's Epistle to the Romans* (Columbus, OH: Wartburg, 1945), 615. In this light (though not stressed in Paul's argument here or in the Old Testament contexts thus far), God does not show favoritism and honors the humble—the Jew or the gentile (Rom. 2:6f). And as Paul argues in Romans 4, all nations were to be blessed through Abraham (Rom. 4:17; Gen. 17:4f). In some instances in the Old Testament, upon hearing of God's power, nations were given the opportunity to *humble* themselves (Jer. 18:8).

The first half of verse 18 summarizes verses 14-17 (and to a lesser degree vv. 6-17) where Paul has defended the merciful nature of God.[42] The second half of verse 18 introduces the concept of God's action of "hardening." While this reference to "hardening" indirectly alludes to Pharaoh, verse 18b also transitions into the next part of the argument, 9:18-23, and hints at the hardening of Israel.[43]

Summary

Paul's midrashic argument, 9:6-18, presents two topics in the form of questions as to whether (1) Israel's unfaithfulness communicates that God's word has failed or (2) whether Israel's unfaithfulness communicates that God is unrighteous. Paul argues that God is faithful and his actions are righteous, for his decision in electing Israel reveals his merciful character and his desire for a relationship with his chosen people. In narrative terms, by choosing Jacob—the son in the lesser position—the older son, Esau, and his descendants were given the opportunity to choose humility and accept God's order of election. They did not. And the younger son and his descendants, the Israelites, were to serve in humility before God and be obedient to his commands. Despite God's merciful decision, they rebelled. Out of this disobedience, God punishes the Edomites, a gentile nation, which sends a merciful warning to Israel to repent. While it seems that Israel deserves greater condemnation because of the gifts afforded

---

42. Paul emphasizes Yahweh's hardening of Pharoah's heart—Exod. 4:21; 7:3; 9:12; 10:1f; 14:8—though Pharoah participated—7:13-14, 22; 8:15, 19, 32; 9:7, 34-35; see also Beale, "Hardening," 145. Furthermore, "Pharaoh" is symbolic in a similar way that "Israel" and "Esau" are; Johannes Munck, *Christ & Israel: An Interpretation of Romans 9-11*, trans. Ingeborg Nixon (Philadelphia: Fortress Press, 1967), 50. Lenski notes that Pharoah attempts to block God—Exod. 10:20, 27; 11:10; 14:4, 5—but Israel's rejecting of the Messiah is worse; *Romans*, 617.

For the possibility of Paul having in mind an identical phrase (οὖν ὃν θέλει) and common theology from Tobit, see A. A. Di Lella, "Tobit 4,9 and Roman 9,18: An Intertextual Study," *Biblica* 90, no. 2 (2009): 263.

43. This "summary-transition" style is not an uncommon feature in Paul's letter writing.

them, God remains patient with them. Yet, a reversal takes place that creates suspense: the "children of the flesh," the descendants of Abraham by birth, are no longer "children of promise"—what then will happen to the nation of Israel?

The election of Jacob expresses something about God's nature. Paul specifically does not infer in this passage that God chooses the son who has *acted* with humility or pride—for in the womb, neither twin had sinned. Nor does the passage suggest that God shows favoritism. Rather, his choice reveals his character in that he chooses the son in the weaker position.[44]

44. Other Old Testament passages support this view. Israel was chosen from all the peoples on the face of the earth to be his treasured possession—the "fewest" of all peoples (Deut. 7:6-8). Israel was not to think more highly of themselves than they ought for God tells them that they did not possess the promised land because of their righteousness but because of the wickedness of the nations and as a fulfillment God's promise to the patriarchs (Deut. 9:4-5). Similarly, the descriptions of Moses' humility do not so much accent his ability but the nature of God in choosing Moses: "Moses was a very humble man, more humble than anyone on the face of the earth" (Exod. 12:3; 3:10f).

Romans 9:6-18 — full text outline

It is not as though the Word of God has failed. 6

  For not all those of Israel are Israel

    Neither are the seed of Abraham all children 7

    but "In Isaac will be called your seed."

    That is, the children of the flesh are not children of God, 8

      but the children of promise will be reckoned into the seed.

      For the word of promise is like this, **"According** 9

      to this time I will come and it will be to Sarah a son."

    Not only but also from Rebekah's womb they will come 10

      having the same father, Isaac.

    For they were not yet born and had not yet done good or evil, 11

      so that the elect plan of God might remain,

      not on the basis of works but by the One who calls

      because it was said, **"The greater will serve the younger"** 12

      just as it has been written, **"Jacob He loved, Esau He hated."** 13

What therefore are we saying, "Is unrighteousness from God?" 14

By no means.

  To Moses He is saying,

    "I will show mercy to whom I will show mercy." 15

  Now therefore, it is not the one desiring neither the one 16

    making effort, but God who is showing mercy.

For scripture is saying to Pharaoh, **"For this reason I raised** 17

you up in order that I might demonstrate My power and

in order that My name might be proclaimed in all the earth.

Now therefore, to whom He wills He shows mercy 18

  and to whom He wills He hardens.

81

Romans 9:19-29 — full text outline

Therefore you say to me,   19

  "Why does he still find fault;

    For who resists his will?"

O man, indeed who are you, the one answering back to God?   20

  Does that which is molded say to the one molding,

    "Why have you made me this way?"

Does not the potter have authority over of the lump of clay   21

  to make it into vessels of honor and also into dishonor?

But if God is willing to demonstrate wrath and to make known his power   22

  bearing with great patience vessels of wrath to be prepared for destruction

    and in order that he might make known the riches of his glory   23

      upon vessels of mercy which he prepared into glory?

Even us whom he also called, not only from the Jews but also from the nations   24

And as in Hosea he says,   25

  "I will call those 'not my people' 'my people'

  and those 'not being loved' 'beloved.'"

And it will be in that place which was said to them,   26

  "'You are not my people'

  They will be called sons of the living God."

But Isaiah cries out on behalf of Israel,   27

  "Though the number of the sons of Israel are as the sand of the sea,

  the remnant will be saved.

  For the Lord will execute his word swiftly and completely."   28

And even as Isaiah prophesied,   29

  "If the Lord of Hosts would not leave us a seed,

    we would become as Sodom,

    and would be likened to Gomorrah."

God's Wrath, 9:19-29

In the latter part of this first midrashic form, 9:19-29, Paul in diatribe style lists a series of questions leading to the conclusion that the gentiles are "in": "*Even us whom he also called, not only from the Jews but also from the gentiles*" (9:24). He then reinforces this main premise with quotations from the prophets, a *testimonia*, 9:25-29. By defining the "remnant" as comprised of Jews and gentiles, and with the introduction of "vessels of wrath" (v. 22) referring to Pharaoh, a foreboding feeling is created at the uncertain outcome of nonbelieving Israel, those who have rejected the Messiah.

Instructional Diatribe, Romans 9:19-29

In "staccato" fashion, Paul continues his use of *diatribe*, 9:19-23, intensifying the rhetorical effect. And while he does not identify his imaginary opponent, his didactic purpose is evident in his conclusion, 9:24, followed by a list of scriptural support:

Question	19
Question	
Question	20
Question	21
Question	22-23
Conclusion	24
OT Support	25
OT Support	26
OT Support	27-28
OT Support	29

In addition to his use of question, Paul incorporates other common language in a diatribe: an interlocutor question, "Therefore are you saying to me?" (v. 19); and the phrase, "Oh man . . ." (v. 20). Paul's questions challenge those who irreverently distrust the goodness of God in his will to harden. Although Paul incorporates a common literary device, his allusions and citations comprise much of the content within the diatribe:

Question	19
Question	
Question – Isa. 29:16[45]	20
Question – Jer. 18:1-12	21
Question – Jer. 18:1-12	22-23

In support of Paul's conclusion—"Even us whom he also called, not only from the Jews but also from the gentiles" (9:24)—Paul selects Old Testament verses from the prophets—Rom. 9:25-28; Hos. 2:23 and 1:10, and Isa. 10:22-23 and 1:9—ones that contain the key words "sons," "seed," and "call," threading the argument back to the beginning theme of this argument, an *inclusio*. He also introduces the key word "remnant" in verses 27 and 28, which thematically connects this portion of the argument to the passages that follow in Romans 9:30—11:32.

Prepared Vessels of Mercy, 9:19-23

Following his statement that God hardens whom he wills, 9:18, Paul speaks directly to those who challenge the sovereign decisions and purposes of God, 9:19-20:

"Therefore you say to me, "Why does he still find fault; for who resists his will?"

O man, indeed who are you the one answering back to God?

Does that which is molded say to the one molding,

  "Why have you made me this way?"

These words are placed in the mouth of an imaginary opponent.[46] A paraphrase of the question in declarative form might make helpful sense: "Since God makes the decision as to who is hardened and who receives mercy, the responsibility is with God, not human failing." Earlier Paul expresses similar logic, 3:5,[47] concerning God's justice,

---

45. The first six words are cited verbatim from Isaiah 29:16 (lxx), but the phase τί με ἐποίησας (9:20) may refer to the phrase τί ποιεῖς in the potter imagery of Isaiah 45:9.
46. Paul may be thinking of Jewish objections; Moo, *Epistle to the Romans*, 600. Romans 9:20-23 should also be understood as wisdom tradition, L. T. Johnson, *Reading Romans: A Literary and Theological Commentary* (New York: Crossroad, 1997), 132–39. The question "Who resists his will?" falls within the domain of wisdom literature, particularly the use of ἀνθίστημι—see also Job 9:19 and Ws. 12:12.

but here, too, he carefully shows reverence by stating that he is applying a "human" argument. This reverent attitude is supported by Paul's allusion to Isaiah's metaphor (Rom. 9:20; Isa. 29:16)[48] where the created object has no right to evaluate the creator.[49] In addition, in the Isaiah context, Judah rebels, which results in impending judgment, a context that supports the direction of Paul's argument for contemporary Israel.

Paul extends his potter imagery and allusions in Romans 9:21-23, which has considerable bearing upon the meaning of this entire section, 9:6-29:

Does not the potter have authority over of the lump of clay   21

    to make it into vessels of honor and also into dishonor?

    But if God is willing to demonstrate wrath and to make known his power   22

    bearing with great patience a vessel of wrath to be prepared for destruction

    and in order that he might make known the riches of his glory   23

    upon vessels of mercy which he prepared into glory?[50]

---

47. The argument of Romans 9:6-18 answers and advances the two theological issues of 3:1-8 concerning God's faithfulness and God's righteousness.

48. See also in Judaism—e.g., Ws. 15:7; Sir. 33:7-13; *T. Naph.* 2:2, 4. Josephus discusses the tension in Pharisaic thought between sovereignty and human will, see *War* 2.8, 14; *Ant.* 18.1-3. Shiu-Lun Shum affirms the connection here with the immediate context of 9:6-18 and sees Paul's purpose in his allusion to Isaiah 29:16 (Rom. 9:20-21) to draw upon the context of Israel's right to challenge their creator's knowledge and wisdom; *Paul's Use of Isaiah: A Comparative Study of Paul's Letter to the Romans and the Sibylline and Qumran Sectarian Texts* (Tübingen: Mohr, 2002), 204–5. Paul's potter-clay imagery differs from Isaiah's emphasis, which is the reason for Paul not having a citation formula here; ibid, 206.

49. It is clear that Paul selects phrases (from Isa. 29:16) to make his point; ibid. Paul's question, "Who are you the one answering back to God?" is likely written in a tone of grief; C. K. Barrett, *The Epistle to the Romans* (London: Hendrickson, 1991), 187. The word πλάσμα can refer to a wide range of materials; for helpful discussion, see Jewett, *Romans*, 593. More importantly, this citation of Isaiah (29:16) reaffirms the paradox of Israel's resistance to God's purposes; J. Ross Wagner, *Heralds of the Good News: Isaiah and Paul "in Concert" in the Letter to the Romans* (Leiden: Brill, 2002), 71.

50. Verses 21-22 are translated literally—an incomplete sentence.

Because of the "vessel phrases," verses 21-23 have received significant debate. In order to better discern Paul's thought flow and meaning, three literary elements need clarification: (a) the potter metaphor of Jeremiah 18:1-12; (b) the "vessel" statements of 9:21-23; and (c) the parallel of 9:22-23 to 9:17. After each aspect is discussed, their contribution to the meaning of the passage as a whole is then explained.[51]

Potter Metaphor, Jeremiah 18:1-12

In biblical times, craftsmen mixed clay with water and other additives to form a mud-like consistency that allowed them to shape clay into pottery. To carry out the normal daily activities, persons depended on these creations, such as bowls, pitchers, lamps, vases, and toys, among others. The potter metaphor was not uncommon in ancient times (see Isa. 29:16; 45:9-11; 64:8; and Jer. 18:1-6). Paul introduces the potter-clay imagery by alluding to Isaiah (9:20; Isa. 29:16—"The one molded does not say to the molder, 'Why have you made me this way?'"). In Romans 9:21-23, Paul extends the imagery by drawing upon the context of Jeremiah 18:1-12, particularly the "vessel" phrases ("vessels of honor and dishonor" and "vessels prepared for destruction and glory").

In Jeremiah, the prophet sees a potter working at the wheel. The pot being shaped from clay was marred in the potter's hands. The potter forms it into another pot, molding it as he thinks is best. The word of the Lord comes to the prophet (18:6-10):

> "Am I not able to form you, O house of Israel, as the potter does?" says the Lord. "As the clay is in the potter's hand, behold, so you are in my hand, O house of Israel. If at any moment, I speak to a nation or kingdom, to be uprooted, torn down, or destroyed, and if that nation

---

51. The use of the verb "mold" (πλάσσω) is commonly used in relation to God's creative actions (e.g., Gen. 2:7-8; Deut. 32:6; Prov. 24:12; Zech. 12:1; *Ant.* 1.32.34). See also *TDNT* 6:256–60.

repents—the one I spoke against—I will relent concerning the disaster I had planned for it. Or if at another time, I speak to a nation or kingdom, to be built up or planted, and if it does evil before me, not obeying [שמע] my voice, then I will relent of the good I had intended for it."

God's *merciful* character is revealed. He is willing to withhold the consequences of judgment if a nation repents and is willing to reconsider the good he intends for a nation if they do not obey him. By aligning the contextual lens in Jeremiah with Romans 9:21-23, not only is God's sovereign will evident, but God's *mercy* and judgment to gentile nations comes into focus.

Yet the thrust of the Jeremiah passage accents God's impending wrath against Israel. Following the potter and clay imagery (Jer. 18:11-23), God tells Jeremiah to ask the other nations if they have heard of anything as horrible as what Israel has done in forgetting God. The Lord then pronounces judgment—invasion and death—to the people of Israel for their idolatry. God is not partial. Israel remains disobedient despite having received the goodness of election.[52]

This scenario resembles the earlier Malachi quotation in Romans 9:16 where God plans to judge Israel after displaying his wrath to a foreign nation, the disobedient Edomites. In Jeremiah and in Malachi, God is patient with Israel and gives them opportunity to repent, sending a clear message by first demonstrating his justice to another nation. By quoting both prophetic texts of Isaiah and Jeremiah, Paul implies that a dramatic fulfillment of judgment will come to a nation who receives the blessings of election but obstinately turns way from God.[53] Therefore, in order to understand

---

52. Paul may also be identifying himself with the Jewish exilic prophet Jeremiah. Smith argues that Paul arrives at a new covenant solution of Jeremiah in Romans 9–11, seeing echoes of Jeremiah 30–31 in Paul's quotation of Isaiah 59:21 and 27:9; Philip Smith, "God's New Covenant Faithfulness in Romans," *Restoration Quarterly* 50, no. 4 (2008): 247.

53. Since Paul often quotes Scripture with reference to its context, and since he places these two prophetic texts adjacent to each other, and since his scriptural verse lists in Romans 9–11 share

Romans 9:19-29, it is important to recognize the contribution of the Jeremiah context: (1) God is impartial in dealing with the nations and Israel,[54] and (2) Israel has been disobedient despite God's mercy extended to them.

The "Vessel" Statements, 9:21-23

The element of apposition in these verses indicates that verse 22 clarifies verse 21, which is likely since Paul's reasoning forms a "chain-like" progression throughout his discussion:

Or does not the potter have authority over the lump of clay to make   21

    (it) into <u>vessels of honor</u> or into <u>vessels of dishonor</u>?

    But if God is willing to demonstrate wrath: 22

    and to make known his power,

      bearing with much patience, <u>vessels of wrath</u> being prepared for destruction

      and in order that he might make known the riches of his glory   23

    upon <u>vessels of mercy</u>, these prepared into glory?

The debate concerning the meaning of the "vessel" statements in verses 21-23 can be summarized in the following question: "Do 'vessels of honor' and 'vessels of dishonor' in verse 21 refer to 'vessels of wrath' and 'vessels of mercy' in verses 22-23?" Paul creates a semantic "merging"[55] by his thought flow and repetition, and it is clear that the vessel statements of verse 21 do refer to the vessel statements of verses 22-23. To show this, the overall progression of

---

particular themes, the assumption that he draws upon the shared context of Isaiah and Jeremiah is reasonable.

54. Also see Joshua 5:13-14.
55. The conditional sentence with a protasis (if clause) but with no apodosis (v. 22) necessitates a contextual search for theological intention.

Paul's argument with respect to the vessel statements is given below as well a discussion of the side-by-side parallel of relevant verses. What seems to be a complicated mingling of contexts is, in fact, a skilled use of literary devices by Paul for the purposes of narrating a "reversal."

Paul introduces the "vessels" phrase in verse 21, but what is important to see (and easy to miss) is the connection between verses 22-23 with verse 17. In other words, Paul integrates the context of his previous explanation concerning God's decided purpose for Pharaoh a few verses earlier—in verse 17—into the potter imagery. Paul's "thought" flow is listed in general terms:

v. 15-16	Exodus context:	God shows mercy to Israel
v. 17	<u>Exodus context:</u>	God hardens Pharaoh's heart
		= mercy to the nations
v. 18	Summary/transition:	God hardens Pharaoh's heart
		= mercy to Israel
v. 19	Question: God's will	
v. 20	Question: Potter imagery	
v. 21	Question: Potter imagery	
	("vessel" phrases introduced)	
v. 22-23	Question: Potter imagery	
	("vessel" phrases <u>elaborate upon verse 17</u>)	

As previously discussed, the Exodus 15 context highlights God's *compassion* to a rebellious Israel, v. 15, and emphasizes God's hardening of Pharaoh's heart, which sends his Name to the gentiles, a *merciful* act, v. 17. Paul transitions in the first half of verse 18 by summarizing the content of 9:6-17 concerning God's mercy to Israel and the nations ("Now therefore, to whom He wills He shows mercy"), and the second half of verse 18 ("and to whom He wills He hardens"), he moves the discussion forward into the topic that follows. Verses 19-23, then, elaborate upon Paul's Exodus quotation concerning God's wrath to Pharaoh.

Paul lists a series of questions in diatribe style, 9:19-23, to (a) reveal God's nature in a reverent tone and (b) to indirectly accuse those who doubt God's character in election. The interrogatives draw from Old Testament concepts without direct answers, which leads the reader into a visual illustration. Paul's midrashic style may seem complicated, but by following his thought flow, his emphasis is powerful and didactive: Paul uses potter-clay imagery in verse 21, likely from Isaiah, to introduce the "vessel" phrases and then merges the well-known potter-clay imagery from Jeremiah into verses 22-23. He then uses this imagery to elaborate upon the Exodus context from several verses before—in verse 17—concerning God's decision to harden Pharaoh. This integration of verse 17 and 21 leading to verses 22-23 will make sense when the parallel of verse 17 and verses 22-23 is demonstrated below.

God's Wrath, Romans 9:17 and 9:22-23

Two principles guide this part of the discussion: First, "wrath" frames these verses, 9:22-23; and second, verses 22-23 parallel verse 17. In verses 22-23, Paul does not make a theological separation between God's mercy and his wrath as if they were two separate entities. Rather, he exposes God's wrath, *which accomplishes both destruction and mercy.* Almost unnoticeably, Paul differentiates "wrath" with the use of the article, 9:22-23, and modifies the demonstration of God's wrath with two purpose clauses:

> But if God is willing to demonstrate [την] wrath   22
>
> and to make known [γνωρισαι] his power
>
>> bearing with much patience vessels of wrath being prepared for destruction
>>
>> and in order that he might make known [ινα γνωριση] the riches of his glory   23
>>
>> upon vessels of mercy previously prepared for glory

The conditional clause, "But if God is willing to demonstrate the wrath," is modified by two subordinate clauses that parallel each other—the infinitive phrase "to make known . . ." parallels the subjunctive purpose clause "in order that he might make known . . ." Again, the point here is to recognize that the "make known" phrases modify the demonstration of God's wrath in the first line, 9:22a.

Not surprisingly, the structure of verses 22-23 aligns with verse 17, and the verses thematically parallel:

17   For this reason I raised you up

     <u>in order that</u> [οπως] I might demonstrate in you my power

     <u>and in order</u> [και οπως] that I might proclaim my name in all of the earth.

22   But if God is wishing to demonstrate the wrath

     <u>and</u> to make known his power

23   <u>and in order that</u> [ινα γνωριση] he might make known the riches of his glory

Grammatically, the conditional clause of verses 22-23—which summarizes the Jeremiah context—does not form a complete thought. But it is interesting that when the two purpose clauses and the vocabulary from the Jeremiah context, verses 22-23, are compared with the two purpose clauses and vocabulary from the

Exodus quotation in verse 17,[56] they show a deliberate and precise thought parallel—the context of wrath and mercy in verse 17 synonymously parallels the context wrath and mercy from the potter imagery in verses 22-23. Both verses concern God's wrath, power, and mercy:

17a   For this reason I raised you up [wrath]

22a   But if God is willing to demonstrate <u>wrath</u>

17b   in order that I might demonstrate in you my <u>power</u>

22b   and to make known his <u>power,</u>

         bearing with much patience,

         vessels of wrath *being prepared for destruction*

17c   and in order that I might <u>proclaim</u> my name in all of the earth,

23   and in order that he might <u>make known</u> the riches of his glory

         upon ***vessels of mercy*** *previously prepared for glory*

In particular, notice how the proclamation of "God's name in all of the earth" in verse 17c (as a result of God's wrath to Pharaoh) is synonymous with God's mercy—"the riches of his glory"—made known to the gentiles in verse 23 (a reference to God's words to Jeremiah concerning his willingness to relent if gentile nations repent). By using the potter metaphor, Paul not only reiterates an explicit text revealing God's mercy to gentile nations but he also

---

56. In verse 17, Paul uses the subordinate conjunction ὅπως for both phrases, though the LXX uses ἵνα and ὅπως respectively; in verses 22-23, Paul uses the conjunction and the infinitive phrase—καὶ γνωρίσῃ—for the first purpose clause followed by a conjunction with ἵνα and the subjunctive—καὶ ἵνα γνωρίσῃ. In this way, Paul wants to show that God's demonstration of power and the proclamation of his name are forms of God's revelation— "making known." See also Romans 16:26.

amplifies an implicit meaning in the Exodus quotation—God delivers Israel by demonstrating wrath to a wicked ruler, sending a *merciful* message to the gentile nations.[57]

A detailed explanation of the comparison of verse 17 to verses 22-23 shows that Paul's *"vessels of mercy"* phrase in verse 23 refers to God's mercy prepared for the gentiles (an important piece in the understanding of the whole argument).[58] When viewing the parallel of verse 17 to verses 22-23, Paul's added comments to the potter imagery stand out (see italics above—*bearing with much patience vessels of wrath being prepared for destruction . . . upon vessels of mercy previously prepared for glory*).

Specifically, Paul's phrases (from the potter imagery—"vessels of wrath" and "vessels of mercy"; see above)—give additional insight into Paul's earlier quotations from Exodus. The phrase "vessels of wrath" in verse 9:22b refers to God's demonstration of power to Pharaoh, 9:17. But the added "vessels of mercy" phrase draws upon the Exodus context of verse 15 (Exod. 33:19). Here God tells Moses that he will cause his goodness, the "proclaiming of his name," to pass in front of him, and then says "I will show mercy to whom I will show mercy." Paul only quotes the latter half of Exodus 33:19 but expects his readers to remember the first half—the "proclaiming of his [God's] name." With this in mind, the "vessels of mercy" phrase in 9:23 draws upon (1) the context of mercy in God "proclaiming his name" *to Moses* (Rom. 9:15; Exod. 33:19) and underscores (2) the context of mercy in God "proclaiming his name" *to the gentiles,*

---

57. The fact that verses 22-23 are not a complete thought (an incomplete conditional sentence) suggests that Paul likely uses the information for his literary point.

58. Also note that the participle "prepared [κατηρτισμένη] for destruction" in verse 22 has a different connotation than the verb "prepared [προητοίμασεν] for glory" in verse 23. Καταρτίζω has an implication of an action performed on something already at hand—to put it in order, indicating the outworking of God's wrath as expressed in 1:18-32; see Dunn, *Romans*, 560. For an interpretation of the vessels in terms of individuals, see Jewett, *Romans*, 594.

which was accomplished through wrath to Pharaoh (Rom. 9:17c; Exod. 9:16). Thus the "vessels of mercy" in verse 23 refers to God's mercy prepared for the gentiles. Now that the connection has been made between the meaning of the vessel phrases of verse 23 and the Exodus context in verses 15-17, the relationship between verse 20 and verses 21-22 is clearer.

In verse 21, Paul in question format affirms God's sovereign right to make "vessels" as he wills in terms of "honorable" use or "dishonorable" use ("Or does not the potter have authority over the lump of clay to make [it] into vessels of honor or into vessels of dishonor?") Paul explains this indirect statement concerning God's power and will by giving an actual example of God's wrath carried out in verses 22-23—building upon the meaning from the Exodus context in verse 17. A paraphrase of verses 22-23 gives this emphasis:

> But God has the authority to demonstrate his wrath, as he did to Pharaoh: (1) for the purpose of making known his power, with great patience, upon vessels of wrath—like Pharaoh who was prepared for destruction; and (2) for the purpose of making known his Name, the riches of his glory, to the gentiles, who are vessels of mercy, prepared for glory.

Thus, the "vessel" phrases in verses 22-23 are framed in the context of a tangible example of God's "wrath." Paul wants to show that God's "wrath" results in God's mercy to the gentiles, which is why he concludes with the following sentence, "Even us whom he also called, not only from Jews but also from the gentiles," 9:24.

Now that three important elements of verses 9:21-23 have been explained—the potter metaphor of Jeremiah, the "vessel" statements, and the parallel to verse 17—Paul's primary emphasis of God's wrath is summarized. First, God's "wrath," which frames Paul's discussion in 9:18-23 reveals the great patience of God as he shows mercy to the obstinate nation of Israel. Second, God's wrath, his power, also

95

results in the proclamation of his name, making known the riches of glory—to the gentiles. Third, Paul's use of the potter metaphor (Jer. 18:1-12) gives a visual illustration of God's sovereign authority to mold as he wills. He is patient with gentile nations, and when he demonstrates His wrath to them, he sends a merciful warning of impending wrath to Israel. In essence, Paul's merging of contexts from Exodus with potter-clay imagery from Jeremiah leads to the conclusion that God molds "Israel" with "gentile" clay, begging the question as to what will happen to those of Israel who remain obstinate.

Gentile Inclusion, 9:24-29

Paul supports his conclusion—God "calls not only from the Jews but also from the gentiles," 9:24—with support from the Prophets.[59] The themes of "remnant" and "seed" tie the argument back to the beginning of this midrashic section (9:7), which creates suspense concerning Israel's outcome.

Scriptural *Testimonia*, 9:25-29

This *testimonia*, 9:25-29, one of four in Romans 9–11, stresses the theme of gentile inclusion into the remnant:

---

59. The semantic emphases build sequentially and logically; in this way, Paul's Old Testament quotations also support his two main conclusions from 9:12 and 16 that refer to God's call apart from human effort.

25 And as in Hosea he says,

   "I will call those 'not my people' 'my people'

   and those 'not being loved' 'beloved.'"   Hos. 2:23

26 And it will be in that place which was said to them,   Hos. 1:10

   "'You are not my people'

   They will be called sons of the living God."

27 But Isaiah cries out on behalf of Israel,

   "Though the number of the sons of Israel are as the sand of the sea,

   the remnant will be saved.   Isa. 10:22-23

28   For the Lord will execute his word swiftly and completely."

29 And even as Isaiah prophesied,

   "If the Lord of Hosts would not leave us a seed,   Isa. 1:9

   we would become as Sodom,

   and would be likened to Gomorrah."

Paul adapts the Scripture citations to his present need. He reverses the order of the sequence in Hosea (2:25; Rom. 9:25-26).[60] And he also alters the initial phrase in the Isaiah quotation to "I will call" (καλέω), linking this text to Paul's earlier quotation from Gen. 21:12 (Rom. 9:7). Paul repeats the key words "sons," "seeds," and "call," with a contextual repetition of the topic of "wrath."

---

60. The placement of the verb "to call" at the beginning requires the clauses (Hos. 2:25) to be reversed; see Hans Hübner, *Gottes Ich und Israel: Zum Schriftgebrauch Des Paulus in Römer 9-11* (Göttingen: Vandenhoeck & Ruprecht, 1984), 56. John E. Toews finds an ABBA pattern (Jews, 24a; gentiles, 24b; gentiles, 25-26; Jews, 27-29); 251. For an explanation of Paul's reversal in 25b and 25c of Hosea, see Wagner, *Heralds*, 81.

A	Gentiles	v.25	Hos. 2:23
A	Gentiles – "sons," "call"	v.26	Hos. 1:10
B	Remnant – "sons" (wrath)	v.27-28	Isa. 10:22-23
B	Remnant – "seed" (wrath)	v.29	Isa. 1:9

Paul's verses from Hosea stress "gentile" inclusion, as do the verses from Isaiah, but implicitly. The Isaiah context introduces a "remnant" theme."[61]

Midrashic Elements

Like a mosaic of words, Paul carefully selects Old Testament citations and places them in a way that underscores particular themes. For example, Paul chooses a verse from Hosea that contains the verb "to call," (καλέω), a repetition of the verb from verse 7, implying that the gentiles are called "sons":

In Isaac will be called (κληθησεται) your seed   v.7

They will be called (κληθησονται) sons of the Living God   v.26

Paul employs a common practice in which Hebrew Scriptures are selected that are comprised of "key" words.[62] The repetition of these words tightens the theological and thematic unity of the midrashic section: "called" (vv. 7, 12, 24, 26), "son" (vv. 26, 28), "seed" (vv. 7-8, 29), and "children" (vv. 7-9). In this way, the use of "seed," "son,"

---

61. The thought rhyme shows balance and symmetry even though the quotations from Isaiah (vv. 27-28) are longer than the verses quoted from Hosea (vv. 25-56).

62. The sonship motif in Romans 9 is a continuation of Paul's argument for gentile inclusion; see George Gianoulis, "Is Sonship in Romans 8:14-17 a Link with Romans 9?" *Bibliotheca Sacra* 166, no. 661 (2009): 82–83. In 9:28, Paul changes "God" to "Lord" as the subject of salvation action, alluding to Christ's role; Wagner, Heralds, 97.

and "called" in the Old Testament verse list, 9:26-29, completes the argument begun in verses 7 and 8.

In the Hosea context, the prophet prophesies God's mercy to the rebellious northern tribes of Israel. The symbolism of the names of Hosea's children, "not pitied" and "not my people" (1:6-9), express the nature of God's mercy in adopting his people again. But Paul is not referring to God's call of only the nation of Israel, 9:25-26;[63] he sees a renewed Israel made up of Jews and gentiles.

Paul then introduces a "remnant" theme (Isa 10:22-23):[64]

> Though the number of the sons of Israel are as the sand of the sea,
>
> the remnant will be saved.
>
> For the Lord will execute his word swiftly and completely.

In the Isaiah context, those of the house of Jacob who have escaped will rely upon the Holy One of Israel—a remnant will return unto God, "the remnant of Jacob" (Isa. 10:20-21). But the context of this prophesy also accents the wrath of God to Israel. Isaiah pronounces the "sentence of the Lord" (10:24). Wrath will be administered to Zion from Assyria in a manner similar to Egypt's cruelty. Furthermore, the imagery of the "sand of the sea" seems ironic in

---

63. See John A. Battle, "Paul's Use of the Old Testament in Romans 9:25:26," *GTS* 2, no. 1 (1981): 115–29.

64. The "remnant" theme introduced here will be expounded upon in 11:5. Romans 9:27b does not closely agree with the first half of Isaiah 10:22 (LXX) but it almost exactly parallels Hosea 1:10. Shum concludes that 9:27-28 supports the phrase "not only from the Jews" in 9:24, and that the inclusive ἡμᾶς identifies Paul and his audience as "vessels of mercy"; Shum, *Paul's Use*, 208—the Hosea and Isaiah texts are skillfully stitched together to show that a small remnant is called to be "vessels of mercy"; ibid. Paul uses Isaiah in Romans 9–11 not simply for rhetorical purposes, but to condemn his unbelieving contemporary Jews, but not absolutely, and to reveal God's grace—11:25-27; Isa. 59:20-21 and 27:9—in an "unexpected" final reacceptance by God; ibid, 297f. In addition, John Paul Heil notices a preliminary climax in Paul's use of the "remnant" of Israel in 9:27 to the hope represented by a "seed" in 9:29—reaching ultimate climax in the salvation of "all Israel"; Heil, "From Remnant to Seed of Hope for Israel: Romans 9:27-29." *CBQ* 64, no. 4 (2002): 703f.

light of God's promise to Abraham—that his descendants will be as numerous "as the sand upon the seashore" (Gen. 22:17). Isaiah's words expose the false belief of their physical descent—those who say "We have Abraham as our father!"—as a means of sufficiency for deliverance.[65]

Similarly, the context of Isaiah 1:9 (Rom. 9:29) is also a declaration of judgment upon Israel.

> If the Lord of Hosts did not leave us a seed,
>
> we would become as Sodom
>
> and be likened to Gomorrah

Here the "remnant" is left among the desolate, devastated, and abandoned; the "daughter who is in Zion needs restoration (Isa. 1:8). The key word "seed" also ties the argument back to the beginning of this midrashic section (9:7; Gen. 21:12), leaving the reader with the question as to what will happen with rebellious Israel.[66]

Summary Insights

Based on Paul's internal connections through key words and his progression of thought in 9:6-29, a narrative interpretation is helpful. After this brief summary, relevant insights are given relating the theological truths in this section to the rest of Paul's argument and his letter.

---

65. Young, *Isaiah*, 1:370. Jewett understands Paul's choice of ὑπόλειμμα (Rom. 9:27) rather than κατάλειμμα (Isa. 10:22) as a softening of judgment; *Romans*, 602.
66. Stegner, "Midrash," 40. Romans 9:29 and Isaiah 1:9 both carry a remnant motif that stresses God's faithfulness.

Narrative Summary

Paul expresses God's heart through grief for his people who were entrusted with covenant blessings, 9:1-5. This shows God's desire for a relationship with a humble, obedient son—the nation of Israel. When God calls Israel—Jacob, the younger son in the lesser position, 9:13—he creates a situation where humility is required from the both sons and their descendants. The older son and his descendants must submit to God's decision in his election of the younger son, Israel, and Israel is to obey God's commands. Even so, Paul, through the use of Old Testament support (Mal. 1:1-2; Rom. 9:12), shows that both sons rebel.

Despite disobedience, God's character is good, patient, and merciful—he desires repentance from both sons (Rom. 9:21-23; Jer. 18:1f). God disciplines the older son—the Edomites—for his disobedience and uses this discipline as a warning to his younger disobedient son—Israel—an expression of love (Mal. 1:1-2; Rom. 9:12). Even so, the nation of Israel disobeys, and God acts with great patience as he shows mercy amidst obstinate resistance, 9:18-23. Out of this disobedience God works mercifully and proclaims the riches of glory to the gentiles, 9:23-25. God's genuine desire to have a relationship with a humble people is realized in a remnant from both Israel and gentile nations, 9:24-29.

The theme of "gentile inclusion" is unique in contrast to rabbinical works, but the theme of a "rejected son" is closely affiliated with messianic overtones related to a rejected "stone" theme.[67] It is

---

67. Not surprisingly, the "rejected son" theme and the "rejected stone" theme were sometimes used interchangeably in rabbinical literature because of the Hebrew wordplay of "stone" (אֶבֶן) and "son" (בֵּן; see Exod. 28:9-29; 39:6-14; Josh. 6:4-21; 1 Kgs. 18:31; Isa. 54:11-13; Lam. 4:1-2; Zech. 9:16; and their Targums; also, *Esther Rab.* 3:1; 7:10. For additional relevant rabbinical texts, see C. A. Kimball's discussion in *Jesus' Exposition*, 184–86). In addition, the theme of the son or sons (Israel) rejecting his father is also present in the Old Testament (e.g., Hos. 11:1-4; Isa. 63:13, and Jer. 3:19-20). It is not surprising, then, that a mixture of "messianic" or "remnant" interpretations from Old Testament Scripture in the New Testament contain a "rejected son"

interesting that this section of Paul's argument, 9:6-29, concerns a called son who rejected the Father's call, and the next section, 9:30—10:21, illustrates Israel's fall, their rejection of the "stone."

Relevant Insights

The election of Israel, 9:6-13, reveals the heart of God and his desire for *humility* from his people. Paul's emphasis on God's election of the son in the weaker position is central to the meaning and purpose of Romans 9–11 and the rest of the letter. God does not show favoritism—he requires humility from all. The gentile believers in Rome must not become proud in their self-estimation. Paul warns them, "Do not boast branches, but if you might boast, you are not bearing the root, but the root bears you . . . Do not be high-minded but fear for if God did not spare the natural branches, neither in anyway will he spare you," 11:18, 21. Paul reiterates this Christ-like attitude when he admonishes the church to offer themselves as a living sacrifice, to renew their minds, and to "not think more highly of themselves than they ought," 12:3.

Based on this desired character, Paul speaks directly to a situation among the Roman Christians. The "strong in faith" are passing judgment on the "weak in faith" who do not feel right about eating meat, 14:1f. Paul warns against this arrogant position of judging a servant of God (see also 2:1f). Instead, Paul refers to Christ's sacrificial death when he encourages them to live and die unto the Lord, 14:8-9, and to bear the weaknesses of others (15:1-3; Ps. 69:9). They are to have the humble mind of Christ, 15:5.

In a general sense, this is Paul's singular purpose—to bring about the humility of Christ in the Roman church, particularly among

---

or "rejected stone" theme (the four significant Old Testament "stone" passages are Ps. 118:22, Isa. 8:14 and 28:16, and Dan. 2:34-45; and those in the New Testament are Mark 12:10; 14:58; 15:29; Luke 20:9-10; John 2:19-20; Acts 6:14; Rom. 9:33; and 1 Pet. 2:7).

the gentile Christians—which involves a multi-purpose effect among different people groups (see 15:14-24; e.g., Macedonians and Greeks, the Christian poor in Jerusalem, Christians in Jerusalem, the Roman believers, the Jews in Jerusalem, and the unreached in Spain). Paul makes it clear early in his letter that his aim depends on working together in humility and faith, 1:12, 17, and since the Roman believers' faith is being proclaimed throughout the known world, it is important that their faith grow without pride. In this way, the gospel will be well represented as Paul evangelizes Rome—when he is there and when he is not—and when he preaches in Spain. In other words, Paul wants fertile soil in Rome, without corrupting pride, so that a harvest of fruit can be born to the neighboring territories.

Paul's narrative argument also emphasizes *disobedience*, 9:11-13, which is an important aspect to understanding God's elective purpose. For example, he ends the body of the argument with the sentence, "For God bound all unto disobedience, so that he might show mercy to all," 11:32. This ending forms a circular argument with the beginning verses (in 9:6-13) concerning God's election of the nation of Israel—the son in the weaker position. It reveals how God works all things together for good—even disobedience—in a manner that results in mercy for all.

And Paul's description of *wrath* against Pharaoh, 9:15-17, clarifies more precisely the result of mercy that comes from it. Paul through his Old Testament support (Exod. 9:16) shows that God's name—his goodness—is proclaimed among the gentile nations when God's wrath is carried out. Paul narrates in this section that a reversal has occurred with Israel now in a position to receive God's wrath, not Pharaoh, which results in mercy to the gentiles (9:25-26; Hos. 1:10 and 2:23)—which Paul explains in more detail in the next section, 9:30—10:21. And this truth about God's nature establishes a theological platform for Paul to warn the gentiles in Rome concerning their pride: "Therefore, behold the kindness and severity of God: upon the ones falling, severity, but upon you, the kindness of God, if you remain in kindness; otherwise you will be cut off," 11:22.

This insight concerning God's wrath also adds to Paul's discussion of wrath in the rest of his letter. Paul's opening words in the body of the letter describe God's wrath being "revealed from heaven against all unrighteousness," 1:17. And this wrath is carried out impartially, for it is stored up for those all those who disobey, 2:8. But this does not mean that God's wrath is not merciful, for God's wrath to Pharaoh results in goodness, 9:15-17—his name proclaimed to the nations. This attribute—of God's goodness resulting from his wrath—is why Paul, after emphasizing that all authority is given by God, confidently writes that the public servant is God's administrative agent to carry out wrath "for your good," 13:4.

God's election of Israel is not a decision based on favoritism but a plan of impartial offering of his grace to all nations. Paul stresses the *impartial nature* of God earlier in his letter, 2:11, but in Romans 9–11, he demonstrates this characteristic of God as he narrates through argument God's dealings with Israel and the nations. In particular, Paul's illusion to the potter metaphor (9:21-23; Jer. 18:1-12) not only gives a visual illustration of God's sovereign authority to mold as he wills, but it also underscores God's gentle patience with the gentile nations and Israel. God relents from his wrath upon any nation who repents—God is impartial in his offering of mercy. And the reversal that occurs—with Israel in a position to receive God's wrath, 9:17-23—shows that God's election of Jacob does not insulate the Israelites from judgment, evidencing God's impartial nature. In this light, God's elective purpose is without favoritism, reserving a *remnant* of Jews and gentiles for himself, 9:25-29.

3

Israel's Failure to Hear, 9:30-10:21

Therefore, what are we saying? That gentiles did not pursue righteousness but they received righteousness and this righteousness by faith. But Israel pursued the law of righteousness; for this law they did not obtain. Why is this? Because they did not have faith; rather, they relied on works. They fell on the stone of stumbling. Even as it is written, "Behold, I placed in Zion a stumbling stone and a rock of offense and the one believing upon him will not be put to shame." Brothers, it pleases my heart to petition God on behalf of you for salvation. For I am witnessing that they have the zeal of God, but not according to knowledge. For they do not know the righteousness of God, and they seek to stand on their own righteousness, and do not submit to the righteousness of God. For the end of the law is Christ into all righteousness, for all the ones believing.

For Moses writes concerning righteousness that comes from the law, "The man doing these, he will live by them." But righteousness speaks by faith, "Do not say in your heart, who might ascend into heaven? (that is, to bring Christ down) Or who will ascend into the abyss?" (that is, to bring Christ up from the dead). But what does he say? The Word is near you, in your mouth and in your heart, that is, the word of faith that we are preaching. Because if you confess with your mouth "Jesus is Lord" and believe in your heart that God raised him from the dead, you will be saved. For the heart believes into righteousness and the mouth confesses unto salvation. For Scripture says, "All the ones believing upon Him will not be put to shame." For there is no distinction between Jew and Greek. For He is Lord of all—riches to all the ones calling upon him, for all the ones calling upon the name of the Lord will be saved.

Therefore, how do they call if they do not believe? How do they believe if they do not hear? How will they hear without someone preaching to them? And how might they preach if no one has been sent? Even as it is written: "Beautiful are the feet of the ones who brings good news." But not all obey the gospel. Isaiah says, "Lord, has anyone believed our message?"

Therefore, faith comes from hearing, and hearing by the Word of Christ.

But am I saying that they have not heard? No, they have. Their voices went out into all the earth; their words to the ends of the world. But again I ask, did Israel not know? First, Moses says, "I will make you jealous by those that are not a nation. I will make you angry by gentiles without insight." Isaiah boldly says, "I was found by those not seeking me; I revealed myself to those not asking for me." But to Israel he says, "I continually extend my hands to a disobedient and stubborn people."

Midrashic Form, 9:30—10:21

After lamenting for Israel, 9:1-5, Paul begins his argument in defense of God's faithfulness, 9:6-29, by narrating, in a sense, the story of the nation of Israel from Abraham to the Exodus, 9:6-18. And he communicates that a reversal occurs, 9:19-29—the gentiles are part of the called remnant—hinting at Israel's hardening. In this second midrashic form, 9:30—10:21, Paul depicts the cause of Israel's stumbling and how they respond unfavorably to God's word.

Since Paul's style is unlike contemporary rabbinical forms of his time, it is important to follow his step-by-step sequence and maintain awareness of his mix of forms, particularly his integration of Old Testament support, in order to better understand God's plan for Israel. In the second midrashic form, Paul incorporates a chiasm, 9:30—10:3, in which within the content of his poetic structure, Paul generalizes the main characters of his narrative—"Israel" represents "works," and "gentiles" represents "faith." At the center of the chiastic arrangement, "Christ," the Messiah, is the stone upon which Israel stumbled.

After his pronouncement of Israel's fall, he states that Christ is the fulfillment of the law, 10:4, and continues his argument by showing how Israel heard the word of God, 10:6-10, and that faith comes by hearing the word of Christ, 10:11-17. Paul supports his conclusion with an Old Testament verse list revealing God's compassionate heart for Israel and foreshadowing the mystery to be unveiled, 10:18-21. Even though this second midrashic form, 9:30—10:21, is one complete unit, the internal divisions are broken down as follows for discussion purposes:

Chiasm	9:30-10:3
Midrashic form	10:4-17
Testimonia	10:18-21

Except for the chiasm, this section shares similarities to the first midrashic form, 9:6-29 (where he began with midrashic argument, 9:6-18, with *diatribe*, 9:19-24 and a *testimonia*, 9:25-29).[1] It also might be helpful to see that this section of Paul's argument, 9:30—10:21, builds upon the previous section, 9:6-29 in theme and content. For instance, in Romans 9:33, at the center of his chiastic arrangement, Paul cites a well-known "son-stone" theme from Isaiah, which has both "messianic" and "remnant" overtones, to support his conclusion. This citation from Isaiah 8:14 connects the second midrashic form, 9:30—10:21, to the first, 9:6-29, where Paul developed a similar theme through the subtle use of key words such as "call," "son,"

---

1. Paul, throughout Romans 9–11, uses questions in such a way that presupposes an audience in diatribe style. Again, these divisions are somewhat artificial, but they aid in explanation.

"seed," and "remnant."[2] Both midrashic forms also accent Israel's failure and gentile inclusion.

In the following paragraphs, the form and then the content of each section of 9:30—10:21 is discussed. For example, the chiasm of 9:30—10:3 is analyzed, followed by the theological discussion of God's relationship to "Israel" and the "gentiles." This same order of form and content analysis is followed for the midrashic argument and *testimonia* sections—10:4-17 and 10:18-21.

Balanced Chiasm, 9:30—10:3

The chart below displays an overview of Paul's chiastic arrangement, 9:30—10:4. The antithetical parallels ("A" and "B" as well as "A" and "A^1") and synonymous parallels ("B" and "B^1") make sense as they are compared side by side. In a similar manner in which form affects meaning in reading a sonnet or some other poetical structure, so a chiasm has basic form elements. The center stanza bears the semantic weight of the unit, and in 9:32 Paul gives the reason for Israel's fall—they "relied on works." While these comparisons may seem a little cumbersome to work through at first, the end result produces clarity of meaning and a respect for Paul's literary skill:

---

2. The phrases "into salvation," "to all those believing," "righteousness of God," and "out of faith," in 10:1-6a repeat elements of Paul's initial theme in 1:16-17. For connection to the resurrection motif, see J. R. Kirk, *Unlocking Romans: Resurrection and the Justification of God* (Grand Rapids: Eerdmans, 2008), 162–63. This ties the solution of Israel's failure to Christ's death and resurrection.

	Question	
A	Gentile	9:30
B	Israel	9:31
	Question	9:32
	Conclusion ("works")	
	OT Proof	9:33
	Intercession	10:1
B^1	Israel	10:2
A^1	Israel	10:3
	Transition	10:4

Romans 10:4 serves as a transition from this chiasm into verses 10:5-17 (in a similar way that Romans 9:18 served as a transition from 9:6-18 to 9:19-29). The full text for the chiasm is written out below (see page 111).[3]

In a typical chiasm, the main topic is in the middle of the poetic structure, and the sentences around the main idea are antithetically or synonymously parallel—which means that the interpreter must think in terms of balanced comparisons. But in this particular arrangement, Paul uniquely creates dual parallels. For example, the first two verses of this chiasm, 9:30 and 9:31, are antithetically parallel: Paul contrasts the "gentiles not pursuing righteousness" with "Israel pursuing the law of righteousness." But he also parallels the "end" stanzas: the first

---

3. Francis Watson sees a slightly different chiasm here with 9:32b-33 as the "B^1" in an ABB^{1}A^1 pattern, and he finds this to be embedded in the larger chiastic structure of 9:30-10:20; Watson, *Paul, Judaism, and the Gentiles: A Sociological Approach* (Cambridge: Cambridge University Press, 1998), 326.

verse of the chiasm concerns the "righteousness" of the gentiles, 9:30, and is antithetically parallel with the last verse, 10:3, concerning the "righteousness" of Israel. In this way, the compact structure exhibits symmetry and thematic stability.

Question	Therefore, what are we saying?	30

A
That gentiles did not pursue righteousness
but they received righteousness
and this righteousness by faith.

B
But Israel pursued the law of righteousness;
for this law they did not obtain.   31

Question   Why is this?   32
Because they did not have faith;
rather, they relied on works.
They fell on the stone of stumbling.

Even as it is written,   33
Behold, I placed in Zion a stumbling stone
and a rock of offense
and the one believing upon him will not be put to shame.

Intercession   Brothers, it pleases my heart,   10:1
to petition God on behalf of you for salvation

B^1
For I am witnessing that they have the zeal of God   2
but not according to knowledge.

A^1
For they do not know the righteousness of God   3
and they seek to stand on their own righteousness
and do not submit to the righteousness of God.

Transition   For the end of the Law is Christ into all righteousness   4
for all the ones believing

Israel's Fall, 9:30–10:4

More specifically, for the purposes of explanation, this analysis begins with a comparison of themes in sequential order—9:30 to 9:31; 10:2 to 10:3. Then the themes from the "end" stanzas are compared: verse 9:30 to verse 10:3, concerning the topic "relationship with righteousness"; and verse 9:31 to verse 10:2, concerning the act of "pursuing the law." These parallel themes encase the conclusion and its support from Isaiah, 9:32-33, regarding the primary indictment that Israel relied on "works" (the first of two main assertions in 9:30—10:21). While Paul's midrashic form and style may seem complicated, when these verses are presented side by side the theological significance of Paul's arguments are not difficult to see.

Righteous Pursuit without Knowledge, 9:30-31; 10:2-3

Paul contrasts two themes–"faith and law" and "pursuing righteousness"–and two people groups–"Israel" and the "gentiles." These contrasts are shown below (underlined and in bold): Israel pursues the law of righteousness (διώκων νόμον δικαιοσύνης), but the gentiles do not pursue righteousness (μὴ διώκοντα δικαιοσύνην). Israel does not obtain the law, but the gentiles receive righteousness by faith.[4]

---

4. For Old Testament support of Israel's pursuit of righteousness, see Deut. 16:20 and Prov. 15:19. "Jew/gentile righteousness," "faith," and "law" have a close correlation to 1:16-4:28; Siegert, *Argumentation bei Paulus, Gezeigt an Röm 9-11* (WUNT 1985), 141. Ulrich Wilckens makes an important point that these chapters discuss Israel's pursuit in light of a Christian situation—in contrast to Romans 1-3 that refers to a "pre-Christian" situation; *Der Brief an die Römer* (Zürich: Neukirchen-Vluyn, 1997), 2.213. It is also apparent that the athletic metaphor should not be overlooked concerning those who did not compete as having won the prize—Paul will build upon this imagery with the stumbling stone, creating a mixed metaphor; Douglas Campbell, *Deliverance of God*, 789. For "law" and "righteousness" as parallel concepts (in Isa 51:7); see Lloyd Gaston, *Paul and the Torah* (Vancouver: University of British Columbia Press, 1987), 127. Interestingly, J. D. G. Dunn sees the emphasis in Romans 9:31 on law, not righteousness; *Romans*, 1:582. This is true concerning "Israel" where Paul seeks to equate "Israel" with "works," but the parallel stanzas in 9:30—10:3 show that Israel has not sought the Person of righteousness. For a helpful discussion on the relationship of "righteousness" and "law," see

Gentiles	the gentiles did not **pursue righteousness**	a	9:30
	but they received righteousness	b	
	and this righteousness by faith	b	
Israel	but Israel **pursued** the law of **righteousness**	a^1	9:31
	for this law they did not obtain	b^2	

After these first two stanzas, Paul gives the reason for Israel's stumble—they relied on works; they fell on the stone of stumbling, 9:32-33. After this pronouncement, the theme of "Israel's lack of knowledge" serves as a synonymous parallel between the next two verses:[5]

Israel	For I am witnessing that they have the zeal of God	a^1	10:2
	but not according to knowledge	b^2	
Israel	For they do not know the righteousness of God	b^2	10:3
	and they seek to stand on their own righteousness	a^1	
	and do not submit to the righteousness of God	a^1	

Israel does not "know" and they do not have "knowledge." These "stanzas" in 9:30-31 and 10:2-3 emphasize certain paired themes: "pursue" and "righteousness," "knowing" and "knowledge," and "law" and "faith." In addition to these sequential parallels, Paul compares and contrasts his themes in the typical chiastic

---

Dunn, "'Righteousness from the Law,'" 216–28; and Brice Martin, *Christ and the Law in Paul* (Leiden: Brill, 1989), 136f.

5. The "a's" and "b's" in the right column show Paul's synonymous and antithetical thought rhymes. These lower case letters will change based on which parallel is being compared ("a^1's" represent the type of "pursuing" or "seeking" that Israel did, and the "b^2's" refer to their "not knowing" or "not obtaining").

arrangement—where the end clauses parallel each other, as do the corresponding clauses as they move closer to the center–9:30 and 10:3; 9:31 and 10:2.

Relational Righteousness, 9:30 and 10:3

Paul mentions "righteousness" in each line of the end stanzas–9:30 and 10:3 (italics below). Five of the six uses of "righteousness" refer to the righteousness of God. The other use of righteousness refers to Israel's attempt to stand on their "own" righteousness" (10:3b; underlined below):

The Gentiles did not pursue *righteousness*	a	9:30	Gentiles
but they received *righteousness*	b		
and this *righteousness* by faith	c		
For they [Israel] did not know the *righteousness* of God	a	10:3	Israel
they seek to <u>stand on their own *righteousness*</u>	b		
and did not submit to the *righteousness* of God	c		

The first three lines describe the gentiles' relationship with Righteousness–they "did not pursue righteousness but they received righteousness . . . by faith," 9:30. The other "end" stanza finds fault with Israel's relationship with righteousness in three synonymous sentences—Israel did not know God's righteousness, they attempted to stand on their own, and they did not submit to God.

Paul demonstrates poetic symmetry by paralleling the first, second, and third lines from each stanza. In light of these comparisons, Paul communicates that neither the gentiles nor Israel knew God's righteousness, 9:30a and 10:3a. However, the gentiles received God's righteousness while Israel sought to stand on their own righteousness,

9:30b and 10:3b. And the gentiles received righteousness by faith, yet Israel did not submit to God's righteousness, 9:30c and 10:3c.

Evidently, *Paul personifies "righteousness" in these verses.* The emphasis is on "who" rather than "what." In other words, the gentiles received the "Gift" by faith, but Israel did not know, pursue, or submit to Him. This personification helps understand why Paul uses the term "righteousness" when referring to the gentiles and the phrase "law of righteousness" concerning Israel in the next comparison–9:30 to 9:31.

Lawful Pursuit, 9:31 to 10:2

The inner stanzas form another direct parallel. Paul describes Israel's pursuit and he elaborates on their failure. Each stanza comprises two antithetical lines (lit. trans.):

but Israel *pursuing the law of righteousness*	a	9:31
<u>by the law</u>, Israel did not obtain	b	
For I am a witness to them that the *zeal of God* they are having	a	10:2
<u>but not according to knowledge</u>	b	

Interestingly, when interpreting the meaning of Israel's "pursuing the law of righteousness" with the synonymous phrase "having the zeal of God" (italics above), it becomes apparent that Paul presents Israel's pursuit in a *less* negative light. Their zeal was for God, but they lacked understanding. Consequently, the synonymous parallel of Israel failing to obtain righteousness "by the law" with having zeal but "not according to knowledge" (underlined above) shows that the knowledge of the law that they practiced was not the knowledge of the law that they needed. In this way, Paul diplomatically affirms their zeal and belief in the goodness of the law, but he reveals their ignorance.[6] And with the mention of the "stumbling stone" as well as the subtle personification of "righteousness" for "Christ" in this poetic structure, it seems that Paul implies their zeal for God did not involve a proper understanding of the knowledge of Christ–a point he will explicitly clarify in the latter half of this midrashic form.

Therefore, we see subtle comparisons with resonating effects. Paul contrasts "knowledge" and "law" exposing Israel's lack of relationship to a Person. Though they knew torah, they did not know, or have a relationship with the "law of righteousness," 10:3. It is important to see that Paul does *not* equate "law of righteousness" with "works." In his second use of the term "law," he clarifies that the practice of torah ("by law") as a means to "righteousness" was not a successful approach, 9:31. Paul selectively chooses his terms to avoid confusion: his use of "law" in 9:31b ("they did not obtain the law") does not contradict the personification of the "law of righteousness" as Christ in 9:31a—"though Israel pursues the law of righteousness, by the law, they did not obtain."

Before looking at the center theme in this chiastic arrangement, 9:30—10:3, a cultural emphasis is worth noting. When Paul writes "law" and "pursuit of law" he appeals to a broader frame of reference than those with a background in Judaism. Paul mentions three times a type of "pursuing" related to law ("pursue" 9:30a, "pursue" 9:31a, "seeking" 10:3b), a popular subject among Romans. The Latin imperial powers were innately zealous in their pursuit of "just" law, and this passionate pursuit infected those around them—a desire to perfect their law for all of the world.[7]

---

6. The Jews reverently understood that the law is good, 7:21, and an embodiment of truth, 2:20, but their breaking the law and boasting in the law as a means to righteousness—2:25 and 3:27—reveals a disconnection with God.

7. Everett Ferguson in paraphrasing A. D. Nock's article—in "Religious Attitudes of the Ancient Greeks," *Proceedings of the American Philosophical Society* 85 (1942): 480—sums up this truth in

Stumbling Stone, 9:32-33

In the first midrashic section, 9:6-29, Paul does not make a direct statement about God's judgment against Israel. He highlights God's judgment against Pharaoh, 9:17, and the Edomites, 9:13. However in 9:32-33, Israel is indicted—the stone that Israel rejected was the Person they did not know. Paul merges phrases and sentences from Isaiah 8:14 and 28:16 to communicate judgment and announce hope.

Behold I place in Zion	Isa. 28:16
a stone of stumbling and rock of offense	Isa. 8:14
and the one believing in Him will not be ashamed	Isa. 28:16

In the Old Testament context of Isaiah 28, the prophet declares God's punishment to Israel. The people of Israel and the rulers of Jerusalem did not listen, and it is prophesied that Israel will be broken, ensnared, and captured. Paul selects two phrases from the Isaiah passage: "*Behold, I place a stone in Zion*" and "*the one who believes will not be ashamed*" (Isa. 28:16),[8] and in place of the hopeful phrase "precious cornerstone" from Isaiah 28:16 ("Behold I place in Zion, a tested stone, a precious cornerstone for the foundation"), he inserts judgment phrases from Isaiah 8:14—"a stone of stumbling and rock of scandal." Yet the context of Isaiah 8 is very similar to Isaiah 28 where the prophet condemns Israel for their unfaithfulness and prophesies

this way: "Rome might look like a theocracy, but it was not, for all was legal. If for Greece the measure of all things was man, for Rome the measure of all things was law. For the east the measure of all things was the king, and it will be seen that for the Jews the measure of all things was God"; Ferguson, *Backgrounds of Early Christianity*, 21.

8. In this same passage, Isaiah prophesies about the remnant: "the Lord becomes a beautiful crown to the remnant of his people" (Isa. 28:5). For a more detailed explanation of this conflation (Isa. 8:14; 28:16), see Christopher D. Stanley, *Paul and the Language of Scripture: Citation Technique in the Pauline Epistles and Contemporary Literature* (Cambridge: Cambridge University Press, 1992), 119f; and Dane Ortlund, "The Insanity of Faith: Paul's Theological Use of Isaiah in Romans 9:33," *Trinity Journal* 30, no. 2 (2009): 369–88.

that many will fall, be broken, ensnared, and captured (8:14b-15).[9] Paul also leaves out the verbal phrase "that makes them fall" from Isaiah 8:14 ("for both houses of Israel, he will be a stone that causes men to stumble and a rock that makes them fall"). By doing so, Paul imputes Israel, pronounces the cause of their stumble—the stone—and imparts hope.[10]

"Stone of stumbling" may be taken to mean "remnant" or it may be refer to the "messiah." Paul's lament begins with the announcement concerning the "messiah" who descends from the patriarchs according to their "seed," 9:1-5. While "messiah" is directly mentioned in 9:4, in the most recent context in 9:6-29, "seed" may instead be a subtle reference to the "remnant" (see vv. 27-28) where Paul emphasizes key words that clue the listener into a "called-son-seed" wordplay. This repetition and the semantic flow of the argument leads the reader into this present midrashic form where a "stone" quotation is selected, 9:33. This theme could have come from a collection of well-known "stone-son" passages from Judaism where "stone-son" imagery refers to the "messiah" or the "remnant." The two interpretations seem interchangeable (in a similar way that Christians speak of "Christ" and "the body of Christ"). Nonetheless, Paul's reference to Isaiah 28:16, a verse that includes the phrase "precious cornerstone," likely refers to the Messiah, as in Romans

---

9. Paul draws from the only two contexts in the Old Testament where the verbatim use of the verbs "broken, ensnared, and captured" (ונשברו ונוקשו ונלכדו) 'are used—Isa. 28:13 and 8:15.

10. The deliberate rearranging of the Isaiah 28:16 text by dropping its middle and inserting two "stone" phrases from Isaiah 8:14 underscores Israel's failure due to their lack of faith; Shiu-Lun Shum, *Paul's Use of Isaiah: A Comparative Study of Paul's Letter to the Romans and the Sibylline and Qumran Sectarian Texts* (Tübingen: Mohr, 2002), 217. Israel's stumble resonates with the context of Isaiah 8:14 and 29:21 (and with Paul's personal experience; Gal. 1:23). For the view of a collection of oral stone texts related to Jesus, see Ernst Käsemann, *A Commentary on Romans*, trans. and ed. Geoffrey W. Bromily (Grand Rapids: Eerdmans, 1980), 279.

9:5.[11] This interpretation also fits with Paul's personification of "Righteousness," 9:30–10:3.

Personification

When Paul describes "righteousness" in six different lines of his chiasm, 9:30 and 10:3, he artistically employs two general literary characters: "Israel" represents the ones who pursue by "works," and likewise, the "gentiles" are the ones who receive righteousness by "faith." It is doubtful that Paul means that "all" Israel are without faith, nor is he suggesting that "all" gentiles pursue the "righteousness of God." If this were the case, the literary use of "Israel" and the "gentiles" would come into direct contradiction with his message, particularly with his recent conclusion that God calls not only from the Jews but also from the gentiles, 9:25, and conflict with his gospel message where a Jew is a Jew because of the Spirit's work in the heart, 2:28-29.

Apparently Paul defines "faith" and "works" in his chiastic arrangement in order to pronounce judgment. Again, he "narrates" Israel's salvation history by using midrashic arguments supported with Old Testament texts. In this way, the "stone of stumbling" causes a division between those who receive "righteousness" by faith and those who pursue "righteousness" without knowledge. In other words, Paul's two domains—Israel as "works"; gentiles as "faith"—create two identities. These different identities *reinforce* the subtle personification of a Person—the "Stone of stumbling" and "Righteousness."

---

11. "Upon him"—which is not in Isaiah 28:16b LXX—refers to the stone laid in Zion, a likely reference to the Messiah in Paul's view. This "divinely appointed means" is based on Paul's Damascus experience; see Shum, *Paul's Use*, 221–22. Interestingly, in Romans 10:13—an allusion to Isaiah 8:14, another "stone" passage—Yahweh is rendered "Lord" in the LXX.

It is important to recognize Paul's literary purpose. He chooses these generalizations concerning the two people groups ("Israel" as "works" and "gentiles" as "faith, 9:30—10:3) to make a theological point concerning the reason for Israel's fall. In a few verses, he will move from the limitations of his literary categories to underscore God's character—"For there is no distinction between Jew and Greek," 10:11-12. As will be explained, this not only adds strength to the case for Paul's use of personification, but it also makes clear his main idea concerning what it means to "hear" the word of Christ, 10:17.

Intercession, 10:1

1   Brothers, it pleases my heart

    also to petition God on behalf of them for their salvation

A personal emphasis from Paul signifies a change of tone concerning the Israel's future. While Paul has inserted an intercessory phrase "Isaiah cries out on behalf of," 9:27, and has referred to God's compassion, 9:26 and 29, he has not made a personal heartfelt expression since his opening lament. In his indictment of Israel for falling upon the "Stone," Paul's heart does seem to lighten—portending a sense of hope for Israel. Rhetorically speaking, if Israel has stumbled, the concern becomes the duration of their plight—"Is it a permanent stumbling?" Paul here in 10:1 expresses a positive energy in his prayer for them.[12]

Paul's zeal to reach the gentiles is influenced by the love for his people, 15:14f. The mystery he reveals (particularly in 11:11f) makes known how God will use gentile inclusion to arrest the attention of

---

12. The "them" obviously refers to "Israel," those who did not know "Righteousness," the stone of stumbling.

the Jews. And as discussed previously, the focus on Paul's personal feelings—9:1-5 and 10:1—also reflects God's heart, as Paul explains the wisdom and compassion of God in these midrashic passages.

From a grammatical perspective, Paul strings together several subordinate clauses introduced by the explanatory conjunction "for" (γάρ; verses 2, 3, 4, and 5). Thus the verses follow in a concatenate manner to elaborate upon Paul's petition for salvation. Such an arrangement suggests several possibilities. First, the latter half of the chiasm, 10:2-3, serves as an explanation of Paul's central point, 9:30-32, concerning Israel's stumble and reliance on "works." Second, compassion, and not merely logical reasoning, influences the progression of these passages. Third, 9:30—10:21 is a complete unit in which each section builds toward or supports Paul's conclusion, 10:17, and in which the main theme of "righteousness" is elaborated on (evidenced by the explanatory conjunction γάρ)." In this way, "righteousness" is related to what occurs in the "heart" of God, of Paul, of Israel in the wilderness, and of the gentiles—10:6, 8-13.

A Roman Suggestion, 10:4

4   For the end of the Law is Christ

into all righteousness for all the ones believing

In the above transition sentence, Paul finalizes the carefully constructed chiasm of 9:30—10:3 and extends his use of personification while reiterating a main theme of his letter—"righteousness for all who believe" (e.g., 1:16 and 4:11). The phrase τέλος νόμου has received considerable scholarly attention and generally means (1) "end" of the Law; (2) "fulfillment" of the Law; or (3) it could carry the dual sense of "end" and "fulfillment."[13]

"End" (τέλος) can mean fulfillment, perfection, or completion. Important here is the Greek understanding. From a Greek mindset, τέλος depicts maturity or perfection as demonstrated in their art and sculptures. It might be that Paul's vision for Israel involves this process of being molded by God, 9:21-23, reaching a "fullness" according to God's grace (see 11:12). However, such a connotation seems narrow.

It might be that Paul interprets Christ as the fulfillment, completion, or perfection of the law in the sense of "moving toward an end." Torah, then, would have been given to Israel at a previous, imperfect stage. Perceiving torah and Christ in this progressive sense may contradict Paul's argument that follows, 10:6-10, that Christ has always been the fulfillment of torah, but now embodies the gospel message, the kerygma.[14] And since 10:4 serves as a transition sentence, the content that follows would give specific insight into Paul's meaning.[15]

13. Much of the discussion focuses on the meaning of τέλος; for overview, see C. E. B. Cranfield, *A Critical and Exegetical Commentary on the Epistle to the Romans* (Edinburgh: T & T Clark, 1975–79), 516f.

14. Based on a comparison to Philo and Cicero, Ira Jolivet posits that Paul meant to be ambiguous for the purpose of harmony between his Jewish and Gentile audiences—he meant to infer both "end" and "fulfillment"; Jolivet, "Christ the TELOS in Romans 10:4 as Both Fulfillment and Termination of the Law," *Restoration Quarterly* 51, no. 1 (2009): 13–30. Rhyne is correct in that the central thrust of this section, 9:30—10:21, concerns the nature of Israel's disobedience and guilt concerning the gospel; Rhyne, "Nomos Dikaiosynēs and the Meaning of Romans 10:4," *CBQ* 47, no. 3 (1985): 499. End as "termination" seems to nullify Paul's scriptural support and does not contribute to the personification of Christ as "Law." However, "termination" does portray a powerful picture of One who has power to do away with the law. M. A. Seifrid offers a compromise: "culmination" of the law, which implies goal and end; *Justification by Faith*, 248. For a thorough review of the debate, see Thomas Schreiner, "Paul's View of the Law in Romans 10:4-5," *Westminster Theological Journal* 55, no. 1 (1993): 113–24. Based on temporal sense and the rest of Paul's usage, Schreiner interprets "end" as the likely intention.

The personification of "Righteousness" should be kept in mind here—Romans 9:4, 6-8. The law points to faith in Christ. There is no proof of justification by works; J. Ross Wagner, *Heralds of the Good News: Isaiah and Paul "in Concert" in the Letter to the Romans* (Leiden: Brill, 2002), 163–64. For the stylistic device, "speech in character," and personification in theses verses, see Thomas Tobin, *Paul's Rhetoric in Its Contexts: The Argument of Romans* (Peabody, MA: Hendrickson, 2004), 343. Martin argues the translation "for righteousness" based on word order; Martin, *Christ and the Law*, 62. Yet it is important to see personification as an indirect emphasis: obedience from faith seems to be the direct covenantal emphasis in Torah contexts (e.g., Deut. 9:4-5 and Rom. 9:6).

Paul does use personification in the verses that follow,[16] and it might be that Paul's word choice of τέλος in relation to the law would appeal to a Roman audience at the center of imperial justice. Though the Romans imitated Greek forms, culture, and art, the Romans adjudicated the rule of law to all imperial peoples. It was the Roman Cicero who promoted the belief that all nations have a core set of values, a natural law (*ius gentium*). And it is interesting that Paul with his audience in mind writes in his letter in a judicious and straightforward manner, pronouncing judgment, 3:17-31, on those whose law is written on hearts. In his reference to the Messiah, personified as the "Stone," he illustrates a forceful picture of the cause of Israel's stumble, 9:30—10:3. Thus the phrase "end of the law" may play upon the concept of the Roman legal system where all legislative authority ends in Rome.

This makes sense in light of the unifying force of the emperor. He became the "supreme judge of appeal" in place of the Roman people as a whole.[17] He could intervene in all areas controlled by the state when necessary (*imperium proconsulare maius*).[18] Paul's recipients, as well as people throughout the empire, observed the political and religious symbolism, which portrayed the emperor as the source of peace, unity, and provision, a personification of Roman virtue.[19] Citizens and peoples throughout the known world worshipped in their private homes during gatherings and banquets by pouring out libations on behalf of the emperor's name.[20] When Paul uses the term

---

15. It is important to note that 9:4 serves as a connection to Paul's initial theme and outline (1:16-17).
16. Richard B. Hays, *Echoes of Scripture in the Letters of Paul* (New Haven, CT: Yale University Press, 1989), 78.
17. Goodman, *Roman World*, 98.
18. Ibid., 139.
19. This is evidenced in the coinage propaganda; see J.R. Fears, "Cult of Virtues and Roman Imperial Ideology," *ANRW* 2, 17, .2 (1981): 895–96.
20. Dio, *Rom. Hist.* 51:19:6-7. Also see, Brent, *The Imperial Cult*, 19f.

τέλος νόμου, he may be supplanting the Roman imperial concept with the truth of Christ's lordship over all, not only as an enforcer of righteousness, but as the Law-giver himself.

Poetic Sequence, 10:5-21

After indicting Israel for not knowing "Righteousness," 9:30—10:3, Paul boldly states that Christ is the end of the law—the one who brings about a righteousness for "all" who believe, 10:4—and then elaborates upon "righteousness" in a "pesher" style midrash, 10:6-8. And in a poetic "stair-step" sequence, he leads the listener to a summary statement: "Therefore, faith comes by hearing, and hearing by the word of Christ," 10:17. In support of his conclusion, he quotes four verses from the Psalms and the Prophets (*testimonia*), which juxtapose the theme of the gospel message being sent to all of the earth against the theme of Israel's hearing but not understanding.[21]

Whereas in the previous midrashic form, 9:6-29, Paul follows his statements with Old Testament verses in order to clarify and explain his main points, in this section, 10:5-21, Paul initiates with Scripture and then gives his commentary. Due to the compact and integrated nature of this passage, this section is divided into five parts for explanation purposes: 10:5, 6-10, 11-13, 14-17, and 18-21.

Below is an overview of Paul's thought flow, which highlights his use of Scriptural support and his major themes—"righteousness," "salvation for all," and "hearing" (in bold):

---

21. In this way, Paul's verse list demonstrates thematic unity with 9:30—10:17.

Transition: Christ is the end of the law	4
Moses writes – **righteousness** of the law	5
Lev. 18:5	
Moses writes – **righteousness** of faith	6-10
Deut. 9:4	
Deut. 30:11-14	
Scripture speaks – **salvation** for *all* who believe, Jew and Greek	11-13
Isa. 28:16	
Joel 2:32	
Preachers are sent to call but not *all* **hear** the gospel	14-17
Isa. 52:7	
Isa. 53:1	
Conclusion: Faith comes by **hearing** the word of Christ	
Verse List: All of the earth **hears**, but Israel does not know	18-21
Ps. 19:4	
Deut. 32:21	
Isa. 65:1	
Isa. 65:2	

What cannot be discerned from the above outline is that Paul strings together themes (or "key words" such as ἐπικαλέω, πιστεύω, ἀκούω, and κηρύσσω) that lead to his main idea concerning the source of faith: hearing the word of Christ, 10:17. It is also relevant to point out the key words in verses 5-14, which are summarized in verses 15-16 in reverse order, poignantly emphasizing for the reader that Israel has not heard.

Paul continues to "narrate" the story of Israel within the overall framework of a lament—9:1-5 and 11:33-36—using logical argument with a mix of literary devices. Paul began the body of his argument with the topics of the "promise" and the "election" of God to the patriarchs, as well as God's deliverance of Israel out of Egypt, 9:6-23. Now he recounts Moses' words to the Israelites on their journey (see the full text of 10:5-21 below).

For Moses writes concerning righteousness that comes from the Law that: 5

  "The man doing these, he will live by them."

But righteousness speaks by faith,   6

  Do not say in your heart

    "Who might ascend into heaven?"

      (that is to bring Christ down) or

    "Who will ascend into the abyss?"   7

      (that is to bring Christ up from the dead)

But what does he say?   8

  "The Word is near you

  in your mouth and in your heart."

    that is the word of faith that we are preaching

  because if you confess with your mouth "Jesus is Lord"   9

    and believe in your heart that God raised him from the dead

      you will be saved.

  For the heart believes into righteousness   10

  and the mouth confesses unto salvation

For Scripture says,   11

  "All the ones believing upon Him will not be put to shame,"

    For there is no distinction between Jew and Greek,   12

    For He is Lord of all,

  Riches to all the ones calling upon him,

  For all the ones calling upon the Name of the Lord will be saved 13

Therefore, how do they call if they do not believe?   14

and how do they believe if they do not hear?

and how do they hear without someone preaching to them?

and how might they preach if no one has been sent?   15

even as it is written:

"beautiful are the feet of the ones who brings good news."

But not all obey the gospel,   16

Isaiah says,

"Lord, has anyone believed our message?"

Therefore, faith comes from hearing, and hearing by the Word of Christ.   17

Hearing Faith, 10:5-17

Righteous Living, 10:5

After referencing Abraham and the Exodus, 9:6-18, Paul now draws from Israel's experience in the wilderness, and at the same time, in verse 5, continues his theme of "righteousness" concerning the law (9:30—10:4).[22]

5   For Moses writes concerning righteousness that comes from the Law that:

"the man doing these, he will live by them."

---

22. Considering the semantic style and structure of Paul's thought flow and support as well as his sequence of subordinate clauses (the use of the explanatory γάρ in verses 5, 6-10, 11-13, 14-17), the argument that follows explains verse 4 leading to the conclusion that "faith comes by hearing and hearing by the word of Christ." Furthermore, Kirk compares the vocabulary between 10:1-6a and 1:16-17 to show a climactic emphasis in chapter 10; see Kirk, *Unlocking Romans*,162f, 206–12. But it might be helpful to note that 1:18 is also an important theme in each section of the letter.

Paul quotes God's words to Moses—"the man doing these, he will live by them" (10:5; Lev. 18:5).[23] Since Paul has concluded that the Messiah brings an "end to the law," he now shows how God's words to Moses *for the Israelites* affirm the means to "righteousness by faith."[24] But Paul's tone concerning the law changes to a more neutral one, since he has not yet set aside the general term "Israel" in relation to "works."[25] He now follows the rabbinic practice of explaining a verse with Old Testament texts and personal comment, 10:6-8.

When Paul's cites Leviticus 18:5, it is not for certain what phrase he stresses for this midrashic argument. He could be emphasizing: (a) the impossibility of attaining life; (b) the interpretation of "the one man" as Christ, accenting Christ's obedience; or (c) the clause "he will live." The first possibility, that Paul might stress a person's inability to attain the law, places the content of verse 5 in contrast with verses 6-8 (strengthened by the use of γράφει in verse 5 and λέγει in verse 6 with the conjunction δὲ). In this way, faith is contrasted with the law, or the impossibility of achieving righteousness by the

---

23. Akio Ito recognizes a relationship between Leviticus 18:5 and Deuteronomy 30 based on orality and literacy; "The Written Torah and the Oral Gospel: Romans 10:5-13 in the Dynamic Tension between Orality and Literacy," *Novum Testamentum* 48, no. 3 (2006): 234–60. Paul understands himself as living and working in the tradition of the "herald" of Isaiah 52, stressing the literacy of Torah when he uses the phrase, "Moses writes" in Isaiah 52.

24. Evidently, Paul extrapolates on the theme of "living" by faith (1:17, 6:4f; 8:4f), but here writes specifically concerning the Israelites. The focus is on Israel's stumble. (For a similar argument concerning his own life, see Phil. 3:9.) Schreiner points out that Paul "does not make a global statement on the relationship between gospel and law here. Instead his point is an exegetical one" ("Paul's view of the Law," 113–24).

25. Here his argument takes a different approach concerning the theme of "life" compared to his first two major sections of his letter (1:17—5:11 and 5:12—8:39). In the opening statement of the body of his letter (1:16), Paul announces that he is not ashamed of the gospel "for it is the power of God unto salvation to all who believe—first the Jew and then the gentile." He then supports the righteousness of God revealed with a quotation from Habakkuk: "the righteous will live by faith" (Rom. 1:17; Hab. 2:4). This life stands in contrast to God's wrath revealed against unrighteousness (1:18—3:20), yet Paul demonstrates that God is impartial in his judgments and righteousness is for all who believe (2:6f; 4:1f). In 5:12—8:39, Paul describes the "righteousness" that comes through Christ for the many who believe (e.g, 5:17-18, 21; 6:4, 22-23; 8:2, 6, 10). And here 10:5-21, Paul emphasizes God's impartiality concerning "life" as it relates to the opportunity of the children of Israel to obey the Law in the wilderness.

pursuit of the law. If this were the case, "termination," the definition of "end" in verse 4, would be likely, making obedience to torah synonymous with "works." However, the pairing of obedience to torah and "works" seems out of context with Paul's emphasis in 10:4, 10:6-8, and with the chiasm of 9:30-10:3.

Paul's argument in 9:30-10:3 distinguishes Israel's behavior, their self-righteousness, and their lack of relationship as the problem, rather than torah observance. As will be shown, in verses 6-8, the law itself contains the gospel message and is not in tension with Christ. Apparently, Paul personifies the "law of righteousness" (9:31), "righteousness" (10:6), and torah (10:7). These literary personifications demonstrate a sense of unity between Christ and the law. To make better sense of Paul's use of the words γράφει, λέγει, and δὲ, it is possible that Paul intended the speakers, Moses and "righteousness," to be compared for the purpose of showing dissimilarity with the content of the Law (Leviticus and Deuteronomy).

It also may be that Paul highlights the "one man"—Christ, his obedience and fulfillment of the law. This makes sense in light of the idea of τέλος in verse 4 as "fulfillment." Yet Paul does not seem to be accenting Christ as a perfect "doer" of the law. This could be misunderstood in the sense of Christ as an example for Israel to earn righteousness, which would lessen the relevance of the latter half of the verse, "he will live in them," in relation to the context of verses 6-8.

It is more likely that Paul chooses this Old Testament citation because of the clause "he will live." Paul seems to imply that the phrase "having done [these]" refers to a doing "by faith." Not only is this interpretation parallel with a major theme of the letter, "the righteous shall live by faith" (1:17), it also elucidates God's character in his covenant relationship with Israel. God did not require perfection from Israel but faith in God's atonement for sin. Paul seeks to show here the congruence between "life" and "law" then, and "life" and "righteousness" in the present. Furthermore, this understanding—"living by faith" as the main emphasis of Paul's citation of Leviticus 18:5—neither contradicts the "unattainableness" of torah nor Christ's perfect obedience. Paul now elaborates on what "living in them" means, 10:6-7.

The Present Word, 10:6-10

In support of his Leviticus quotation ("he will live"), Paul quotes from Deuteronomy 9:4 and 30:11-14. In both Deuteronomy contexts, Moses speaks to the Israelites before they cross the Jordan River. In Deuteronomy 9:4, Moses wants the people to know that as God goes before them and defeats stronger nations, each person is "not to say in his heart" that their righteousness caused God to do this. Instead, God acts because of the wickedness of the nations.

Paul merges this imperative, "Do not say in your heart," from Deuteronomy 9:4 into the citation from Deuteronomy 30:11-14. Apparently, *Paul inserts the theme of "heart" to form a clear parallel to the verses that follow* ("heart" with regard to looking beyond to the resurrection in verses 6-7; and "heart" with regard to the "word of Christ" unto righteousness in verses 8-10, *as this fits with the Deuteronomic context of loving God with all of the heart*). Moses tells the Israelites that "life" and prosperity or death and disaster are set before them. If they turn to God, even if in exile, he will bless them. He will cleanse their hearts and their children's hearts, so that they will be able to love him and "live." Moses assures them that the commandment to love God with all of their heart and mind is not too difficult or far removed (Rom. 10:6-10; Moses' words are in bold):

But righteousness speaks by faith: 6

Do not say in your heart, "Who might ascend into heaven?"

(that is to bring Christ down) or

"Who will descend into the abyss?"   7

(that is to bring Christ up from the dead)

But what does he say?   8

"The Word is near you in your mouth and in your heart"

that is the word of faith that we are preaching

because if you confess with your mouth "Jesus is Lord"   9

and believe in your heart that God raised him from the dead,

you will be saved

For the heart believes into righteousness   10

and the mouth confesses unto salvation

Paul's running commentary and use of personification demonstrate that the "law" that Moses gave and the "word of faith" that Paul preaches carry the same message concerning Christ.[26] God desires a humble people who do not pursue self-righteousness (Rom. 10:6; Deut. 9:4) for it is through Christ and his resurrection (Rom. 10:6-7; Deut. 30:12-13) that righteousness has been made known. Paul

---

26. Steven R. Coxhead, "Deuteronomy 30:11-14 as a Prophecy of the New Covenant in Christ," *Westminster Theological Journal* 68, no. 2 (2006): 315f. The running line-by-line Pesher commentary is similar to Qumran exegesis (1QpHab) in which the community looks forward to Christ (whether they knew it or not); Hays, *Echoes*, 79. But Paul here uses the Old Testament more so as a basis for principles; see Seifrid, "Paul's Approach "Paul's Approach to the Old Testament in Rom 10:6-8," *Trinity Journal* 6, no. 1 (1985): 3–37. Romans 10:5-10 functions as an intense paradox of Israel's unbelief and God's grace, with the Messiah identified with Torah and Wisdom (e.g., Bar. 3:29-30); ibid., 80–82. For a more in depth look at Paul's citation in Romans 9–11, see Stanley, *Paul and the Language of Scripture,* 103–71.

intentionally replaces the word "sea" from the Old Testament text (Deut. 30:13) with the word "abyss" (Rom. 10:7) and by doing so personifies torah (a common literary practice in wisdom literature).[27]

Paul clarifies that "the word near you" described in Deuteronomy is the "word of faith" that he and other Christians proclaim. Paul explains that the "word in your mouth" is the act of confession—"Jesus is Lord"—and this "word in your heart" is the act of believing that God raised Jesus from the dead. Acting upon the word results in salvation, 10:8-9. Paul restates this truth, "For the heart believes into righteousness, and the mouth confesses unto salvation," 10:10.

Thus with literary style, Paul contrasts the knowing of the Person of Jesus ("Righteousness") with Israel's not knowing the "Righteousness" of God.[28] In the preceding passage, 9:30—10:3, Paul contrasts gentile "righteousness by faith" with Israel's "pursuing the law of righteousness" by works. For Israel stumbled on the stumbling stone, 9:33—Christ—who is the "end" of the law, 10:4. In order to show how torah—righteousness from the law—proclaims and embodies Christ, 10:5-6, Paul discontinues his comparison between the "gentiles" and "Israel." He quotes Leviticus and Deuteronomy to demonstrate that obedience results in "life," and in a step-by-step manner, explains the phrase "in your heart" (Deut. 9:4 and 30:12) in relation to the "word of Christ." Thus it is important to see (1) that Paul associates "righteousness from the law" with "life," not with the selfish ambition of the Israelites, and (2) how torah speaks about this "Righteousness" as personal and relational. Through preaching, this

---

27. "Sea" and "abyss" are closely related; Douglas J. Moo, *The Epistle to the Romans* (Grand Rapids: Eerdmans, 1996), 655.
28. The phrase "Lord of all" (v. 9) is a formulation proclaiming "Christ as the one replacing the emperor in establishing a new realm of plentitude in which all are treated equally"; Robert Jewett, *Romans: A Commentary*, ed. Eldon Jay Epp (Minneapolis: Fortress Press, 2007), 622.

faith in the resurrection is received, resulting in a confession of Jesus' lordship.[29]

Called Remnant, 10:11-13

Since the gentiles have received "righteousness" by faith, 9:30, and those who believe receive "righteousness" through the proclamation of the "word" of faith, 10:8-10,[30] it may appear that Paul stresses the point that the gentiles are "in" and Israel is "out." But this is not the case.

Paul alludes to three different sentences in the Old Testament that refer to "all" who call on or believe in the Lord (Isaiah 28:16, Psalms 86:5, and Joel 2:32).[31] Significantly, Paul adds the word "all" (πᾶς) in verse 11, which is not in the Isaiah 28:16 text. This addition, along with the content of his comments in between his quotations, reinforce a central theme of Paul's letter—"all who believe":

29. Hays understands Deuteronomy 30 as a "metaphor" for Christian proclamation in Romans 10:5-10. The "present" word of God is the same word of God to Israel in Torah—the function here is to intensify Israel's unbelief; Hays, *Echoes*, 83. For Romans 10:8-13 and 10:4 as Christological and resurrection, see Kirk, *Unlocking Romans*,172–80. Desta Heliso argues for 9:30—10:13 as expansion and explication of Romans 1:16-17; *Pistis and the Righteous One: A Study of Romans 1:17 against the Background of Scripture and Second Temple Jewish Literature* (Tübingen: Mohr Siebeck, 2007), 191f.

30. Jewett notes the connection between the "Personified Righteousness by Faith" in relation to "all" in 10:11 and Paul's use of honor and shame language in 1:14; *Romans*, 622.

31. Isaiah 28:16 does not have "all" (πᾶς) but "the one believing" (ὁ πιστεύων), which connotes a sense of "everyone who believes." See also 9:33.

For Scripture says,	11	
For everyone [πας] who believes upon him will not be put to shame		Isa. 28:11
For there is no distinction between Jew and Greek,	12	
For he is Lord of all [πας],		
Riches *to everyone [πας]* who calls upon him.		Ps. 86:5
For everyone [πας] who calls upon the name of the Lord will be saved.	13	Joel 2:32

Paul quotes Isaiah 28:16 for the second time. Earlier he wrote, *"Behold, I placed in Zion a stumbling stone* and a rock of scandal, *and the one believing upon him will not be put to shame"*—that supported the central theme of his chiasm, 9:30—10:3, that Israel fell on the stumbling stone. But here in 10:11-13, Paul corrects the limitation of his previous metaphor, 9:30—10:3, where all "Israel" was stigmatized with the label "works" incurring judgment, 9:32-33, and now establishes hope for them, creating coherency in this section, 9:30—10:21.[32]

Paul's repetition of words and his thought pattern demonstrate a sequence of parallels. Paul affirms the relationship between "righteousness of the law" and "life," and at the same time contrasts the "righteousness of the law" with "righteousness of faith" that places emphasis on the heart—10:5-6 (see thought rhyme below):

32. The phrase ἐπ' αὐτῷ (Rom. 10:11) is not in the LXX (Isa. 28:16b). This phrase refers to the stone laid in Zion, the Messiah; Shum, *Paul's Use,* 221. In essence, Paul applies monotheistic language to Christ (Rom. 10:12); ibid., 223. Isaiah sees the triumphant home coming occurring in Zion; Motyer, *Prophecy of Isaiah,* 416.

a	righteousness of law	5
b	live in them	
a	righteousness of faith	6
b	in your heart	

Paul then adds commentary to the Deuteronomic context (see thought pattern outlined below) concerning the resurrection and this leads to the bold statement that whoever confesses Jesus Christ as Lord and "believes" in his heart will be saved, 10:10:

a	righteousness of <u>faith</u>	6
b	in your heart	
c	—resurrection of Christ	6b-7
b	in your heart, in your mouth	8
c	—the word of <u>faith</u> that we preach	
b	in your heart, *confess* and <u>believe</u>	9
c	—resurrection unto **salvation**	
	the heart <u>believes</u> unto righteousness,	10
	confess unto **salvation**	

"Righteousness of faith" ("a") is described in parallel phrases as "in your heart" ("b's") concerning the "resurrection," which is the "word of faith that we preach" ("c's"). Thus in verse 10, Paul brings together several key thoughts: "faith" or "believing"[33] (underlined above), "confessing" (italics), and "salvation" (bold).

33. To support this, Paul cites Scripture that contains the word "believe" (πιστεύω—Rom. 10:11; Isa. 28:16).

In verses 11-12, Paul continues his stress on the act of "believing" by repeating the main theme of God's impartial call—"there is no distinction between Jew and Greek" (e.g., 1:16, 2:11, and 3:22). Notice the repetition of the words "all" and "call" in the abbreviated outline below:

All who believe	11
no distinction between Jew and Greek	12
Lord of **all**	
riches to **all** *who call*	
For **all** *who call* on the Lord will be saved	13

In this way, Paul summarizes the Lordship of Christ from the torah contexts, 10:9-10, and emphasizes the theme "all who believe" by stating that Christ is "Lord of all."[34]

It is likely that Paul also alludes to Psalm 86:5 with his phrase "riches to everyone who calls upon him." Interestingly, in the first mention of "riches" in his letter, Paul reprimands the Jew for showing contempt for the "riches of God's kindness" and for God's forbearance and patience, 2:4. Paul's use of "riches" in Romans serves as a synecdoche for the characteristics of God. Likewise, in Psalm 86:5, the Psalmist speaks to the Lord, "For you, Lord, are kind, gentle, and great in mercy to *all those calling upon you*." Thus, Paul in his

---

34. Notice that Paul uses the identical adjective in the phrase "the *same* Lord of all." The adjective πᾶς (10:11) is not in the LXX or MT of Isaiah 28:16. For theological significance, see Hyon Suk Huang, *Die Verwendung* πᾶς, 235 and 264. Furthermore, "all" with the phrase "not being put to shame" (καταισχύνω) carries the sense of vindication on the last day; Dunn, *Romans*, 619. Cranfield stresses that "all" references Jews; *Critical and Exegetical Commentary*, 533; and Dunn stresses gentile inclusion, *Romans*, 620. Gentile inclusion is Paul's point in vv. 11-13; Räisänen, *Paul and Law*, 175. E. P. Sanders, on the other hand, understands Paul's line of argument in 9:30–10:13 to stress lack of faith in Christ versus doing the law; *Paul, the Law, and the Jewish People* (Philadelphia: Fortress Press, 1993), 42.

mention of "riches" refers to God's mercy, and his allusion to the Psalmist's phrase "who call upon him" indicates Paul's intentional thought rhyme in a string of parallels.[35]

Yet the primary import rests not on human initiative but upon God's act of calling. Paul makes this point clear earlier when he discusses God's election and calling of the remnant, made up of both Jew and the gentile, 9:11-29. Here in 10:13, Paul quotes the prophet Joel's words—"all those who call upon him will be saved," Joel 2:32—but what Paul seems to be elucidating with the quotation is that God's "call" remains unchanged—in Joel's day, in Moses' day, 10:6-8, and in his own time. Interestingly, Paul does not state explicitly the latter part of the verse, which concerns the remnant (Joel 2:32):

> And it will be that all who call upon the name of the Lord will be saved,
>
> for on Mount Zion and in Jerusalem there will be deliverance,
>
> as the Lord has said,
>
> *among the survivors whom the Lord calls*

Likely, he implicitly underscores God's character in calling a "remnant."[36]

---

35. It is difficult to dismiss an imperial context here. Claiming that Christ is "Lord of all" not only implies that Christ shares the nature of God (9:5) but plays upon the Roman slogan of "Caesar as Lord." Paul's phrase "all those who call upon him" echoes the cultural phrase of "calling upon a god or Caesar," a common act of worship. Paul's two-front approach in looking at the imperial context in addition to the Old Testament context makes sense of his personification in 10:4 where Paul announces Christ as "end of the Law," 10:4.

36. "Survivor" (שריד) is used synonymously for the "remnant." Also, the phrase "among the survivors whom the Lord calls" affirms the theological reality of predestination, Rom. 8:30.

Christ's Word, 10:14-17

After faulting "Israel" for not knowing "righteousness, 9:30—10:3, and after exalting Christ as Lord for all who believe, 10:4-13, Paul shifts his focus to "hearing" in verses 14-17.

Therefore, how do they call if they do not believe?	14
How will they believe if they do not *hear*?	
How will they *hear* without someone preaching to them?	
and how will they be preached to if they are not sent?	15
Even as it is written,	
Beautiful are the feet of the ones bringing good news.	16
But not all *obey* the gospel,	
Isaiah says,	
"Lord, has anyone believed our message?"	
Therefore, faith comes by *hearing*	17
and *hearing* by the word of Christ.	

Paul may be synonymously summarizing the content of 10:6-13 in verses 14-15a:

v.14a	"call"	v.13	"all those who *call* upon him"
v.14b	"believe"	v.11	"all those who *believe*"
v.14c	"hear"	v.10	"confess"
v.14d	"preach"	v.8	"*preaching*"

But regardless of whether this is an intended "reverse" thought rhyme, he does follow a stair-step thought pattern in vv. 14–15 (as demonstrated in the abbreviated pattern below):[37]

	call, believe	14
	believe-hear	
	hear-preach	
	preach-sent	15
	beautiful feet-good news	
	"Not all obeyed [υπακουω] the good news"	16
	"Who believed our message [ακοη]"	
Conclusion	Faith from hearing [ακοη],	
	and hearing from word [ακοη] of Christ	17

In essence, Paul presents credible evidence that Israel has not "heard" (10:16)—a verdict of disobedience. Several phrases in 10:14–17 contain the root "hear" (ακου- or ακοα-; underlined below):

. . . and how will they believe if they do not <u>hear</u>? How will they <u>hear</u> without someone preaching to them? . . . beautiful are the feet of the

37. Paul's stair-step pattern in verses 14-18 leads to a grievous reality that Israel has heard. Paul's arrangement by key phrases forms an unbroken chain of pairs: call upon, call upon (ἐπικαλέω, 13-14), believed-believe (πιστεύω, 14), hear-hear (ἀκούω, 14), preach-preach (κηρύσσω, 14-15), "sent" (ἀποστέλλω) paired with the thought rhyme of "how beautiful are the feet who bring good news," gospel-gospel (εὐαγγελίζω and εὐαγγέλιον, 15-16), obey with its root hear of hearing (ὑπακούω) and message with its root (ἀκοή, 16), and believed-faith (πιστεύω and πίστις, 16-17). This leads to the last clause where "hearing" paired with "hearing" results in the conclusion that Israel "did not hear" the word of Christ (ἀκοῆς, διὰ ῥήματος Χριστοῦ, 17). The scriptural quotation from Isaiah 53:3 is reversed to make the parallel work. Verse 16 seems to break the poetic chain, but it does not. Verse 16a continues the "gospel" theme of v. 15b, and introduces disobedience. Verse 16a and 16b are synonymous (statement with Old Testament proof); therefore, the thought rhyme of 16a, "not all obeyed" thematically pairs with the question "has anyone believed our message?" in 16b.

ones bringing good <u>news</u>. But not all <u>obey</u> the gospel. Isaiah says, "Lord, has anyone believed our message?" Therefore, faith comes by <u>hearing</u> and <u>hearing</u> by the word of Christ.

In order for there to be confession, the gospel must be sent and heard, v. 15. Notably, Paul omits "hearing" in verses 5-13, but then in his summary verses 14-15, he repeats different cognate nouns and verbs for "hearing." The sentences leading to the conclusion and the conclusion itself continue the repetition of the root for "hearing" in such a manner as to build, a crescendo.[38] This omission juxtaposed with repetition seems to suggest that Paul intentionally makes an indirect statement against Israel concerning their lack of hearing/ obeying. In other words, the "all" who are called, who believe, and who confess, 10:5-13, does not include some who disobey—those who do not *hear* the word of Christ, 10:14-17.

More significantly, Paul identifies with the prophet Isaiah in proclaiming that only a few experience salvation. The Isaiah context behind Paul's quotation—". . . beautiful are the feet of the ones who bring good news" (Rom. 10:16; Isa. 52:7)—refers to the Lord's comfort and deliverance of those in Jerusalem among the ruins. Apparently, Paul seeks to highlight Isaiah's prophetic blessing and to prove that messengers were sent—Israel is condemned for her unbelief.[39]

---

38. "Obedience of faith" is the result of justification. Each of the major sections explains what this phrase means—chapter 4, chapter 8, and here in chapter 10. Chapters 14–15 describe a practical application of "obedience of faith" in Rome.

39. Shum, *Paul's Use*, 224. Paul omits the latter half of 52:7; Hays, *Echoes*, 45–46. Paul's use of "all" (see v. 10f) gives an eschatological import, and the order of election—first to the Jew and then to the gentile—reaffirms God's plan carried out. Based on specific citations and allusions from suffering servant passages in Isaiah, Luke Timothy Johnson affirms that the "word of Christ" (v. 17) is the "message concerning the messiah" that was preached by Isaiah; *Reading Romans: A Literary and Theological Commentary* (New York: Crossroad, 1997), 173. Concerning Paul's change from the Old Testament singular to the plural use, "the feet of those bringing good news," Moo understands the words to apply to Israel; *Epistle to the Romans*, 662-63.

Paul concludes this section of the argument with the clause—"Faith comes by hearing and hearing by the word of Christ"—that brings together several semantic elements. The "word near you" that Moses speaks about in Exodus is now explicitly stated as "the word of Christ." The four formulas in 10:5, 6, 8b, and 11 that introduce scriptural support in this section, 10:5-17, lead the reader to the conclusion of verse 17:

	Introductory Formula	Topic
5	Moses writes	Live in righteousness of law
6-8a	From faith, righteousness says	*Christ* and resurrection
8b-10	But what is he saying?	*Word of faith*; believe resurrection
11-16	For Scripture says	*Hearing* and obeying
17	Faith comes by *hearing* and hearing by the *Word* of Christ	

In other words, "faith," "hearing," and the personified "Word of Christ" summarize the content of verses 5-16.

Previously the question was asked whether verses 6-8, 5-13, or 5-21 elaborate upon 10:4—"Christ is the end of the law." Paul explains that "righteousness" of the law is lived by faith, 10:5. Moreover, Moses explains how this "word" is near, which Paul equates with the message of Christ that he preaches, 10:6-8, and personifies the word as Christ, something to be believed inwardly and confessed openly, 10:9-13. This "word of faith" that embodies the person of Christ is to be heard and obeyed, 10:14-17, bringing an "end" to the law—a fulfillment of righteousness (3:21-28; 4:13-16; 6:14-15, 7:1—8:1f).[40] In this way, the phrase in verse 4—"end" of the

---

40. "Hearing through the word of Christ" (ἀκοὴ διὰ ῥήματος Χριστοῦ) summarizes the "hearing" in verse 14—this poetic repetition then explains some of the awkwardness in Paul's connected list. The concept of "listening" or "hearing" (שמע) in Hebrew means "obey." Personification

law—unifies the midrashic section, transitioning the chiastic structure of 9:30—10:3 to 10:5-21—which means that *the "Righteousness" that Israel stumbles on is sent to the nations, the gentiles.*

Now that the thematic and structural unity of 9:30—10:21 has been demonstrated, several reasons are given to support Paul's use of subtle personification—for the Person of Christ serves as his lens for interpreting Hebrew Scripture. First, by contrasting "not knowing" in relation to the "law of righteousness," Paul personifies the "law of righteousness," 9:30—10.3, and more directly refers to the "stone of stumbling" as Christ, 9:33. Second, "the end of the law" also intends the emphasis of Christ as the fulfillment of "Law," 10:4. Third, "Righteousness" speaks, 10:6. And fourth, the expression—"torah speaks" parallels the Christian kerygma, 10:7-8.[41]

Continual Mercy, 10:18-21

Now that Paul has argued that the word of Christ comes from a hearing faith,[42] Paul asks the question whether Israel has heard, to which he emphatically answers, "They have."

---

in light of wisdom literature does suggest a clear parallel with 10:5-7; see Joseph Dodson, *The "Powers" of Personification: Rhetorical Purpose in the Book of Wisdom and the Letter to the Romans* (Berlin: Walter de Gruyter, 2008), 211.

41. Christ is the content of proclamation, the proclaimed Word. In a similar way that the "messiah" and the "remnant" share a semantic domain, so does the fulfillment of "law" and "Christ," and "Christ" and the "message preached." The Person of Christ is "in" the spoken "word." For example, Paul quotes a passage from Isaiah (Rom. 10:16, Isa. 53) that portrays the suffering of the messiah—"Has anyone heard our message?" The words of the messiah are foretold, an embodiment of Christ's Spirit.

42. The Hebrew שמע is translated "hearing" or "obeying." With this close connection, a "hearing" faith is an "obedient" faith. Thus Paul's two uses of "obedient faith" (ὑπακοὴν πίστεως)—1:5 and 16:26—encapsulate Paul's message in Romans, and this phrase finds its clearest referent here in 10:17.

But am I saying that they have not heard? No, they have.   18

Their voices went out into all the earth

their words to the ends of the world.

But again I ask, did Israel not know? First, Moses says,   19

"I will make you jealous by those that are not a nation

I will make you angry by gentiles without insight."

Isaiah boldly says,   20

"I was found by those not seeking me

I revealed myself to those not asking for me."

But to Israel he says,   21

"I continually extend my hands

to a disobedient and stubborn people."

He supports this truth with a quotation from Psalm 19:4 (Rom. 10:18): "Their voice went out into all the earth; their words to the ends of the world." These sentences describe the continuous nonverbal messages about God's nature that are sent throughout the world.[43] More significantly, not only do the key words "voice" and "words" (τὰ ῥήματα) relate to the midrashic explanation of verses 5-17 where God's word is sent, but the context in Psalm 19 involves the expression of God's general revelation in creation *that parallels God's Law.*[44] In the last half of the psalm, the psalmist declares how the law of the Lord is perfect—it revives the soul and gives joy to the heart. He prays that the words of his mouth and the meditation of his

---

43. This emphasis upon the continuous nature of God's revelation echoes Paul's initial theme (1:17).
44. The noun term "word" (ῥῆμα) connects verse 17—"hearing the word of Christ"—and verse 19—"their words to the ends of the earth." This subtle poetic thought rhyme implies that Israel has heard the gospel.

heart be pleasing to his Rock and Redeemer. These expressions share a similar context with the explanation in 9:30—10:17.

In Romans 10:19, Paul repeats his introductory formula and question:

> But I say, "Have they not heard?" Indeed.   18
>
> But I say, "Does Israel not know?"   19

He then foreshadows the content of the mystery that will follow with his quotation from Deuteronomy: "First, Moses says, I will make you jealous by those that are not a nation. I will make you angry by gentiles without understanding" (32:19). In this way, God communicates a message to Israel, not through the law or through nature, but through their own inner "jealousy" toward the gentiles. In the Deuteronomic context, Moses proclaims the name of the Lord, the Rock, telling of God's care and love for his people and how he will display his wrath for their disobedience according to his covenant. Moses warns them to "take to heart all the words" in order to obey the words of the law—"not just idle words—they are your life" (Deut. 32:47).

In the next two verses, Paul quotes Isaiah (65:1-2):[45]

---

45. This repetition of listing four quotations is distinctive (also 9:25-29 and 11:7-11) creating a balanced and integrated style of thought parallels.

Isaiah boldly says,   20

   "I was found by those not seeking me

   I revealed myself to those not asking for me."

But to Israel he says,   21

   "I continually extend my hands

   to a disobedient and stubborn people."

The Isaiah context is one of impending wrath to Israel but also a promise to the remnant. The prophet speaks of a messianic age in which God gathers descendants from Jacob and from Judah, his chosen servants who will sing out of joy in their hearts. The hopeful promise to the remnant contrasts the predicament of those who will cry out from anguish of heart and wail in brokenness of spirit. The reference to those "not seeking" and "not asking" (Rom. 10:20; Isa. 65:1) antithetically parallel Paul's previous verse where, in the Deuteronomic context (Rom. 10:19; Deut. 32:19), the gentiles are the ones without insight and understanding—"I will make you jealous by those that are *not a nation*; I will make you angry by gentiles *without insight.*" Thus Paul reverses the Old Testament context concerning the referent for "gentiles" by making his context in Romans refer to "Israel." This reversal fits neatly with his general terms in his literary chiasm, 9:30—10:4, where "Israel" represents "works" and "gentiles" represent "faith." Furthermore, the emphasis of gentiles as the ones "not asking" or "not seeking" also thematically unifies the two midrashic sections together, 9:6-29 and 9:30—10:21, since both sections end with quotations accenting gentile inclusion—9:25-26 and 10:20.[46]

---

46. "It will be in the place that was said, 'you are not my people.' There they will be called the sons of the living God" (Rom. 9:26 and Hos. 1:10). Shum notes that Paul concurs with the original

Theologically speaking, the phrase "I continually extend my hands" (10:21; Isa. 65:2) punctuates the continual nature of God's communication,[47] especially when interpreted in light of the communication imagery in Psalm 19:4 (Rom. 9:18). In addition, the message of "jealousy" is, in a sense, synonymous with God extending his hands to Israel. In other words, even though Israel has heard, disobeyed, and remained obstinate, God continues to reach out to them through jealousy.

In this *testimonia*, 10:18-21, Paul returns to his literary names: "Israel," referring to those who hear but do not know; and the "gentiles," referring to those who hear and believe the word of Christ. In 10:18-21, Paul reveals Israel's character—"Israel" has not heard, a fitting testimony to "Israel's" lack of relationship with "righteousness," 9:30—10:4, and their lack of "faith" in the Christ proclamation, 10:5-17. Likewise, Paul in these verses, 10:18-21, underscores God's revelation to the gentiles. For (a) God has been made known to all the earth, v. 18; (b) he has revealed himself to the gentiles, which results in jealousy, v. 19; and (c) those not seeking him (the gentiles) have been found by him, v. 20.

For in all of this, God's character is consistent as he continually extends his hands to Israel, v. 21. Thus Paul infers that acceptance of the gentiles sends a compassionate message to Israel. This "jealousy" theme serves as a transition into the next section of Paul's argument, 11:1-24, which is the key to the mystery revealed.

Summary

Based on Paul's sequence of thought and literary unity in 9:30—10:21, a narrative summary is given. After this, relevant

---

context (Isa. 65:2), but Paul reiterates here that the words of Isaiah point not to the rejection of the nations but Israel's rejection of Christ; *Paul's Use*, 231f.

47. This is a point Paul makes at the beginning of the body of his letter in 1:17-18.

insights are discussed relating the theological truths in this section to the rest of Paul's argument and his letter.

Narrative Summary

Paul proves that God's plan in electing Israel included the gentiles, 9:6-29. As a result of Israel's fall, the gospel message is sent into all of the world, 9:30—10:21. Paul asks the question as to whether Israel has heard the word of Christ. He attests that Israel has heard but did not obey; they did "know"—have a relationship with—the Messiah.

A pattern emerges in Paul's argument, 9:6—10:21. God's decision to show mercy to Israel, 9:11, demonstrates his mercy toward Esau and his descendants. For the "older" was to serve the "younger," requiring humility and dependence on God. Despite God's election, both nations rebel. The descendants of Esau incur God's wrath for their sins, 9:12, yet God's character is revealed in his patient desire for repentance. Israel, it seems, should have received greater condemnation for their wickedness, for they were granted the blessings of election, 9:4. But God first sends a visual demonstration of punishment for disobedience, a warning to Israel, by carrying out his wrath against the Edomites.

Despite this expressed love, Israel rebels. God sends his Son, and Israel rejects him, 9:32. Their fall ought to have brought them to a place of humility and realization of their need for relationship with Righteousness, their salvation. Yet they remain obstinate. Consequently, God reveals himself to the gentiles, and by blessing the gentiles, God's purpose is to make Israel jealous, 10:19. This raises a logical question that Paul will answer with the mystery revealed—"If God's mercy is revealed to the gentiles as a response to Israel's disobedience, how much more will God's blessing to the gentiles result in mercy to Israel?"[48]

Relevant Insights

For the first part of this section (9:30—10:3), a precise chiasm is outlined. Paul creates dual parallels with not only the opposite end lines and middle lines parallel (such as 9:30 with 10:3 and 9:31 with 10:2), but he also writes his thoughts so that they parallel each other in immediate sequence (9:30 with 9:31; and 10:2 with 10:3). Paul's form shows beautiful symmetry and thematic consistency.

Several points are worth repeating. First, in verses 9:30-31, Paul contrasts two themes—"faith and law" and "pursuing righteousness—and he contrasts two people groups—"Israel" and the "gentiles." The conclusion is that Israel pursues the "law of righteousness" but they do not obtain this law. The gentiles do not pursue righteousness but they receive righteousness by faith. Paul uses these general labels—"Israel" and "gentiles"—for instruction purposes. He is not implying that all Jews have rejected the messiah nor that all gentiles have received righteousness.

Second, in 10:2-3, Paul reiterates the reality that Israel did not have "knowledge" or "know" the righteousness of God. Paul repeats "righteousness" three times in each of the end verses (9:30 and 10:3) and it becomes apparent that Paul personifies "Righteousness" (the emphasis is on "who" rather than "what"). In other words, Israel did not know Jesus Christ. This personification of "Righteousness" contributes to a more relational understanding of "justification by

---

48. Paul's reference to Pharaoh is an important piece of information in Paul's logical sequence. This as follows—(1) initial election of younger son, Israel, (mercy to Israel) before disobedience is also merciful decision for the older son and his descendants; (2) Gentile disobedience results in a merciful warning to Israel (Malachi quotation); (3) Israel's disobedience results in mercy shown to gentiles; and then (4) how much more will mercy shown to the gentiles result in mercy shown to Israel. Concerning Pharaoh and Paul's elaboration in 9:17-23, God demonstrates wrath to a gentile that results in deliverance for Israel from the Egyptians, but it also is merciful in that God's name is proclaimed to the nations. This, on the one hand, builds suspense so the reader asks the question, "Is Israel's fall permanent like Pharaoh's?" And on the other hand, Paul's reference to Pharaoh completes the logical possibilities concerning God's mercy—wrath to disobedient Pharaoh (gentiles) results in mercy to the gentile nations.

faith" in the letter. For example, believers are not slaves to a quality or virtue of "righteousness," but slaves to the person of Jesus Christ (6:18-20).

Third, at the center of the chiasm, Paul selects two phrases from two verses from Isaiah and replaces a hopeful phrase—"precious cornerstone" from Isaiah 28:16—with a judgment phrase—"a stone of stumbling and rock of scandal" from Isaiah 8:14. By doing so, Paul imputes Israel pronouncing the cause of their stumble—the stone, the Messiah. In this way, Israel by their own choice rejects faith in the Messiah, choosing pride instead by trying to attain purity through self-effort. This raises the concern whether Israel has *heard* the gospel.

Paul argues that the "law" that Moses gave and the "word of faith" that he (Paul) preaches carry the same message concerning Christ (10:6-17). He associates "righteousness from the law" with "life" and not with selfish ambition, and he explains how torah speaks about this "righteousness" as personal and relational. Thus, God's election of Israel and his continued interaction with his people reveal that God has revealed "Righteousness" to them. Paul shifts momentarily from his generalized labels of "Israel" and "gentiles" (10:11-13) to stress God's *impartial nature* in that "all" who call upon the Lord will be saved, for there is "no distinction between Jew and Greek." In order for there to be confession, the gospel must be heard, and faith comes by hearing the word of Christ (10:14-17).

This definition of faith—hearing the word of Christ—confirms Paul's interest in seeing the Roman Christians remain faithful in their humble attitude. Based on Paul's repetitive use of words containing the root "hear/obey" (ακου- or ακοα- ; 10:14-17), it seems that Paul makes an indirect statement concerning Israel's lack of hearing/obeying. In other words, the "all" who are called, who believe, and who confess, 10:5-13, do not include some who disobey—those who do not hear the word of Christ, 10:14-17. Paul's purpose is to strengthen believers so that they continue in "obedient faith" (see 1:5 and 16:19).

In his *testimonia* (10:18-21), Paul returns to his use of the literary names: "Israel" who hear but do not know; and the "gentiles" who hear and believe the word of Christ. Paul's use of Old Testament support from Psalms, Exodus, and Isaiah, reveals Israel's character in that she did not choose a relationship with "Righteousness" (9:30—10:17); in contrast, God reveals himself to the gentiles (vv. 18 and 20). But this, too, results in a merciful response from God. His grace to the gentiles causes Israel to become jealous (v. 19), a compassionate decision.

4

———

The Grace of God for Israel, 11:1–32

Therefore I am saying, "Did God reject his people? By no means." For I am an Israelite, from the seed of Abraham, the tribe of Benjamin. Did God reject His people that he foreknew? Do you not know what Elijah said in Scripture as he interceded to God with anger toward Israel? "Lord, they have killed your prophets. They have cut down your altars, and I have been left alone and they are seeking my soul." But what does the oracle say about him? "I have left for myself seven thousand men who have not bowed their knee to Baal." Therefore, in this same manner and in this present time there is a remnant according to the called grace of God. But if by grace, it is not by works, otherwise grace would no longer be grace. Why therefore? What Israel sought, they did not achieve, but the called achieved and the rest were hardened. Even as it is written, "God gave them a spirit of stupor; eyes not seeing, ears not hearing, all the day long." And David said, "Let their table be a trap and a snare, a stumbling block and retribution to them. Let their eyes be darkened so as not to see and their backs bent over forever."

Therefore I am saying, "Did they trip in order that they might fall?" By no means. But their sins result in salvation to the Gentiles in order that the Gentiles might make them jealous. But if their sins means riches to the world and their failure riches to the nations, how much more their fullness?

But to you Gentiles I am speaking. Therefore, in as much as I am an apostle to the gentiles I will boast in my ministry if somehow I might make my brothers jealous and save some of them, for if the their casting away means reconciliation of the world, what about their reception if not life from the dead? But if the first fruits are holy then the whole batch is holy, and if the root is holy also the branches. But if some of the branches were cut out and you wild olive branches were grafted into them and now share in the nourishing sap of the olive tree root, "Do not boast, branches!" But if you might boast you are not bearing the root but the root bears you.

Therefore, you are saying, "They were cut out in order that I will be grafted in." Well, in unfaithfulness they were cut out but you have stood in faith. Do not be high minded, but fear! For if God did not spare the natural branches neither will he spare you.

Therefore, behold the kindness and severity of God. Upon the ones falling, severity, but upon you, the kindness of God, if you remain in kindness, otherwise you will be cut out. And also if they do not remain in unfaithfulness they will be engrafted. For God is able to engraft them again. For if you, according to nature, were cut out of a wild olive and were engrafted into the cultivated olive tree, how much more will these according to the natural be grafted into their own olive tree?

For I wish that you would not be ignorant, brothers, of this mystery in order that you might not think of yourselves too highly, because the partial hardening in Israel has happened until the fullness of the gentiles might come in. And likewise, all Israel will be saved. Even as it is written, "From Zion comes the One who delivers he will turn Jacob from godlessness. And this is by my covenant with them, I will forgive their sins. According to the gospel, enemies on account of us; according to the elect, beloved on account of the fathers. For God's call and gifts are irrevocable. For just as you were disobedient to God, now you have been shown mercy by their disobedience; likewise, those who have presently disobeyed resulted in your being shown mercy in order that now they too might be shown mercy. For God bound all into disobedience, in order that he might show mercy to all.

Overall Outline, 11:1-32

Paul's cohesive literary style exhibits intellect. After he demonstrates God's inclusion of the gentiles, 9:6-29, and the reason for Israel's fall, 9:30—10:21, Paul clarifies the meaning of his terms that he has used for Israel in a transition section, 11:1-10. He then encases the "mystery" within a poetic structure, 11:11-24, integrating logic, balanced parallels, and extended metaphor.

11:1-10	Clarification: Remnant Israel and Hardened Israel
11:11-24	Poetic Structure:
11:11-15	Balanced Parallels ("Reconciliation")
11:16-24	Olive tree metaphor and Imperatives
11:25-32	Summary Section

Furthermore, Paul's summary of the revealed mystery, 11:25-32, thematically brings together the whole argument of Romans 9:6—11:32, an *inclusio*.

Prophetic Identity, 11:1-10

In Romans 11, Paul reveals the "mystery" concerning Israel's future. But he first delineates what he means by "Israel," since up to this point in his argument he has used different terms for "Israel" that refer to different groups: In his first midrashic form, 9:6-29, Paul defines the "remnant" as called sons comprised of Jew and gentile. In his second midrashic form, 9:30—10:21, he describes "Israel" as those who have heard the message of the Messiah, stumbled, and have become hardened. So, here in 11:1-10, Paul juxtaposes these two identities, "remnant" Israel and "hardened" Israel, for the purpose of clarification—"remnant" Israel is called by grace, 11:5, and "hardened" Israel sought to obtain their goal through "works," 11:6-10. This definition and repetition prepare the reader for what is about to be unveiled, 11:11-32.

In the first half of this section, 11:1-6, Paul identifies and compares his present situation, as an Israelite lamenting for Israel, to Elijah's circumstances in the Old Testament where the prophet speaks to God against Israel. Paul does this to reinforce a main point: "in this present time there is a remnant called by grace," 11:5. Logically speaking, the more parallel the factors are—between Paul and Elijah; and "Israel-then" and "Israel-now"—the more true his conclusion is concerning the "remnant" called by grace, 11:5. The outline below makes it easier to follow Paul's thought structure (for full text see next page):

1	Did God reject his people?	A
	Paul as a remnant Israelite	B
2	Did God reject His people that he foreknew?	A
	Elijah as a remnant Israelite	B
3-4	1 Kings 10:14, 18	
5-6	Conclusion: remnant called by grace, not by works	C
7	Israel is hardened	X
8	Deut. 29:4	x
9	Isa. 29:10	x
10	Ps. 69:22	x
	Ps. 69:23	x

In the latter half of this section, 11:6-10, Paul reintroduces his "works" theme when describing "Israel" (see 9:11, 32) and contrasts the "remnant according to the called grace of God" with those of Israel who have been hardened (this topic shift is represented by the "x's" in the outline above)—"What Israel sought, they did not achieve

. . . and the rest were hardened," 11:7. Paul quotes verses from the Torah, the Prophets, and the Writings,[1] 11:8-10, which contain a thought rhyme supporting the truth that God has caused a hardening of Israel—part of God's plan from the beginning: " . . . spirit of stupor . . . eyes not seeing . . . let their table be a trap . . . eyes darkened."

Prophetic Identification, 11:1-10

11:1   Therefore I am saying,

Did God reject his people? By no means!

For I am an Israelite,

from the seed of Abraham,

the tribe of Benjamin.

2   Did God reject His people that he foreknew?

Do you not know what Elijah said in Scripture

as he interceded to God with anger toward Israel?

3   **"Lord, they have killed your prophets.**

They have cut down your altars,

and I have been left alone

and they are seeking my soul."

4   But what does the oracle say about him?

"I have left for myself seven thousand men

who have not bowed their knee to Baal."

---

1. Verses 19-21 comprise a Haraz; E. Earle Ellis, *Paul's Use of the Old Testament* (Edinburgh: Oliver & Boyd, 1957), 186.

5   Therefore, in this same manner and in this present time there is a remnant

according to the called grace of God,

6   but if by grace, it is not by works,

otherwise grace would no longer be grace.

7   Why therefore?

What Israel sought, they did not achieve,

but the called achieved and the rest were hardened.

8   Even as it is written,

"God gave them a spirit of stupor,

eyes not seeing, ears not hearing, all the day long."

9   And David said,

"Let their table be a trap and a snare,

a stumbling block and retribution to them.

Let their eyes be darkened so as not to see

and their backs bent over forever."

As previously mentioned, Romans 11:1-10 serves as a "transition" section. It brings together the two identities elaborated on in the first two midrashic forms[2]—"remnant" Israel, 9:6-29, and "hardened Israel," 9:30—10:21, forming a thematic platform from which the "mystery" in Romans 11:11-24 is presented. Yet in order to interpret the mystery in 11:11-24 with confidence, three topics from 11:1-10 deserve explanation: (a) Paul's "intercession" for Israel, 11:2; (b) the

---

2. The "rejected stone" and "rejected son" imagery also provides a literary connection between the two midrashic forms. For Paul's use of possible catch words in his question in relation to other Jewish sources, see B. J. Oropeza, "Paul and Theodicy: Intertextual Thoughts on God's Justice and Faithfulness to Israel in Romans 9-11," *NTS* 53, no. 1 (2007): 73f.

meaning of the phrase "his people," 11:2; and (c) the context of wrath in 9:6—11:1-10 in relation to Israel's "hardening," 11:6-10. As these matters are explained, it becomes apparent that Paul is consistent with his definition and argument.

Paul's "interceding against" Israel and the phrase "his people" are discussed first (11:2; "Did God reject *His people* that he foreknew? Do you not know what Elijah said in Scripture as he *interceded* to God with anger against Israel?") Then follows a discussion of the third topic, God's wrath in relation to Israel's hardening, 11:7-11.

Remnant Intercessor

Paul likely alludes to an Old Testament lament when he frames his argument with a repetitive question implying the objection, "God did not reject *His people*?" (11:1-2).[3] The content of this first question and his emphatic answer, "By no means!" (11:1a), emphasizes God's mercy (a view congruent with the rest of his letter—e.g., 3:21-26; 5:12f; 12:1f; 15:7f). Paul then identifies himself as an "Israelite" from the seed of Abraham and the tribe of Benjamin:

Therefore I am saying,

Did God reject his people? By no means!"   A (Lament Question)

For I am an Israelite,   B (Paul)

from the seed of Abraham,

the tribe of Benjamin.

---

3. Paul may be alluding to 1 Samuel 12:22 or Psalm 94:14 (93:14 LXX) in which he frames the question as an objection—Psalms 94 is a personal lamentation for deliverance; Joseph Fitzmyer, *Romans* (New York: Doubleday, 1993), 603. In both the context of 1 Samuel and Psalm 94, God does not reject or abandon his people.

He repeats his question with a declarative statement and describes Elijah's words and circumstances as a response to his initial rhetorical question (11:2-3).

God did not reject His people that he foreknew?   A (Lament Question)

Do you not know what Elijah said in Scripture   B (Elijah)

as he interceded to God with anger against Israel?

"Lord, they have killed your prophets.

They have cut down your altars,

and I have been left alone

and they are seeking my soul."

Paul authenticates an analogy by weaving two contexts together—Elijah's and his own. In other words, by describing himself as an "Israelite," a Benjamite, and a descendent of Abraham, Paul strengthens his identification with Elijah as a "remnant" Israelite. And in the present context of Paul's lament, he speaks against them, as one who has experienced God's presence, in a similar manner as Elijah. But a closer look at Paul's quotation of 1 Kings and Elijah's context shows that Paul, unlike Elijah, sees God's compassionate mind in both contexts.

In verse 2, Paul writes, "Elijah intercedes against Israel . . ." (Rom. 11:2; 1 Kgs. 19:10).[4] Noticeably, the word "intercede" (ἐντυγχάνει) is not in the Greek Old Testament passage of 1 Kings 11, which means that Paul chooses this word to make a specific inference concerning Elijah's attitude against Israel. Elijah, pursued and dejected, grieves

---

4. The verb ἐντυγχάνω with the preposition κατά carries the idea of "plead against" in a negative sense of complaint or denounce—e.g., 1 Macc. 10:61, 63 and 11:25. Ernst Käsemann understands a court metaphor; *A Commentary on Romans*, trans. and ed. Geoffrey W. Bromily (Grand Rapids: Eerdmans, 1980), 300.

for himself, it seems, as he protests. Amidst this complaining, God personally reveals himself to Elijah, "Go stand on the mountain in the presence of the Lord for the Lord is about to pass by . . ." (1 Kgs. 11:11f). Paul likely expects the believers in Rome who are listening to the reading of his letter to remember the Old Testament context.[5]

Although Paul interjects the word "intercede against" (or "plead against"), it seems that he does not want to show that God has rejected Israel. Rather, Paul decides to present Elijah's attitude in contrast with God's heart in order to highlight God's compassionate response to Israel.[6] This becomes clear when taking into consideration the similarities of both contexts (1 Kings 11 and Romans 11): God judges Israel as guilty, God reveals his Person to the one interceding, and God reserves a *"remnant"* by grace. But unlike Elijah, Paul does not complain. In fact, Paul writes to prepare the reader for what he will soon disclose: God's wise and *merciful plan* for Israel (see 11:11f—the hardening of Israel results in gentile salvation, causing Israel to become jealous, which then leads to Israel's repentance).

More specifically, Paul stresses God's character by directing attention to what God says about himself to Elijah—that he has left (καταλείπω) a faithful remnant for himself (Rom 11:4; 1 Kgs. 19:18):

---

5. Yet an apocalyptic stress should not be dismissed (e.g., ἑπτακισχιλίους, 11:4); Otto Michel, *Der Brief an die Römer* (Göttingen: Vandenhoeck & Ruprecht, 1963), 340.
6. Michael G. Vanlaningham finds more agreement between Paul's text and the MT, rather than the LXX and sees a close analogy between Paul's situation and Elijah's; Vanlaningham, "Paul's Use of Elijah's Mt. Horeb Experience in Rom 11:2-6: An Exegetical Note," *Master's Seminary Journal* 6, no. 2 (1995): 224f. For parallels between Elijah and Moses, see William Dumbrell, "What Are You Doing Here? Elijah at Horeb," *Crux* 22 (1986): 15–17; Childs, "On Reading the Elijah Narratives," *Interpretation* 34 (1980): 134–35; and Cohn, "The Literary Logic of 1 Kings 17-19." *JBL* 101 (1982): 341–42. While Paul's arrangement is not precisely linear, portions of his argument follow a historical sequence—the patriarchs (9:6-13); Israel's deliverance from Pharaoh (9:17); Israel before crossing the Jordan (10:6-8); Israel during the exile (11:1-5).

> But what does the oracle say about him?
>
> **"I have left for myself seven thousand men**
>
> **who have not bowed their knee to Baal."**

The repetition of the root word "left/leave" (λείπω) in the first half of this section, 11:3-5, indicates Paul's intentional topic—the remnant. Having just quoted Elijah's words that he was the only one "left" (11:3, ὑπολείπω), and God's words that he has "left" (11:4, καταλείπω) for himself seven thousand men, Paul identifies with Elijah by concluding that God has reserved for himself a "remnant" (11:5; λεῖμμα) in this *present time*!

This raises the question as to what Paul means by the "remnant" and how this definition fits with the meanings of "Israel" in the preceding passages. Since 11:1-10 serves as a summary-transition section for the first two midrashic sections, Paul (a) repeats themes from these sections and (b) clarifies his definitions.

Concerning a repetition of topics, he brings together his "not by works" theme in relation to "hardened" Israel, and the "grace of God" theme in relation to the "remnant." The first section articulated the inclusion of the gentiles into the "remnant," those who are "called" by God, 9:6-29,[7] and the second section described how Israel stumbled and was "hardened," those who attempted to achieve justification by "works," 9:30—10:21. Not surprisingly, Paul's concluding statement in his transition section weaves these topics together, 11:5-6:

---

7. For "called" (ἐκλογή) see 9:11, 11:5, 7, and 28.

5   Therefore, in this same manner and in this present time there is a <u>remnant</u>

according to the <u>called</u> grace of God,

6   but if by grace, it is not by <u>works</u>

otherwise grace would no longer be grace.

Paul's specific emphasis is noteworthy. He continues the "remnant" topic, 11:5, from the first midrashic section, where he listed two verses from Isaiah to underscore the salvation of the remnant (9:27; Isa. 10:22—ὑπόλειμμα), which includes gentiles, and to show God's action in leaving descendants (9:29; Isa. 1:9—ἐγκαταλείπω) so that Israel is not destroyed. Furthermore, he contrasts grace with "works," 11:6, which highlights both a central theme of the letter ("not by works": 3:20, 27–28; 4:2, 6) and repeats his topic in the first midrashic section concerning the character of God in his election of Jacob—"not by *works* but by the one *calling*," 9:11.

In addition, Paul's "not by works" statement, 11:6, along with his direct claim that "Israel" was "hardened," 11:7, serves as a summary of the second midrashic section, 9:30—10:21:

7   Why therefore?

What Israel sought, they did not achieve

but the called achieved and the rest were hardened.

Paul began his second section with a chiasm, 9:30—10:3, which equated (1) the "gentiles" with "righteousness by faith" and (2) "Israel" with pursuing righteousness through "works of the law." Paul stated that Israel pursued the law of righteousness by the law, but "Israel did not obtain it," 9:31. Even though Paul does not discuss "law" in 11:1-10, he again connects "Israel" with "works," 11:7, and its end result—a "hardening." Thus in 11:1-10, Paul clarifies two people groups—"Israel" who represents those who have been hardened, and the "remnant," which signifies those who are called by grace. This thematic repetition prepares his audience to know with clarity *who* he is speaking about as he reveals the "mystery," 11:11-24.

"His people"

When Paul indirectly states that, "God did not reject His people (τὸ λαὸν) that he foreknew" (11:2) he may be referring to the "remnant" made up of Jews and gentiles (see 9:6-29) or he may be referring to "hardened" unrepentant Israel (9:30—10:21 and 9:18-23). It seems that Paul is intentionally not clear. On the one hand, Paul punctuates the theme of election—"remnant according to God's grace," but on the other hand he keeps silent, at this point, concerning the final outcome of obstinate Israel—though he seems to hint at their salvation with the wordplay "the rest" (οἱ λοιποὶ).[8] The likely reason for this? By delaying making a clear statement on the future of "hardened" Israel, Paul momentarily builds suspense. In other words, the reader should not be quick to judge or conclude that God has rejected "hardened" Israel.

Israel's "Hardening"

For the first time in his argument, Paul explicitly mentions that Israel has been hardened (11:7; πωρόω). Immediately following this statement, Paul defines what he means by "hardened" with a list of Hebrew Scriptures that illustrates God's action, 11:8-10.[9]

---

8. Paul uses the phrase οἱ λοιποὶ whereas Jeremiah reads "κατάλοιπος " for the remnant (Jer. 43:5; 50:5; and 52:16 LXX).

9. The connotation of hardening ranges from "to petrify," "make dull," or "to blind;" BADG, s.v. "πωρόω." Paul cites from Deuteronomy 29:3 (LXX), Isaiah 29:10, and Psalms 68:23 (LXX). "Spirit of stupor" is inserted into Deuteronomy 29:3 from Isaiah 29:10—God withholds understanding "until this very day" (Deut. 29:4), a context of future hope.

7   Why therefore? What Israel sought, they did not achieve

but the called achieved and the rest were hardened.

8   Even as it is written,

"God gave them a spirit of stupor;   Isa. 29:10

eyes not seeing, ears not hearing, all the day long."   Deut. 29:4

9   And David said,

"Let their table be a trap and a snare,   Ps. 69:22-23

into a stumbling block and retribution to them.

10   **Let their eyes be darkened so as not to see**

and their backs bent over forever."

From a literary standpoint, the imagery in the Isaiah passage, "eyes not seeing," and the imagery in the Psalms quotation, "eyes darkened," form a synonymous thought parallel. And the word "stumbling block" (σκάνδαλον, 11:9) repeats the earlier reference where God lays down a stone of stumbling, a rock of "offense" (9:33; σκάνδαλον).[10] This repetition reinforces Israel's guilt and the consequential judgment. But more importantly Paul in his verse list draws from Old Testament contexts to reinforce the reality of Israel's hardening as well as God's mercy.

Concerning Israel's hardening, the quotations in each of the verses—one from Torah, one from the Prophets, and one from the Psalms—supports the connected themes that God has blinded Israel, that she has acted disobediently despite his deliverance, and that Paul's petition is against Israel—for God's wrath is to be meted out. In Deuteronomy 29:4 (Rom. 11:8a), Moses delivers the words of the

---

10. In Psalms 69, the psalmist cries out to God for deliverance against his enemies. In Paul's present context, "Israel" is the referent, underscoring the reversal of 9:6-29.

covenant to Israel before crossing the Jordan and reminds them of *God's actions* to Pharaoh and his leading them through the wilderness despite their rebellion.[11] In Isaiah 29:10 (Rom. 11:8b), the prophet Isaiah gives the primary reason for Israel's blindness—it is *God's decision*—before using potter imagery to instruct his listeners concerning God's sovereign actions. And in Psalm 69, Paul cites the psalmist's suffering and his prayer for *God's wrath to be carried out* against those causing him suffering, which in a prophetic sense refers to those who killed the Messiah (Israel).[12]

Nonetheless, Paul's selected quotations do not adequately answer the obvious question that is in the mind of the reader: "Is this a permanent hardening?" Contextually, it helps to see how the word "hardened" in 11:7 compares to Paul's other uses of God's "wrath" in his argument, 9:6—11:10. "Wrath" does not necessarily imply eternal perdition. Earlier, when Paul refers to God's wrath in 9:12, "God 'hated' Esau," he drew upon the Malachi context in which Edom would experience God's wrath for their continued prideful response to God (Mal. 1:4). Interestingly, the result of this judgment sends a message of God's power and magnificence *beyond the borders of Israel*, also an act of mercy. At the same time, God's wrath against Edom precedes the impending judgment against God's covenant people for their disobedience, revealing God's patience and faithfulness. And although the Malachi context illustrates God's continual wrath against the Edomites for their belligerent and hostile attitude toward God and his people, it is important to interpret this reference of

---

11. Isaiah's words, "a spirit of deep sleep" (29:10) is harsher in tone than the language of Deuteronomy; Shiu-Lun Shum, *Paul's Use of Isaiah: A Comparative Study of Paul's Letter to the Romans and the Sibylline and Qumran Sectarian Texts* (Tübingen: Mohr, 2002), 233. The use of "deep sleep" suggests a temporary state (see Gen. 2:21f) as well as the phrase ἕως τῆς σήμερον ἡμέρας . Romans 11:8 hints at the possibility of resuscitation; ibid., 234.

12. The New Testament writers interpreted the rejection of the psalmist in Psalm 69 in relationship to Christ's suffering and life—Matt. 27:34, 48; Mark 3:21; 15:36; Luke 11:35; 23:36; John 2:17; 15:25; Acts 1:20; Rom. 15:3; and Heb. 11:26.

wrath (Rom. 9:12; Mal. 1:2-3) in light of Paul's following argument where Israel's fall results in God's mercy extended to all gentile nations—which would seem to include the Edomites.

Paul expresses a more fearful demonstration of God's power when he quotes God's words to Moses: "God hardens whom he wills" (σκληρύνει, Rom. 9:18; Exod. 33:19), which Paul then explains as vessels "prepared for destruction" (Rom. 9:22-23). Evidently, "hardening" refers to Pharaoh, and in this instance, it would denote eternal destruction. But what Paul stresses in 9:19-23 is that God's wrath was against Pharaoh, not Israel. By not passing judgment on Israel in the first midrashic section, 9:6-29, the listener ponders as to what will happen to Israel, the ones who rejected the messiah—"Will they be cursed as Pharaoh was?"

Therefore, when Paul begins this transition section with the question "Has God rejected His people?", he responds to the reader's concern that was first initiated by an allusion to God's wrath against Pharaoh, 9:17, and then compounded by the subsequent feelings of uncertainty caused by Israel's stumble, 9:30—10:21. Hence, Paul's limited explanation of God's wrath, God's "hardening," accomplishes two purposes: (1) it allows Paul the opportunity to emphasize God's bestowing of grace upon the remnant, 9:6-29 and 11:5; and (2) it gives him an effective means of building suspense in this "narrative" argument by withholding the final verdict concerning God's sentencing of "hardened" Israel, 9:30—10:21 and 11:7-10.[13] Paul prepares his readers for the mystery that reveals the outcome of those who have rejected the Messiah.

---

13. If the context of Exodus 32–34 is taken into consideration, Brian Abasciano suggests that Israel had lost their election, as in the time of the worship before the golden calf. In this case, God does not restore Israel; rather, he punishes the guilty and grants them existence and a measure of blessing, which includes their priority of the gospel; see Abasciano, *Paul's Use of the Old Testament in Romans 9:1-9: An Intertextual and Theological Exegesis* (London: T & T Clark, 2005), 104. Abasciano also lists the objections to this parallel; Ibid., 214 n.20.

Poetic Form, 11:11-24

With literary beauty Paul pens a poetic "mosaic" revealing the grace of God, 11:11-24. He meticulously weaves together logical patterns, metaphors, and imperatives in a style different from any of his previous paragraphs, a *hapax legomenon*. Paul begins with two synonymous stanzas—verses 11-12 and 13-15—built around a "jealousy" theme introduced earlier: "I will make you jealous by a nation that is not a nation," 10:19. Paul reveals the sequence of God's plan using "how much more" language concerning the future "fullness" of Israel, 11:11-12, and then parallels this truth by demonstrating how he participates in Israel's reconciliation, 11:13-15 (a positive response to grief):

A		Israel's fullness	11-12
A		Paul's participation	13-15
		Transition	16
C	x	"If" statement	17
	y	Imperative	18
D	x	"Gentile" statement	19-20
	y	Imperative	21
CD		Summary	22
CDA		Conclusion	23-24

In verse 16, Paul employs agricultural imagery—"first fruits" and "root"—to transition from the topic of Israel's future fullness, 11:11-15, into the practical imperatives addressed to the gentiles among the Roman believers, imperatives embedded within an extended olive tree metaphor, 11:17-22. The olive tree metaphor imagery illustrates the kindness of God toward the gentiles as a result of Israel's disobedience, framing Paul's bold command to the church in Rome: "Be humble!" In the final verses, Paul summarizes this whole section, 11:11-24, by integrating similar form and elements from 11:11-15 and 11:17-22, particularly the "how much more" language from verses 11-15 with the olive tree imagery of verses 17-22.

Romans 11:11-24 is one arrangement, and the full text with the parallel demarcations demonstrates Paul's poetic structure that encases the revelation of the "mystery":

11   Therefore I am saying,

Did they trip in order that they might fall? By no means

But their sins result in salvation to the Gentiles   a

A   in order that the Gentiles might make them jealous   b

12   But if their sins means riches to the world   c

and their failure riches to the nations,   c

How much more their fullness?   d

13   But to you Gentiles I am speaking,

Therefore, in as much as

A   I am an apostle to the Gentiles I will boast in my ministry   a

if somehow I might make my brothers jealous and save some of them   b

15   for if the their casting away means reconciliation of the world   c

what about their reception if not life from the dead?   d

16   But if the first fruits are holy then the whole batch is holy

and if the root is holy also the branches

17   But if the branches were cut out   x

and you wild olive branches were grafted into them

and now share in the nourishing sap of the olive tree root

18   Do not boast branches   y

but if you might boast

you are not bearing the root

but the root bears you

19   Therefore, you are saying,   x

              "They were cut out in order that I will be grafted in"

20   Well, in unfaithfulness they were cut out

              but you in faith have stood

              DO NOT BE HIGH MINDED BUT FEAR   y

21   For if God did not spare the natural branches

                neither in any way will he spare you

22   CD   Therefore, behold the kindness and severity of God,

                upon the ones falling, severity,

              But upon you, the kindness of God, if you remain in kindness,

                otherwise you will be cut out

23   CDA   And also if they do not remain in unfaithfulness they will be engrafted

                For God is able to engraft them again

24   For if you, according to nature, were cut out of a wild olive

              and were engrafted into the cultivated olive tree

                How much more will these according to the natural,

                  be grafted into their own olive tree?

Revealed Mystery, 11:11-24

Paul's Boast, 11:11-15

In Romans 11:11a, Paul responds in a straightforward manner about what has been withheld up to this point: Israel's fall is not forever.[14] "Therefore I am saying, "Did they trip in order that they might fall? By no means," 11:11a. Since Paul directly addresses "gentiles" in this section, 11:13, and since the word "trip" is not used in the Greek Old Testament, it is likely that his initial question, "Did they trip in order that they might fall" echoes a well-known story from the *Aeneid* in which a "trip" does not reference permanent fall, but a blessing.[15] In addition, Paul's use of purpose clause "in order that" (ἵνα) indicates that God does not determine Israel's sin nor did he purpose a terminal fall.[16]

In Romans 11:11b-15, Paul now lays out God's plan for Israel in general terms, 11:11-12, and then personalizes the context to show how his ministry is an example of *how* God's plan works, 11:13-15.

---

14. Based on context, the meaning of "fall" (πίπτω) in verse 11 implies forever even though the same word is used in verse 22 to indicate a temporary fall.

15. Stanley Stowers argues for an echo of the footrace imagery of the funeral games for Patroclus in Book 23 of the *Iliad*; Stowers, *A Rereading of Romans: Justice, Jews, and Gentiles* (New Haven, CT: Yale University Press, 1994), 314–15; however, the footrace in Book 5 of the *Aeneid* seems to make better sense, since "tripping" results in blessing to two people groups—the Trojans and Greeks; see Wallace, *Gospel of God*, 171-72. For a "dominance" of the foot race metaphor in 9:30—10:21, see also, David Southhall, *Rediscovering Righteousness in Romans: Personified Dikaiosyneē Within Metaphoric and Narratorial Settings* (Tübingen: Mohr Siebeck, 2008), 160–61. Paul in his lament-midrash describes two people groups—Israel and gentiles—stemming from the same "root," which is probably meant to counter the ideology of the Aeneid where two people groups "branch from the one blood"; Wallace, *Gospel of God*, 174–80. Yet in the *Aeneid* the emphasis is on Roman pride.

16. Interpreting the ἵνα clause as "so as to" is a better interpretation; William Sanday and Arthur C. Headlam, *A Critical and Exegetical Commentary on the Epistle to the Romans* (Edinburgh: T & T Clark, 1898), 321. C. E. B. Cranfield discusses the other possibilities, particularly in relation to ἔπταισαν—if the use of ἵνα was final, it would be the subject of ἔπταισαν and refer to divine purpose; *A Critical and Exegetical Commentary on the Epistle to the Romans* (Edinburgh: T & T Clark, 1975–79), 544. In addition, taking πέσωσιν as what has actually happened is not a preferred meaning; ibid.

To see the direct parallel between these verses, notice below that Paul substitutes "sins resulting in salvation to the gentiles," (v. 11b) with his ministry and "apostleship to the gentiles," (v. 13b):

11b	But their sins result in salvation to the Gentiles	a
12	in order that the Gentiles might make them jealous	b
	But if their sins means riches to the world	c
	and their failure, riches to the nations	d
	How much more their fullness?	
13	But to you Gentiles I am speaking,	
	Therefore, in as much as	
	I am an apostle to the <u>Gentiles</u> I will boast in my ministry	a
14	if somehow I might make my brothers jealous and save some of them	b
15	for if their casting away means reconciliation of the world	c
	what about their reception if not life from the dead?	d

Central to the meaning of the mystery and the catalyst for change in this theological equation is "jealousy," a theme introduced earlier from an Old Testament quotation (10:19; Deut. 32:21).

It is important to highlight the "cause-effect" relationship in more detail, with specific reference to the subtle phrase that "some" of Israel "will be saved" (11:14).[17] The logical flow of the parallel within verses 11-12 is demonstrated as follows:

---

17. The words "some" and "save" are relevant to the discussion, especially concerning what Paul means by "all" Israel being saved, 11:26.

11   Israel's sins → Gentile salvation → Jealousy

12   Israel's sins → Gentile riches → Israel's fullness

Paul's point is clear—on account of Israel's sins, God mercifully blesses the gentiles, which then causes jealousy, resulting in Israel's fullness. Interestingly, Paul uses a rare but important word in verse 12: "failure" (ἥττημα), which can also be translated "loss."[18] Israel's persistent disobedience puts them in a position of weakness and needing to call upon God (ironically, they did not remember their low position from which God had called them; 9:11-13).[19]

The phrase "their fullness" (τὸ πλήρωμα αὐτῶν) can be translated "full number."[20] The antecedent for the pronoun "their" needs to be identified to clarify the meaning of "fullness." "Their" refers to either: (1) those of Israel who have rejected Christ and will repent, or (2) all of ethnic Israel. In other words, when Paul speaks of "fullness" he either means the full number of all of the ethnic Jews or the full number of some of the Jews.[21] Paul follows this internal parallel of 11:11-12 by giving additional information as to what he means by "their fullness."

---

18. BADG, s.v. ἥττημα." This word is only used twice in the New Testament (the other use means "defeat"; 1 Cor. 6:7). Ἥττημα is derived from ἔτταομαι which means to be defeated or be inferior, and Cranfield suggests ἔτταομαι can be interpreted as "to be lesser" or "to be weaker"; 557. C. K. Barrett is open to the meaning of "smaller" or "lesser"; *The Epistle to the Romans* (London: Hendrickson), 214. Käsemann suggests "failure to meet God's demands," which runs contrary to the context of Romans 9–11; *Commentary on Romans*, 305. James D. G. Dunn states that Paul wanted a -μα word, which would serve as another expression of Israel's plight; *Romans*, 654.

19. "Casting away," 11:15; "sins," 11:12; and "failure," 11:12 are structurally parallel.

20. BADG, s.v., "πλήρωμα." Sanday and Headlam do not see the exact meaning to be ascertained but suggest "full and completed number"; *Critical and Exegetical Commentary*, 322; Similarly Cranfield, *Critical and Exegetical Commentary*,558; and "compliment, or full strength"; Barrett, *Epistle to the Romans*, 214.

21. Concerning ethnic Israel, Paul either means the faithful Jews throughout history or the Jews at the moment in time of the parousia.

In 11:13-15, Paul repeats a similar theological "cause-effect" pattern from 11:11-12. First, he substitutes the phrase "gentile ministry," 11:13, instead of the phrase "Israel's sins," 11:11-12. By doing this, he makes a personal application of his ministry in relation to God's plan for Israel. Rather than experiencing grief (e.g, 9:1-5), he now gives his audience insight into how blessing results from Israel's sin, and insight into how the outreach to the gentiles causes Israel to be jealous—a blessing:

11	Israel's sins → Gentile salvation → Jealousy		
12	Israel's sins → Gentile riches	→ Israel's fullness	
13-14	<u>Gentile ministry</u> → Jealousy	→ *some of Israel saved*	
15	Israel's sins	→ Gentile riches → *Resurrection of Israel*	

Second, in verses 13-15 (italics above), Paul equates "some" of Israel's salvation with resurrection language—"life from the dead."

Paul's reasoning in these parallel sentences is simple: since Israel's failure results in riches[22] to the Gentiles, Israel's repentance will result in a "greater" or "full" return of Israel to God. This hope and expectation is made clear with two questions at the end of each stanza: "How much more Israel's fullness?" (v. 12) and "their reception, if not life from the dead?" (v. 15).[23] Paul's description of his priestly participation—his ministry (διακονία) to the gentiles (11:13; also 15:16)—carries an internal significance (in a similar way that Paul

---

22. "God has chosen Israel to be a channel of salvation for all nations"; Terence Donaldson, "Riches for the Gentiles (Rom 11:12): Israel's Rejection and Paul's Gentile Mission," *JBL* 112 (1993): 98. This infers that "Jew" and "gentile" are equal terms; ibid.

23. Building upon the notations of other scholars in a comparison of the language of 11:15 to 5:10, J. R. Kirk emphasizes God's hand in bringing life out of death with his Son and the subplot of Israel's death turning from death to life; Kirk, *Unlocking Romans: Resurrection and the Justification of God* (Grand Rapids: Eerdmans, 2008),185. He notes this thought pattern in 11:30-32 also.

experiences Christ being made great in him for the advancement of faith in others; see Phil. 1:21). Here in Romans Paul's ministry (τὴν διακονία μου) is magnified for the purpose of making his ethnic people (μου τὴν σάρκα) jealous, resulting in the salvation of some of them.

Two points need to be made in support of this view. First, Paul uses three different words for Israel's disobedience—trespass, failure, and casting away (11:11-12)—that result in salvation, riches, and reconciliation for the gentiles. This mirrors Paul's explanation about how even though through one man sin entered the world affecting all persons, through Christ's obedience grace abounds more, resulting in life, 5:18-19.[24] Though not explicitly stated, Paul understands that Christ is working within him to bring about an increase in "ministry" and salvation among his people. Second, Paul does explicitly state this reality at work within his ministry—"For I will not dare to speak anything except what Christ has worked out through me in the obedience of the Gentiles by word and deed," 15:19.

Paul conspicuously states that his aim is that "some of Israel" will be saved (v. 14) through his ministry to the gentiles. This "some" cannot mean the complete number of ethnic people who accept the Messiah, for he soon asks "how much more their fullness?" (11:15). Paul's reasoning leads the reader to expect an exponential result based on part-to-whole thinking. It might be that Paul wants his readers to see something "beyond" ethnic Israel in this section, 11:11-15. For example, in verse 15, Paul leaves out the possessive pronoun "their" in the last line and uses resurrection language—"life from the dead," 11:15 (literal translation):

24. "Trespass" is used seven times in 5:15-20 and twice in 11:11-12. The only other use in Romans is in 4:25 where Paul writes concerning Christ being delivered up for our trespasses and raised to life for our righteousness.

Verse 12	Verse 15
But if *their* trespasses,	For if *their* casting away,
riches of world;	reconciliation of the world
and *their* failure,	
riches of nations;	
How much more *their* fullness?...	What about their reception
	if not life from the dead?

He may do this to make an indirect reference to Jew and gentile believers, rather than ethnic Israel. In addition, Paul's use of the phrase "from the dead" (ἐκ νεκρῶν) is only used in Romans in reference to the resurrection of Christ or the resurrection power of God in the believer (1:4; 4:24; 6:4, 9, 13; 7:4, 8:11, 34; 10:7, 9; 14:9). Thus the sentence (literal translation)—"What reception, if not life from the dead"—could either refer to a complete number (not limited to the "some" from Paul's ministry to the gentiles) of ethnic Jews, or it refers to the total number of Jews and gentile believers who experience the power of Christ's resurrection through faith.

And since Paul conveys the idea that the resurrection power is at work—"fullness" (v. 12) and "acceptance, if not life from the dead" (v. 15)[25]— it is possible, at this point in the argument, to contend that he means that "all" of ethnic Israel could be saved.

It is also important to know that this resurrection imagery, 11:15, mirrors Paul's theology in his letter thus far. In the life of the believer, exponential grace occurs where sin increased, 5:21,[26] and the believer

---

25. The connotations for πρόσληψις include: "taking in addition," "taking into oneself," or a sense of "acquisition"—Paul must be thinking of the final resurrection at the end of the age (see also 5:10 and 11:15 that refer to the death of Christ; Dunn, *Romans*, 657 and 670). Again, Kirk sees the resurrection motif as the key lens to interpret Paul's emphases in Romans. His parallel of 11:15 to 5:10 is worth viewing; *Unlocking Romans*, 185.

participates by being baptized with Christ in his death and raised to life with him, 6:4. This power of the Spirit who raised Christ lives in the believer who dies to sin, 8:10-11. In Romans 9–11, Paul experiences grief and is given wisdom to see how the resurrection power of God is applicable to individuals *and nations*—Israel and the gentiles. From a missiological perspective this makes great sense, for Paul's zealous pursuit of gentile salvation functions as part of God's agency for reaching Israel. In other words, the more kindness bestowed upon the gentiles, the greater the volume of God's message—through jealousy—will be sent to Israel: "Repent!" Thus, Paul grieves sincerely for his people (e.g., 9:1-5 and 10:1), and his ambitious desire to evangelize Spain and the world, 15:20, is, in part, because of his deep love and motivation for his Jewish brothers.

In 11:11-15, Paul understands that "some" (or "part") leads to the impact of the "whole." If this is his aim, and if his style of knitting themes together in his argument is consistent, then he will continue to instruct his audience in this way.

Agricultural Imagery, 11:16-24

Although the sentence in Romans 11:16 may appear to be a style break in the argument,[27] it serves a more pivotal purpose in the poetic arrangement of this section (11:11-24):

> 16   But if the first fruits are holy then the whole batch is holy
>
> and if the root is holy also the branches

---

26. For the parallel of 5:10 and 11:15, see also Wright, "Letter to the Romans," 682. "Out of dead" refers to the final resurrection; Dunn, *Romans*, 658; This could involve eschatological and apocalyptic reference to the end—salvation history; Douglas Moo, *The Epistle to the Romans* (Grand Rapids: Eerdmans, 1996), 695. Kirk understands that God will bring Israel back from the dead; *Unlocking Romans*, 188–89.

27. The internal break between 11:15 and 11:16 seems appropriate, but dividing 11:12 and 11:13 seems inappropriate. For a threefold argument: v.18b, 19-22, 23-24, see Dunn, *Romans*, 652.

Paul just boasted in his ministry to the gentiles, 11:13—a role that he sees as a priestly service of sanctification.[28] Now in verse 16, Paul uses two "part-to-whole" metaphors that parallel each other for the purpose of emphasizing "holiness": (1) a holy "first fruits" means that the "whole" is holy, and (2) the holiness of a root means the branches are holy, too. Thus, Paul associates *root* and *first fruits* in relation to their state of "being made holy."

By following Paul's thought flow—from verses 11-15 to verse 16—it is evident that Paul stresses degree. In 11:11-15, through the use of question and "how much more" language, Paul punctuates Israel's repentance and the degree of their salvation. Here in 11:16, Paul emphasizes, in some sense, the degree of holiness—if part of the whole is holy then "how much more" holy will the "whole" be? The ambiguity of this verse, then, has more to do with what Paul means by "first fruits" and the "root." In other words, do these metaphors refer to the "gentiles" or "Israel"?

"First fruits"

By referring to the "first fruits" as gentiles who believe in Christ, Paul secures the hope for Israel's salvation.[29] In the transition of

---

28. For a similar boast, see 15:16.
29. The basic meaning is "consecrated before the rest"; BADG, s.v. "ἀπαρχή." Seven of the nine uses in the New Testament are in Paul's letters, and he uses the term in various ways. In essence, the sacrifice of the part affects the blessedness of the whole, as the whole of the grain harvest is consecrated by the offering of the first sheaf (e.g., Num. 15:19f); see G. M. Burge, "First Fruits, Down Payment," *DPL*, 300. The "first fruits" was offered based on the requirements of God's law, such as in Exod. 22:28; 23:19; 25:2-3; Lev. 2:12; 23:10; Num. 15:19-20. Interestingly, other olive tree metaphors do not suggest the "whole" tree as holy (Jer. 11:16 and Hos. 14:6). Cranfield emphasizes that nowhere does the Old Testament say that this offering hallows the rest of the dough; *Critical and Exegetical Commentary*, 563. For New Testament uses referring to gentiles, see Rom. 16:5, 1 Cor. 16:15, and James 1:8. Other representative interpretations include "Christ" or "remnant" as "first fruits"; Cranfield, *Critical and Exegetical Commentary*, 564. Ἀπαρχή could refer to the "patriarchs" and those who first responded to the gospel; as a reference to Christ, this is unlikely; Dunn, *Romans*, 659. Barrett traces the origin of "first fruits" to Numbers 15:20, where the offering de-sanctifies for general consumption. He understands the "lump and branches" to signify Israel and the "first fruit and root" to refer to the first Jewish

verse 16, Paul introduces "gentiles" here, leading into the olive tree metaphor. His purpose in using the symbol "first fruits" is to show that the gentiles are made "holy." Paul makes the case concerning God's plan for Israel that the gentiles who have come to believe in Christ are God's "first fruits" with respect to the outcome from Israel's disobedience. Even though it is "disobedience" that has occurred, Paul makes it clear that the gentile offering—the "first fruits"—is a "holy" offering. It is not the first time in Romans Paul discusses the nature of God's mercy in relation to human sin (e.g., where sin increases, grace abounds more, 5:20f; 8:28). Likewise, with Israel's disobedience, God works out mercy in terms of gentile "holiness" (or blessing), which will also result in Israel becoming jealous, 11:14. This same idea is expressed more clearly at the end of his letter as he speaks of his role as an apostle: ". . . in order to be a priestly-servant of Christ Jesus for the gentiles, ministering the gospel of God, in order that an offering might be made of the gentiles pleasing, being sanctified (ἡγιασμένη) in the Holy Spirit" (15:16). In essence, Paul implies, "If the first fruits [gentiles] are holy, *how much more* will Israel be made holy!"

It is important to make the distinction that "first fruits" does not explicitly refer to the "remnant." Following the natural thought progression from 11:1-10, "remnant" may appear to be the appropriate referent. Earlier Paul defined the "remnant," 9:6-29, in terms of gentile inclusion in order to prepare the reader for the mystery he is about to unfold, 11:11f, but here in the olive tree metaphor, 11:16-24, Paul temporarily sets aside the identifications of "remnant" Israel and "hardened" Israel from 11:1-10, and returns to

---

Christians, not the patriarchs, as a pledge of the eventual salvation of Israel; 216. Robert Jewett sees a parallel to Philo, *Sacra AC*; *Romans: A Commentary*, ed. Eldon Jay Epp (Minneapolis: Fortress Press, 2007), 107. For a helpful summary of varying views, see Thomas Schreiner, *Romans* (Grand Rapids: Baker Books, 1998), 600f.

the more general terms—"gentiles" (representing "faith") and "Israel" (representing "works"; see 9:30—10:3).

He does this for literary congruency—to make the olive tree metaphor work. By using the term "gentiles," Paul removes "Jewish Christians" from the metaphorical picture so that "gentiles" receives the semantic weight in the discussion. In other words, if "remnant" was used here (representing Jewish and gentile Christians), God's blessing of the gentile would not be clearly delineated.[30] Paul is not underscoring the Jews "being made holy" as an agent for Israel's salvation; rather, he emphasizes the conversion of the "gentiles" so that the mystery concerning God's merciful and wise character is made plain—his mercy to the "gentiles" (not Jewish converts) provokes "Israel" to jealousy, causing Israel's repentance. Thus, in the first clause of this transition sentence—"But if the first fruits are holy then the whole batch is holy"—Paul uses Levitical-agricultural imagery to summarize what he has said about God's blessing of the gentiles as a means of making Israel jealous, 11:11-15. In a similar way, the "root" in the second clause of this transition ("and if the root is holy also the branches," 11:16b) introduces the "patriarchs" into the agricultural imagery of the olive tree in the verses that follow, 11:17f.

"Root"

Based on the context of Romans 9–11, the "root" of the tree refers to the "patriarchs" for several reasons:[31] First, while "root" and "first fruits," 11:16, are both within the semantic domain of agricultural

---

30. "Israel" represents hardened Israel and "gentiles" represent Christian gentiles. By using the label "gentiles," Paul emphasizes God's decision to bless gentiles who believe. The general term "gentiles" does not include non-Christian gentiles. See the explanation in chapter 3 on Romans 9:30—10:3.

31. "Root" as patriarchs; e.g, Sanday and Headlam, *Critical and Exegetical Commentary*; Dunn, *Romans* (1988); John Murray, *The Epistle to the Romans* (Grand Rapids: Eerdmans, 1968); Leon Morris, *The Epistle to the Romans* (Grand Rapids: Eerdmans, 1988). Also see *Jub.* 21:24. For "root" as Jewish Christians, see Barrett, *Epistle to the Romans*.

imagery, the term "root" does *not* synonymously parallel "first fruits." "First fruits" refers to the converted "gentiles"—pointing back to what Paul says in 11:11–15—while "root" moves the imagery forward by introducing the olive tree metaphor, a reference to the "patriarchs" from which engrafting and "cutting out" takes place (see discussion below, v.17).[32] Second, in 9:6–19, Paul made a sequential reference to God's elective purposes, which included the gentiles[33]—"children of promise" *from the seed of Abraham* (9:8; "The children of the flesh are not children of God, but the children of promise will be reckoned into the seed."). Thus, "root" symbolizes the patriarchs, highlighting God's order of election, particularly referring to a spiritual origin for believers based on faith in God's promise—a faith that is not limited to a people group. Third, the referent for the "root" as "patriarchs" also makes sense with Paul's mention of Jacob in the verses that follow the olive tree metaphor, "concerning [Israel] they are beloved on account of the patriarchs," 11:28. Fourth, this interpretation agrees with Paul's earlier thought progression where "patriarchs" comes first in the order of discussion: "they are the *fathers* [οἱ πατέρες] and from them comes the Messiah according to the seed," 9:5.

In 11:16, Paul's words give the reader assurance concerning Israel's salvation. He shows that (1) the "root," the fathers of the nation Israel, is holy and (2) the first fruits, the gentile Christians who benefited from Israel's disobedience, are holy. Therefore, if the patriarchs are holy and if the gentiles are also made holy then "how much more according to the natural branches will they [Israel] be engrafted into their own olive tree?" (11:24b)

---

32. This takes place from the "tree" in verses 23–24. Despite all of the criticism, there is a good possibility that Paul draws from a real life arboricultural practice; see A. G. Baxter and John Ziesler, "Paul and the Arboriculture: Romans 11:17–24," *JSNT* 7, no. 24 (1985): 25–32.

33. This presupposes that "engrafting" is a synonym in the olive tree metaphor for God's elective decisions.

God's Kindness and Severity, 11:17-22

The purpose of the olive tree metaphor is didactic as well as revelatory. The cutting and engrafting represent the actions of God, and in this way God's character is demonstrated. Using parallel thought, Paul enlightens his recipients concerning the kindness and severity of God in election—the cutting and engrafting—in order to prevent pride among them (11:17-21):

17	Kindness to the gentile	x	C (kindness)
18	Imperative against pride	y	
19-20	Severity to Israel as example	x	D (severity)
21	Imperative against pride	y	
22	Behold the kindness and severity of God		CD

Verses 17-18 parallel verses 19-21: "kindness" (x), imperative (y), "severity" (x), imperative (y). Verse 22 restates the themes "kindness" and "severity" of God.[34]

Verse 17 begins with a conditional clause followed by a description of God's mercy in relation to the wild olive branches, the gentiles:

> But if some of the branches were cut out
>
> and you wild olive branches [gentiles] were grafted into them
>
> and now share in the richness [mercy] of the olive tree root . . .

---

34. While "kindness" and "severity" may be connected with "faith" and "unbelief" (see Barrett, *Epistle to the Romans*, 219), it is more likely that Paul highlights the nature of God's "mercy" and "wrath," a continuing theme from the beginning of his letter; particularly see 1:18 and 2:4.

These words encapsulate what Paul has asserted concerning the gentiles up to this point in his argument: "They are included!" Paul then commands the gentile Christians to choose humility (v. 18):

Do not boast branches

but if you might boast

you are not bearing the root

but the root bears you

The phrase "the root bears you" does not place emphasis on the merit of the fathers but on God's election of Abraham and his descendants. Paul's use of agricultural imagery—the sequence of "root" and "wild branches"—indirectly reiterates his thesis concerning the order of God's election—"salvation to the Jew first and then the gentile" (1:16; 2:9-10)—admonishing the believers to respect God's wisdom. The gentiles are not to boast in their status as if it produces some self-advantage, but they are to boast in the spiritual benefit through God's election of the patriarchs.[35]

After this imperative, Paul in *diatribe* style places words in the mouth of a proud gentile and follows these words with the reason for Israel's fall—unfaithfulness (11:19-20a):[36]

---

35. In the first century, Judaism placed considerable emphasis on the merits of the patriarchs as a type of "grace" in which they remained in the covenant (see E. P. Sanders, *Paul and Palestine Judaism: A Comparison of Patterns of Religions* [Philadelphia: Fortress Press, 1977]).

36. Paul uses this same technique in his reprimand of the Jew who boasts hypocritically (2:17f). Furthermore, his use of the olive tree metaphor in relation to actual Mediterranean practices suggests that Paul undermines the pretensions of the Greek Christ followers in Rome; Philip Esler, "Ancient Oleiculture and Ethnic Differentiation: The Meaning of the Olive-Tree Image in Romans 11," *JSNT* 26, no. 1 (2003): 103f.

Therefore, you are saying,

"They were cut out in order that I will be grafted in"

Well, in unfaithfulness they were cut out

but you in faith have stood

In parallel fashion, 11:20c, Paul synonymously repeats an imperative against gentile "high-mindedness" (ὑψηλὰ φρόνει) but antithetically warns of God's judgment:

Do not be high minded but fear   20c

for if God did not spare the natural branches   21

neither in any way will he spare you

Paul's pattern — statement, imperative, statement, and imperative — intensifies the charge to the gentiles. It is interesting that the climactic part of his argument in Romans 9–11 instructs the gentiles' attitudes, begging the question as to their own status before God.[37] Paul weaves these corresponding imperatives into his literary mosaic, 11:11-24, for a particular purpose—to warn the gentiles in Rome to be humble. This gives priority to the main purpose of his letter: to engender fertile, "humble" soil among the gentile believers in the Roman congregation, 1:13.

In verse 22, Paul ties together his previous four stanzas by using two synonyms for God's mercy and wrath—his "kindness" (χρηστότητα) and "severity" (ἀποτομίαν):

---

37. The problem in Rome is among "Christians" and not with Jews; see N. A. Dahl, "The Future of Israel," in *Studies in Paul: Theology for the Early Christian Mission*, ed. G. W. Bromiley (Minneapolis: Augsburg Publishing House, 1977), 158.

> Therefore, behold the kindness and severity of God,
>
> upon the ones falling, severity,
>
> But upon you, the kindness of God, if you remain in kindness,
>
> otherwise you will be cut out.

These terms make sense in light of the rest of the letter. In the first pages of his letter, 2:3-4, Paul expresses God's "kindness" in contrast to coming wrath. He stresses the enduring patience of God that leads people to repentance—an attribute not naturally exhibited in humankind (3:12; Ps. 14:1).[38] Only here does Paul use the term "severity" (ἀποτομία) which is synonymous with the imagery of being "cut out" (ἐκκόπτω) of the olive tree.[39]

Foreshadowed Grace, 11:23-24

Paul summarizes verses 11-22 in verses 23-24 in a manner that generates hope. He merges (1) his logic from v. 11-15 ("*if gentiles . . . then how much more Israel*") and (2) the specific phrases from the imperatives of verses 16-21.

---

38. In other words, as a characteristic of God, "kindness" is to be lived out in the believer's life through the Spirit; see 2 Cor. 6:6; Gal. 5:22; Eph. 2:7; Col. 3:12; Tit. 3:4.
39. The concept of "cutting out" may very well share similarity to the connotation of God's wrath as depicted as a "handing over"—1:18, 24, and 26. The degree of separation is not explicitly stated.

> 23 And also *if they do not remain in <u>unfaithfulness</u> they will be engrafted*
>
> *For God is able to engraft them again*
>
> 24 For if you, according to nature, were cut out of a wild olive
>
> and were engrafted into the cultivated olive tree
>
> How much more will these according to the natural,
>
> be grafted into their own olive tree.

Notice in verse 23 that Paul accents Israel's *unfaithfulness* by repeating his previous statement a few sentences before: " . . . in unfaithfulness they were cut out," v. 20a—but in place of judgment (being "cut out") Paul substitutes hope—"*if they do not remain in unfaithfulness they will be engrafted*," v. 23a. Then Paul emphasizes God's resurrection power at work—"*For God is able to engraft them again*"—a restatement of verse 11:15b ("for if their casting away means reconciliation of the world, what about their reception if not life from the dead?")

Similarly in verse 24, when Paul expresses God's kindness to the gentile—"For if you, according to nature, were cut out of a wild olive tree and were engrafted into the cultivated olive tree . . ."—he reiterates what he said in 17b—"But if some of the branches were cut out and you wild olive branches were grafted into them." And in Paul's final sentence of this section (11:24c), he alludes to verse 12:

> 12c How much more their fullness?
>
> 24b How much more will these according to the natural
>
> be grafted into their own olive tree?

Therefore, in verses 23-24, Paul threads back through his topics from verses 11-22 to summarize the mystery of God's election. However, where verses 17-22 contrast the severity and kindness of God, *verses 23-24 express only the grace of God.*[40]

Interestingly, in the olive tree imagery, the gentiles believe in Christ first and then the Jews follow. Paul's imagery reverses the order of salvation from the initial theme of his letter—"For I am not ashamed of the gospel, it is the power of God unto salvation, *first to the Jew and then to the gentile*," 1:16. This reversal evidences God's impartiality in election. Sequence and order do not mean superiority or less in significance. God is the God of the Jew and the gentile, 3:29; and there is no distinction between Jew or Greek, for the Lord is Lord of all, 10:12. The focus of the midrashic argument turns to God's character in election—he chooses those in humble circumstances. This reversal—repentant gentiles before the repentant Jews —is congruent with the "engrafting" imagery of the olive tree metaphor. The order of election is not negated; rather, the olive tree imagery emphasizes God's impartiality—order does not suggest favoritism. Furthermore, Paul does not eliminate ethnic distinctions or do away with God's order. Thus, the whole argument has less to do with "equality" and more to do with God's character in election (e.g., choosing the son in the humble situation and blessing those who remain in faith).

Paul's warning and encouragement evidences his aim to address a particular situation in Rome. For he bolsters the purpose of his letter: to effect humility in a context of grace. Now Paul ends the body of his argument in Romans 9–11 with a summary and final statement concerning "all Israel."

---

40. The repetition of the phrase "how much more" as well as the thought rhyme *"their* fullness" indicates that Paul refers to those of ethnic Israel who return to God.

Thematic Outline, 11:25-32

In this final section of the body of his argument, Paul brings together all of the elements thus far, 9:6—11:24. He summarizes what has been said, 11:25-32, with his themes and conclusions, rather than bring in new ideas, with the exception of the Old Testament support from Isaiah, which serves a thematic purpose. An overall outline of these verses is as follows:

Summary of Olive Tree Metaphor	25-27
Isa. 59:20-21	
Isa. 27:9	
Summary of Midrashic Sections	28
Inclusio	30-32

It might be helpful to see the full text and corresponding verses that summarize retrospectively:

25 For I wish that you would not be ignorant, brothers, of this mystery

in order that you might not think of yourselves too highly   **Summary of**

because the partial hardening in Israel has happened   **Olive Tree**

until the fullness of the gentiles might come in   **Metaphor**

26 and likewise all Israel will be saved.   **(11:11-23)**

Even as it is written,   **Support**

"From Zion comes the One who delivers   **Isa. 59:20-21a**

he will turn Jacob from godlessness

27 and this by my covenant with them

I will forgive their sins."   **Isa. 27:9**

Summary of Sections

28 according to the gospel, enemies on account of us   **(9:30—10:21)**

according to the elect, beloved on account of the fathers   **(9:6-29)**

29 For God's call and gifts are irrevocable

30 For just as you were disobedient to God   **Inclusio**

now you have been shown mercy by their disobedience

31 Likewise, those who have presently disobeyed   **(11:22-23**

resulted in your being shown mercy   **to 9:6-12)**

in order that now they too might be shown mercy.

32 For God bound all into disobedience

in order that he might show mercy to all.

After the meaning of these verses is explained, the content of this summary passage, 11:25-32, is discussed, which then makes clear the theological import of the phrase "all Israel."

Israel's Salvation, 11:25-32

In Romans 11:25-26a, Paul summarizes his olive tree imagery, bringing together the sum of his argument:

> For I wish that you would not be ignorant, brothers, of this mystery
>
> in order that you might not think of yourselves too highly
>
> because the partial hardening in Israel has happened
>
> until the fullness of the gentiles might come in.
>
> and likewise all Israel will be saved

The phrases and words in these verses deserve explanation—"brothers," "partial hardening," "fullness of the gentiles," "likewise," and "all Israel"—for their semantic significance is relevant to the meaning of the whole argument. And the parallels and possible meanings of these terms are discussed below to determine their contribution to the meaning of the phrase "all Israel."

Gentile Humility, 11:25a

> For I wish that you would not be ignorant, brothers, of this mystery
>
> in order that you might not think of yourselves too highly

Paul boldly states the purpose of this mystery:[41] to produce humility—a theme that Paul vigorously supports in his arguments, 9:6—11:24. Paul's commands against pride—"Do not boast branches . . . Do not be high minded" (11:18 and 21)—come after a lengthy midrashic narrative leading to this practical conclusion. For Paul demonstrates how even though the Father desires a humble, obedient son in the nation of Israel, they did not know the righteousness of God, nor make the humble confession of "Jesus as Lord" (see 10:2-9). And through the use of Old Testament support, Paul reveals how God defeated proud Pharaoh for the purpose of displaying power, and to send his Name to all the nations—a call for humility and at the same time a warning of impending judgment for those who do not repent (see 9:13-24). Paul also reveals God's character in the choice of the son in the lesser position in order that God's elective purposes might remain—not based on works but by the character of the One calling (9:12).[42]

In 11:25, Paul addresses his listeners as "brothers," a term he uses for two different groups of people. Earlier, Paul uses "brothers" in reference to his race, those of the nation Israel who have rejected the Messiah, the Israel for whom Paul grieves, 9:1-5 and 10:1. However

41. The "mystery" is revealed. "Mentioned twenty or twenty-one times in Pauline corpus . . . [it] denotes characteristically in the New Testament not something which must not be disclosed to the uninitiated (which is its connotation in extrabiblical Greek, when used in connection with mystery cults), but something which could not be known by men except by divine revelation, but with which though once hidden, is now revealed in Christ and is to be proclaimed so that all who have ears to hear my hear it."; Cranfield, *Critical and Exegetical Commentary*, 573. The word has strong apocalyptic associations; however, the content of this revelation is from the Old Testament, carrying a prophetic sense, discerned in light of gospel events; ibid.

42. In chapter 2, Paul reprimands the "Jew" who arrogantly passes judgment on those who break the law, yet they themselves break the law that they preach against. It is this hypocrisy that Paul seeks to change in the minds of the Roman believers, making this issue a situational one, addressed throughout the letter. Also, it is not surprising that this theme of humility is carried into his admonition section, 12:1—15:13. Paul warns the Roman believers—"Do not think more highly of yourself than you ought!" 12:3. And based on the situation among the Roman household churches, Paul reminds the believers who are strong in faith not to be prideful in choosing to pass judgment on the person who is weak in faith, 14:1—15:7.

in 11:12, Paul directly addresses gentile Christians as "brothers," an address that continues through to the end of the argument. Thus in 11:25, Paul refers to gentile "brothers," those whose "fullness" will be a catalyst to Israel's salvation.[43]

"Partial Hardening," 11:25b —"because the partial hardening in Israel has happened"

While verse 25a reiterates the purpose for revealing this mystery—"in order that you might not think of yourselves too highly"—verses 25b-26 summarize the content of the mystery described in verses 11:23-24 (and the olive tree imagery of 11:11-22, respectively). But Paul omits any mention of "jealousy," 11:25-26,[44] letting the listeners supply in their minds this relevant piece of information from the olive tree metaphor—"the partial hardening in Israel has happened until the fullness of the gentiles might come in [caused by jealousy], and likewise all Israel will be saved."[45]

---

43. Yet his address in 11:25 would not exclude Jewish Christians. Both sections, 9:30—10:3 and 11:11-24, are written within a metaphorical context and should be understood in light of their literary purpose. Paul's references to "gentiles" as "faithful Gentile Christians" and "Israel" as representative of "works" accent the righteousness of God and Israel's pride. Since not all gentiles have faith and neither are all Israelites hardened, it is clear that Paul does not intend these labels to be stringently applied. It would make little sense for Paul to address the Israelites as "brothers" in the context of his ministry and the olive tree metaphor, 11:12-24, if they have not repented.

44. The key to the mystery—jealousy—is not mentioned here. In one way, this hiddenness adds to the meaning of the "mystery" revealed.

45. A demonstrative pronoun (ὅτι), most likely expresses "what" the mystery consists of and immediately follows the purpose clause (ἵνα); BADG, s.v. "ὅτι." Paul's effective use of a variety of literary devices such as omission, inversion, and suspension demonstrate his intellectual skill.

11:11-15	Israel Sins	Israel hardened	Gentile Blessing	Jealousy	Israel's Salvation
11:23-24	Israel Unfaithful	Israel cut out	Gentiles Engrafted	——	Natural branches engrafted
11:25-26	Israel Sins	Israel hardened	Gentile Blessing	——	Israel's Salvation

Consequently, verses 25-26 follow Paul's parallel sequence found in verses 11:11-15 and verses 23-24 (remember that verses 23-24 are written using olive tree imagery):

In these summary verses, 11:25-26, Paul adds new information—"partial" (ἀπὸ μέρους)[46] hardening. By doing so, he eliminates the concern the readers may have concerning a permanent hardening of Israel. The word "partial" restates Paul's earlier phrase, "Their trip was not a forever fall," 11:11. Also, when Paul writes partial "hardening" of Israel, he makes a slight literary distinction. Paul has completed his use of the olive tree imagery, 11:17-23, and does not need the generalized labels he used earlier—"Israel" representing "works" and "gentiles" representing "faith," 9:30—10:3 and 11:11-24. He now returns to the defined identity of "hardened" Israel, 11:7-10, referring to the Israelites who have rejected Christ, whose disobedience God uses to bless the gentiles.

Gentile "fullness," 11:25c —"until the fullness of the gentiles might come in"

Paul, for the first time in his letter, writes the phrase "fullness of the Gentiles."[47] (In 11:12, he uses the word "fullness" but he does this

---

46. Paul is placing a "numerical limitation" on Israel's hardening; Moo, *Romans*, 717.

with respect to Israel's salvation.) Logically speaking, "fullness" either means absolutely every gentile or a complete number of "some" of the gentiles. Since the context of this letter does not agree with the reading "every gentile" (see 1:18f; 9:27),[48] the other possibility refers to "less than every gentile." And based on the context of Paul's argument, he defines this group as those believers who are called (10:13 and 11:5). Therefore, "fullness" implies the number of those gentiles whom God calls—those who call upon Him. The mystery, then, consists of God's temporary hardening of Israel until God's full number of called gentiles comes in.

More specifically, the contrast between "partial" and "fullness" accents God's ability: a "temporary" hardening (of Israel) results in "eternal" blessing (of the gentiles). The natural thought progression would then be: "Since God is able to take what is 'partial' and negative[49]—disobedience—and work out what is 'eternal' and positive—blessing—then how much more, with God, will 'fullness' result in 'fullness'?" Yet, interestingly, in Paul's climactic statement concerning "all Israel," 11:26, he intentionally omits the "how much more" language. Either Paul omits the phrase "how much more" for the reader to supply it, or he omits the phrase because he is referring to "all Israel" with a particular nuance in mind.

47. The connotation is that which is brought into fullness or completion—full number; BAGD, 672.

48. Paul does not argue for a universalistic principle. For the idea of the "full number intended by God," see Dunn, *Romans*, 680 and 691; Delling, *TDNT*, 6:302. Pressing the nearness of an eschatological completion, Mark Nanos sees no reason for a numeric quality here; see *The Mystery of Romans: The Jewish Context of Paul's Letter* (Minneapolis: Fortress Press, 1996), 266.

49. The terms "negative" and "positive" are used in a mathematical sense for illustration.

"All Israel," 11:26a — *"and likewise all Israel will be saved"*

Paul expresses *how* God works out the salvation of "all Israel":[50] the "fullness of the gentiles come in" (v. 25c) after the partial hardening of Israel has happened (v. 25b).[51] Thus verses 25b-26a can be interpreted as follows: "The purpose of this mystery is to encourage humility. This mystery consists of God's partial hardening of Israel until the fullness of the gentiles comes in, and likewise 'all Israel' will be saved."[52]

With the completion of the olive tree metaphor in 11:24, Paul returns to the defined identities of "remnant" Israel and "hardened" Israel, 9:6—11:10. He defines "remnant" Israel as those who are called by grace, 11:1-6, made up of both Jew and gentile, 9:6-29. He defines "hardened Israel" as those who have heard and rejected the gospel, 9:30—10:21, and who have been hardened, 11:7-10.

It was for the literary purposes of the olive tree metaphor in 11:17-24 (and the poetical structure of 9:30—10:3) that Paul employed the *general* terms "gentiles" and "Israel." He used these

---

50. The use of the conjunction καὶ with the adverb οὕτως intends a modal emphasis. Neither BAGD or LSJ lists a "temporal" sense. While Paul's gospel here expresses a Jewish concern, it is important to remember that his gospel answers the dilemma in a manner that respects God's order of election ("first the Jew and then the gentile") in relation to God's impartiality. Thus while the use of οὕτως signifies the manner in which God acts, the context of the argument as a whole implies a general "sequence" as to what follows—process and time are involved.

　　Nanos argues for a two-step pattern upon which the mystery is not "all Israel saved" but *how* they become saved (based on Acts 28:15, 24-28; 13:40-41, 46-48; and 17:1-2); see *Mystery of Romans*, 256–60.

51. "Until" (ἄχρι) introduces a dependent clause and should not be separated from the preceding ὅτι clause. On the other hand, Cranfield sees this sentence as broken down into three rather than two clauses: (1) πώρωσις . . . γέγονεν, (2) ἄχρι οὗ . . . εἰσέλθῃ, (3) καὶ οὕτως . . . σωθήσεται; with "καὶ οὕτως " having the meaning "and thus"; *Critical and Exegetical Commentary*, 574.

52. Israel's salvation was a common theme of Jewish eschatology (Deut. 30:1-5; Neh. 1:9; Jer. 23:3; 29:14; Ezek. 11:17; 36:24; and Amos 9:11-15); Dunn, *Romans*, 681. Based on a reference in the Mishnah ("All Israelites have a share in the world to come," *m. Sanh.* 10:1). Morris interprets that Paul refers to the Israelites as a whole, and that some Israelites will not participate; *Epistle to the Romans*, 421. For a history of interpretation in light of patristic and medieval exegesis, see Cohen, "The Mystery," 247–81.

labels to elucidate the character of God in his blessing of the gentiles as a means of Israel's salvation.[53] This means that in Romans 9:6—11:25, Paul refers to "Israel" in four different ways: (1) ethnic Israel, 9:5-6; (2) "Israel" as a literary term symbolizing "works"—9:30—10:3; 11:17-24; (3) "hardened" Israel, 11:7-10; and (4) the "engrafted branches" (or "repentant" Israel) who return to God following the gentiles receiving blessing, 11:23-24.[54] Several factors warrant consideration before an appropriate conclusion can be drawn as to what Paul means by "all Israel": (a) the parallel verses to 11:25-26, (b) the supporting Old Testament quotations from Isaiah, 11:27, and (c) the Old Testament idiom "All Israel."

Parallel Verses

The reading of "all Israel" as "all those of hardened Israel who repent" makes logical sense. The content of verses 11:25-26 parallel the poetical thought sequences of 11:11-15 and 11:23-24. Notice particularly verses 12 and 24:

---

53. With great fervor Paul argued that gentiles are called sons, too (9:6-29). He painted a metaphorical picture of the gentiles as "faith" (9:30—10:3), and he employs a pesher type midrash to prove that God's mercy has always been extended to the gentile as well as the Jew. In 10:19, Paul clues the reader into the significance of God's blessing. By blessing the gentiles, God arouses the jealousy of Israel.

54. The clause "all Israel will be saved" is interpreted to mean several possibilities: (a) Jew and gentile Christians, comprising the remnant; (b) the nation of Israel saved based on the covenant, apart from faith in Christ; or (c) future salvation of historical Israel at the parousia. The majority view seems to be a reference to elect Jews and gentiles in a spiritual sense; see also John Calvin, *The Epistles of Paul the Apostle to the Romans and the Thessalonians*, eds. Ross Mackenzie, David W. Torrance, and Thomas F. Torrance (London: Oliver & Boyd, 1961), 255. For the argument of a future redeemed Israel based on Galatians 6:16 and Romans 11:26, see S. Lewis Johnson, "Paul and 'The Israel of God': An Exegetical and Eschatological Case-Study," *Master's Seminary Journal* 20, no. 1 (2009): 49f. It is difficult to argue for a definition of "all Israel" as something more than "remnant" because of Paul's explicit language in 11:4 and the Old Testament context of Elijah. Paul's initial midrashic section of 9:6-29 intimates gentile inclusion in the remnant, reinforced in 11:1-10.

11:12   a   if their <u>sins</u> ... (no olive tree imagery)

b   means riches to the world ...

c   how much more their fullness

11:24   a   if they do not remain in <u>unfaithfulness</u> they will be engrafted ...

b   if you were cut out and engrafted into cultivated olive tree

c   How much more will these be grafted into their own olive tree

In the above parallels, Paul does *not* write that the (a) sins of Israel and the (b) blessing of the Gentiles result in the "fullness of the remnant." Rather, he refers to the "fullness" of hardened Israel—their repentance—in these verses. If Paul intended to extend the logical parallel of 11:12 and 11:24 to 11:26 in this way, then "all Israel" would refer to those of ethnic Israel who "repent."[55]

11:25-26   a   because the partial hardening in Israel has happened

b   and the fullness of the gentiles might come in

c?   and likewise all Israel will be saved (repentant ethnic Israel?)

In the first lines of each verse above, Israel's disobedience is expressed synonymously as "sins," "unfaithfulness," and "partial hardening." In the second lines of each verse, gentile blessing is expressed synonymously as "riches to the world," "engrafted into cultivated olive tree," and "fullness of the gentiles." When comparing the third lines, Paul uses the conjunction and adverb "and likewise" (καὶ

---

55. Christopher Zoccali names this group the "total national elect," which is defined as "the complete number of elect from the historical/empirical nation"; Zoccali, "'And So All Israel Will be Saved': Competing Interpretations of Romans 11.26 in Pauline Scholarship," *JSNT* 30, no. 3 (2008): 303.

οὔτως; or "and in this way") in verse 26 instead of the "how much more" phrase:

12	c	how much more their fullness
24	c	how much more will these be grafted into their own olive tree
26	c?	and likewise all Israel will be saved

Paul might be omitting the "how much more" reasoning so that the listener supplies this phrase—"how much more will all Israel be saved."[56] If so, Paul in a similar way omitted the word "jealousy" in the olive tree metaphor in 11:14-15 just after he explained the mystery concerning the catalyst of "jealousy" (the reader is expected to supply this piece of information when Paul explains that the exponential return is a result of jealousy in response to the "fullness" of the gentiles coming in, 11:26b). Based on the first two parallels above, 11:12 and 11:24, the final sentences refer to "repentant" Israel—Jews who turn to Christ. If this parallel carries over to 11:26, then "all Israel" refers to all of the "repentant" Jews, which could mean either (a) the return of every "ethnic" Jew, or (b) a "full number" of Jews who repent and turn to Christ, but not every Israelite.

Helpful to this discussion may be Paul's description of his personal role as an apostle to the gentiles: to make his own people jealous so that "some" of Israel might be saved, 11:14-15, a statement preceding

---

56. I have demonstrated up to this point how Paul's narrative and sequence of reasoning in his lament-midrash is balanced, creating suspense and expectation concerning Israel. His logical structure can be summarized as follows (with "X" referring to Israel and "Y" referring to gentiles) and with representative verses listed: mercy to X → mercy to Y (9:11-12); wrath to Y→ mercy to X (9:13); wrath to X→ mercy to Y (9:22-24; 9:30—10:13); therefore, "how much more will" mercy to B→ mercy to A (10:19; 11:11-16, 24-25)? I have left out the Pharaoh element but it, too, adds to the "how much more" line of reasoning concerning mercy to Israel: "wrath to Y (gentile ruler representing a gentile nation)→ mercy to Y (9:16-17), then how much more would mercy to Y→ mercy to X?" If strict logic was used in this case, "all Israel" would refer to the nation, but Paul does not use the phrase "how much more" in 11:26, leaving the meaning open to contextual interpretation.

the olive tree imagery. When Paul follows the clause "some [of Israel] might be saved" (11:14) with resurrection language—"if their rejection [unbelieving Jews] means reconciliation of the world, what about [their?] reception if not life from the dead," 11:15—he refers to the aggregate saved, not just the "some" as a result of his own personal ministry. With this is in mind, "all Israel," 11:26, means more than the "some" that results from Paul's ministry, and with the use of a resurrection theme, he may be referring to all of ethnic Israel returning.[57]

However Paul does not use the resurrection theme in his letter in a "Jewish only" context, but in relation to believers, made up of Jews and gentiles. For example, Paul stresses that the promise came to Abraham by faith so that by grace "all" would be saved—"not only to those who are of the law but also to those who are of the faith of Abraham," 4:16-24. He reminds his readers of God's promise to Abraham as the "father of many nations," describing Abraham's faith in the "God who gives life to the dead." For Abraham, without weakening in faith though his body was as dead, believed in God's power to do as he promised. Paul then applies this to his *present audience* by saying righteousness is credited to "us" who believe in him who raised Jesus our Lord from the dead.[58] Paul's resurrection language in 11:15 references converted Jews who believe in the Messiah, but could also include gentile believers.[59] Thus based on

57. Johannes Munck makes clear that "some" (τινες) can simply mean less than "all" (πάντες) rather than imply a small number; *Christ & Israel: An Interpretation of Romans 9-11*, trans. Ingeborg Nixon (Philadelphia: Fortress Press, 1967), 124.

58. For a two-covenant interpretation in which only the gentiles are in need of salvation through Jesus Christ, see Lloyd Gaston, *Paul and the Torah* (Vancouver: University of British Columbia Press, 1987), 135–50; and Stowers, *Rereading Romans*, 285–316. This view places emphasis on the Sinai covenant as the means for Israel's future salvation, apart from faith in Christ, which deviates from the message of Paul's gospel—3:21-26.

59. Paul aims to reach the gentiles so that "some" of the Jewish people return to God. This part of his ministry leads the reader to expect an exponential result. In 11:11-15, Paul asks two questions that apparently refer to a repentant ethnic Israel—"How much more their fullness?" and "What will acceptance [be], if not life from the dead?" However, the second question

the logical parallels above and Paul's resurrection motif in 11:15, the phrase "all Israel" refers to a full number of "repentant" Jews, which might also include believing gentiles.

General Term

There is little doubt that Paul echoes the well-known Old Testament idiom "All Israel."[60] By doing so, he borrows from the connotative meaning, a unified body of Israel (but not necessarily every member).[61] It is important to remember that Paul thematically summarizes respective portions of his argument in this final section of the body, 11:25-32. Significantly, in 11:26, he completes a circular argument (an *inclusio*) with the phrase "all Israel"(πᾶς Ἰσραὴλ) which he initiated in 9:6: "*not* all [born] *from* Israel [referring to Jacob] *are from Israel*" (οὐ γὰρ πάντες οἱ ἐξ Ἰσραὴλ οὗτοι Ἰσραήλ). His statement in 9:6 not only excludes some Israelites by birth, but Paul's argument that follows, 9:6-29, implies that some of the gentiles are included as children of promise by faith. Thus, not all of the Israelites who were born by natural means are Israelites born by faith. This is why Paul concludes his first midrashic section in 9:24—and "God called not only from the Jews but also from the gentiles." Therefore, according to Paul's circular and thematic style of argument—particularly his definition of Israel at the beginning of the

may intend something "beyond" only ethnic Israel to include the gentiles. Paul leaves out the possessive pronoun "their" in the second question and instead of the "how much more" phrase uses resurrection language—"life from the dead," 11:15. Interestingly, Paul only uses the phrase "from the dead" (ἐκ νεκρῶν) in Romans in reference to the resurrection of Christ or the resurrection power of God in the believer in Romans (1:4; 4:24; 6:4, 9, 13; 7:4; 8:11, 34; 10:7, 9; 14:9). Thus Paul refers to a complete number of ethnic Jews and possibly to the total number of Jews and gentile believers who experience the power of Christ's resurrection through faith.

60. See 1 Sam. 25:1; 1 Kgs. 12:1; 2 Chron. 12:1.
61. Barrett, *Epistle to the Romans*, 33; Käsemann, *Commentary on Romans*, 300; Sanday and Headlam, *Critical and Exegetical Commentary*, 335; Cranfield, *Critical and Exegetical Commentary*, 577; Morris, *Epistle to the Romans*, 419. Barrett points out that in the Sanhedrin (10:1), "all Israel" shares in the world to come, but this reference does not mean every Israelite, since there is a long list of exceptions that follow this statement; *Epistle to the Romans*, 223.

argument, 9:6—the interpretation of "all Israel" in 11:26 encompasses the connotation of a unified body of Israel that excludes some of ethnic Israel.

Furthermore, based on Paul's use of the general term "Israel" in 9:6—11:24, the meaning of "Israel" in 11:26 should *not* be confused with the rendering "ethnic Israel." In the olive tree metaphor, 11:17-24, Paul uses the labels "Israel" and "gentiles" as a means to emphasize the active character of God in Israel's hardening and gentile blessing, which then results in mercy to Israel. Throughout Romans 9–11, the identity of "hardened" Israel—the Jews who reject the Messiah—shares the same characteristics with the general literary term of "Israel" (a general reference to ethnic Jews who relied on "works" and did not know "Righteousness"). But *some of Paul's Jewish brothers are presently believers in Christ* and would not be described accurately under the general literary term "Israel." In fact, when Paul directly addresses his "ethnic" brothers, he expresses grief, 9:1-5, in the context of "not all of them," 9:6 (which agrees with his conclusion that God calls those not only from the Jews but also from the gentiles, 9:24). It would seem contrary to the purpose, theme, and direction of Paul's letter to perceive Paul as supporting a nationalistic emphasis. For example, in the early sections of his letter, Paul defines a Jew in a radical way: "a man is a Jew inwardly, circumcised of the heart by the Spirit," 2:29, and he teaches that grace is guaranteed to all those who have the faith of Abraham, the father of many nations, 4:16-17.

It does not make sense then that Paul would suddenly change theological direction by referring to "all Israel" as all of ethnic Israel. And for "all Israel" to refer to only those of "hardened Israel" who repent seems to hold rigidly to the constructs of the Old Testament idiom without any new sense given to the meaning of the phrase. In other words, it seems awkward in light of the theology of Paul's letter to reference the *old* idiom in the *old* sense of only "hardened" Israelites who repent. Rather, by interpreting "all Israel" with a *new* sense given to the phrase—as made up of Jew and gentile believers—Paul redefines "Israel" in the same way he redefines a "Jew" in a spiritual connotation, 2:29.[62]

If Paul does intend that "all Israel" refers to ethnic Israel, he is communicating one of two possibilities. He may expect the reader to "fill in" the exponential emphasis from the previous parallels (11:12 and 24) so that as the full number of gentiles comes in, a "how much more" of the nation of Israel will return. Or he might have intentionally left out the "how much more" language in 11:26 to focus *less* on the exponential result and more on a "summation" emphasis—that gentile fullness results in a full return of repentant Jews (a full number of repentant gentiles *plus* a full number of repentant Israelites equals "all Israel"). In either possibility, Paul's reference to "repentant" Jews refers to a full number.[63] Paul's Old Testament support from Isaiah clarifies his meaning.

Old Testament Support — Isaiah

Paul's quotations in support of the clause—"all Israel will be saved"—strengthens the interpretation for "all Israel" to mean "all of hardened Israel who repent." At the same time, based on the Old Testament context, Paul amplifies a "remnant" theme. Standing in apposition to Paul's assertion "all Israel will be saved" are quotations from Isaiah—59:20-21 and 27:9—which all contain "Jacob" as a syndoche for a future repentant Israel, 11:26b-27:

---

62. See also . Wright, "Letter to the Romans," 691–93.
63. Since the resurrection occurred decades before Paul writes, and since Paul believes that Christ will return sometime in the near future (13:11-12 and 16:20; also 1 Thess. 4:15f and 1 Cor. 15:51-52), the events that Paul writes about are occurring during his ministry and he perceives that they will come to completion in the near future. Thus a temporal aspect is not as significant as the import of the events revealing God's character—his merciful decisions. Also, Paul's use of νὖν (in 11:5, 30, and 31) affirms Paul's urgent expectation of these events. See also Dunn, Romans, 687; and Moo, *Epistle to the Romans*, 735.

Even as it is written,

"From Zion comes the One who delivers   **Isa. 59:20-21a**

he will turn Jacob from godlessness

and this by my covenant with them

I will forgive their sins."   **Isa. 27:9**

These passages comprise rich covenantal language. In the context of the first quotation (Isa. 59:1-21), Israel has committed rebellion and treachery against God (vv. 1-16). God repays wrath to his enemies (vv. 17-19), and *from Zion*,[64] the dwelling place of God most High, comes the Messiah, the Redeemer (v. 20).[65] This reference in Isaiah to the "Deliverer" does not signify the salvation of the whole nation, but deliverance comes to the seed according to election, the group of hardened Israelites who repent.[66] Interestingly, Paul draws upon the context of God's covenant with Abraham and the patriarchs in relation to a "remnant" (Isa. 59:21; Gen. 9:9 and 17:4), for Paul's quotation does not refer to a "new" covenant, but a new administration of the covenant once made with the fathers. It is

---

64. Paul uses ἐκ rather than ἕνεκεν (LXX), which is more of a directional emphasis than "on account of."

65. "The one who delivers" may be interpreted as God or the Messiah. In the MT, Isa. 59:20, the "One" may be understood as referring to God Himself while other rabbinical interpretations render "the One" as the Messiah. In the latter case this is probably understood as the second coming; Cranfield, *Critical and Exegetical Commentary*, 576. Concerning the time of redemption, there is no hint; Stanley, "'The Redeemer Will Come ek Ziōn': Romans 11.26-27 Revisited," in *Paul and the Scriptures of Israel*, eds. Craig A. Evans and James A. Sanders (Sheffield: JSOT, 1993), 118f.

    In 11:26-27, Paul conflates Isaiah 59:20-21 and 27:9. In these contexts, the "removal of sin" is a repeated theme and thus likely significant to Paul's aim here. Shum notes three things achieved: removal of sin resulting in salvation, removal of sin linked to the covenant, and the mysterious will of God; *Paul's Use*, 244. The phrase καθὼς γέγραπται—used seventeen times to introduce proof texts—is used to repeat what has already been said, either explicitly or implicitly, and not for further detail; ibid.

66. Young, *Isaiah*, 3:441.

because the Lord made this "eternal" covenant with Abraham that he will come to Zion (59:21):

> "As for me, this is my covenant with them," says the Lord.
>
> "My Spirit, which is upon you, and my words which I have put in your mouth,
>
> will not depart from your mouth,
>
> or from the mouths of your descendants,
>
> or from the mouths of their descendants from now and forever."

Thus "Jacob" in 11:26 refers to "repentant Israel" in the context of a "remnant." Notice also, that the Isaiah context affirms both God's faithfulness concerning his words[67]—the primary theme of Romans 9–11 (see Rom. 3:1f and 9:6)—and repeats the emphasis of God's people confessing the words of God with their mouth—a reference also in Paul's arguments to the remnant of believing gentiles and Jews (see Rom. 10:8-9; "The word is near you, in your mouth and in your heart. . . and if you confess with your mouth . . .").

In the second prophetic passage, Isaiah 27:9, God remains faithful to His covenant with Israel by forgiving "Jacob" of their sins. But the context of this verse portrays God's mercy amidst a people incurring judgment. They are likened to a desolate city in the wilderness with bare branches. The people are without God's favor, so he will thresh among the nations and gather his people one by one to worship him in the holy mountain in Jerusalem (Isa. 27:9-13). Paul's support from

---

67. Romans 9–11 answers Paul's original questions of his letter—3:1f. Paul raises the question as to whether there is an advantage in being a Jew if circumcision is of the heart by the Spirit. His immediate response concerns God's words—"Much in every way, for they [the Jews] have been entrusted with the very *words* of God." He then addresses the logical issue of God's *faithfulness* in relation to chosen people who act in unbelief (3:3). Paul elaborates on what this means in 9:30—10:21, particularly explaining how the "word" of God was near them and in their "mouth" (10:8; Deut. 30:14). Paul's quotation of Isaiah 59:21 and its context summarize his reasoning in a succinct manner.

Isaiah depicts a "remnant Israel" returning based on God's faithful mercy.[68]

Based on several factors—Paul's parallel thought, the Old Testament support, and the meaning of Paul's particular phrases, such as "partial hardening," "fullness of the gentiles" and the adverb "likewise"—it seems most likely that "all Israel" refers to a full number of "hardened" Israelites who return to God. But taking into account Paul's inclusion of the gentile in his interpretation of what it means to be a Jew, 2:29, in his definition of *who* "Israel" is, 9:6 and 24, as well as in his clarification of the "remnant," 11:5-6, he may intend an emphasis for "all Israel" to include Jews and gentiles. A closer look is needed at Paul's use of the "remnant" theme as well as his agricultural imagery in verse 16 in light of the above information to deduce that the latter interpretation is accurate.

"Remnant" Israel—Jews and Gentiles

The interpretation of "all Israel" as a reference to the "remnant"—made up of Jews and gentile believers—takes into account Paul's argument as a whole. If true, Paul chooses to use the adverb "likewise" (οὕτως or "in this way") instead of the "how much more" language to provide a summary of not only verses 23 and 24 but for the entire argument, 9:6—11:24. In this light, the coming in of the full number of gentiles who believe in Christ provokes jealousy among the Jews, and as a result a full number of Israelites believe in Christ. The "remnant," or "all Israel," returns to God for their salvation (repentant Israel + repentant gentiles = the remnant or "*all Israel*"; 11:25-26):

---

68. However, the earnestness of Paul's mission and desire to affect "some" of his own people gives the indication that in the end "some" of his own people, ethnic Israel, may not be saved; otherwise, why would he be zealous in the first place? The argument can then be made that he simply wants to participate in God's process of salvation, believing that "all" of the Jews will be saved in the end. But then his grief for them (9:1-5) would be for literary purposes.

> a   because the <u>partial hardening</u> in Israel has happened
>
> b   until the <u>fullness of the gentiles</u> might come in,
>
> ab and likewise all Israel will be saved (remnant)

This parallels Paul's imagery in verse 16 where Paul used a seemingly unorthodoxed analogy of a whole batch made holy:

> But if the first fruits are holy then the whole batch is holy   16
>
> and if the root is holy then also the branches

It was previously demonstrated that "first fruits" refers to the repentant gentiles and that the "root" refers to the "patriarchs." Therefore, the "whole batch" references *the total number of repentant gentiles and repentant Israel*. Likewise, "the branches" refers to the converted gentiles and converted Jews, those of Israel who are grafted into their own olive tree. In essence, the whole tree is made holy: "But if the first fruits are holy [gentiles] then the whole batch is holy [gentile and Jewish Christians; or "all Israel"]."

The body of Paul's argument progresses toward a "remnant" theme. This is first made clear when the "gentiles" who "were not God's people are now "God's people," included in the remnant of God, 9:26-27. Then after Paul demonstrates that the nation of Israel chose disobedience despite having been given the words of God, 9:30—10:21, Paul identifies with Elijah concerning the "remnant," 11:1-5. Yet Paul's understanding carries a greater appreciation for God's compassionate heart, and he defines the "remnant" with Jews and gentiles in mind—"Therefore, in this same manner [οὕτως] and in this present time there is a remnant according to the called grace of God. But if by grace, it is not by works, otherwise grace would no longer be grace" (11:5-6).[69] It is not surprising then that Paul uses the adverb οὕτως in 11:5 to show *how* God brings together both converted people groups. It is also interesting, that when Paul uses the adverb οὕτως in Romans, he refers to *how* God works in relation to "all" or "many."[70]

For this final interpretation to make sense concerning "all Israel" as referring to the Jewish and gentile remnant, Paul presupposes a logical step in his sequenced pattern. Paul does *not* explicitly mention the "fullness of repentant Israel" in 11:26[71](which might have been expressed as the partial hardening of Israel results in the fullness of gentiles which results in the *fullness* of Israel). Reading "all Israel" as the return of "hardened" Israel shows sequence and how God works, but so does reading "all Israel" as the aggregate of those who repent, both Jew and gentile, but not every Jew and gentile.

Paul's descriptive use of the word "all" leading up to the phrase "all Israel," 11:26 (and the summary in 11:32) guides the reader toward a "summation" nuance concerning the "remnant"—made up of converted Jews and gentiles. Paul's initial theme includes a proclamation of the gospel for salvation to "all" who believe—Jew and

---

69. This description of the "remnant" complements Paul's definition of a Jew as an inward, spiritual action—a circumcision "of the heart by the Spirit," 2:29, and it also aligns with his discussion concerning believers as the sons and children of God (8:14-21 and 9:29) and children of promise, 9:8.

70. The instances of οὕτως in Romans include: Paul is under obligation to preach to all and "in this way" (οὕτως) he plans to come and preach to those in Rome (1:15 and 15:19); Abraham will become the father of many nations and "in this way (οὕτως) so shall your descendants be" (4:18; Gen. 15:5-6); how (οὕτως) through one man death works into all men, and the grace of God through Christ (5:12, 15, 18-21); with reference to believers (6:4, 11, 19, and 12:5), and how God is able to respond with mercy or wrath to whomever he wills—for does the thing being made say to the potter, "Why have you made me this way (οὕτως)?" (9:20; Job 16:3).

  This composite thinking can also be observed in the final verses of his argument (with the use of οὕτως and the accompanying ἵνα clause). Paul has both gentiles and Jews in mind concerning God's mercy, 11:30-31: "For just as you were then disobedient to God, you have now been shown mercy because of their disobedience. Likewise (οὕτως), they also have now been disobedient, but because of the mercy shown to you, (ἵνα) they also may be shown mercy. For God bound all into disobedience in order that all might be shown mercy."

71. Paul's use of omission can also be seen in verses 24-25 with the understood term "jealousy."

gentile (see also 4:11, 16, 5:18, and 8:32). In the body of his argument, 9:6—11:32, Paul in particular emphasizes that whoever believes in Christ will be saved, 10:11, and that there is "no distinction between Jew or Greek, for the same Lord is the Lord of *all* . . . and *all* who call upon him will be saved," 11:12-13 (see also 10:4). And since Paul is concerned from the beginning of his argument with *who* comprises Israel (e.g., "not 'all' of Israel are Israel," 9:6), it would make sense that as he summarizes his argument in 11:26 with the clause "all Israel will be saved" he answers the issue of God's righteousness and God's faithfulness based on faith in the Messiah (e.g., 9:5, 10:5f and 17).

Furthermore, it makes sense that Paul would leave out the "how much more" language and choose the adverb and conjunction, "and likewise" (καὶ οὕτως) for a reason. It is important to see that in chapter 5, Paul uses the "how much more" phrase to accent the nature of God's grace through Christ concerning sin—5:9, 10, 15, and 17. Where sin—disobedience—abounds, grace abounds much more. The discussion refers to "many" but not everyone. In Romans 8:34, Paul uses the word "more" in a similar way with respect to God's reconciliation of the elect through the death and resurrection of Christ.[72] Not surprisingly in Romans 9–11, Paul accents the "how much more" nature of God concerning his plan for Israel and the nations. He uses disobedience to bring about mercy to all (11:12, 24). But Paul does not include the "how much more" language in 11:26 and instead uses the adverb "likewise" (οὕτως), which accents the result of the "whole" (see 11:16). In contrast, the emphasis of "how much more" in verse 11:12 and v. 24 concerns "repentant" Israel. By choosing the adverb "likewise" rather than the phrase "how much more," Paul moves away from an ethnic emphasis for "all Israel" and stresses *how* God is faithful to a people who believe in the Messiah by

72. The NET translates the meaning with this sense, "Christ is the one who died (and more than that, he was raised) . . ."

faith. In other words, Paul adjusts an old idiom to communicate new understanding.

In a similar manner, Paul's content and arrangement in Romans 9–11 follows the pattern of an Old Testament lament (an address, lamenting, turning to God, petitioning. and a final praise) with new significance. Paul establishes his right to speak and lists God's covenantal gifts to Israel, 9:1-5, but does not directly invoke God to act on Israel's behalf. In the first two sections of Paul's argument, 9:6-29 and 9:30—10:21, he does not accuse God, but Israel for their loss. He bases his reasoning on God's character in his election of Abraham, Isaac, and Jacob, and defends God's faithfulness by showing that God's *impartial* decision in electing Jacob results in a plan for "all Israel"—repentant Jews and gentiles—to return, based on a faith that comes from hearing the word of Christ.[73]

Paul's lament focuses on God's character. And the verses that follow, 11:28-32, summarize the content of his argument.

Romans 11:28-29

according to the gospel, enemies on account of us	28a
according to the elect, beloved on account of the fathers	28b
For God's call and gifts are irrevocable	29

In these first two lines—v. 28a and v. 28b—Paul summarizes his two previous midrashic forms with respect to Israel. When Paul writes, "according to the gospel, [they are] enemies on account of us," he restates the sum of his second midrashic form, 9:30—10:21, where Israel rejected the gospel and remains obstinate. When Paul writes, "according to the elect, [they are] beloved on account of the fathers,"

73. Thus the praise for God's infinite wisdom, 11:33-36, is not limited to God's decisions for the nation of Israel only.

the latter phrase refers to those of ethnic Israel in his first midrashic form, 9:6-29, who did not believe in the promised seed. The "elect" in 9:6-29 refers to both Jew and gentile believers, not the nation of Israel.[74] So, the phrase "beloved on account of the fathers" emphasizes God's covenantal faithfulness and compassion to an obstinate Jewish nation.[75]

Therefore, it is true—"God's call and gifts are irrevocable," 11:28. When God made his compassionate and wise decision to choose Israel as His son, 9:4-5, he did not withdraw His love, despite their rejection of the Messiah. Paul develops his arguments in Romans 9–11 in such a way as to play on the possibility that Israel might be cursed as a nation forever because of their lack of faith in Christ. So when he writes "irrevocable" (ἀμεταμέλητα)[76] he does not imply that all Israel will be saved due to their calling as a nation; rather, he emphasizes God's *mercy* in that God's hands are continually extended to them.

74. See also 11:5.
75. It might seem that the gospel and election stand in contradiction here because of what seems to be an antithetical parallel in 11:28a and 11:28b. Cranfield mentions that these are two contrasting parallel statements are not in equilibrium—the addition of the latter statement limits the validity of the former; *Critical and Exegetical Commentary*, 579. On the contrary, both election and the gospel reveal God's desire for the character of a humble obedient son—a parallel thought that is more synonymous than it is antithetical.
76. "Without feeling regret"; BAGD, 45. Also, see *TDNT* 4:627.

Romans 11:30-32

Now just as you then were disobedient to God,   30

but now have been shown mercy because of their disobedience.

Likewise, those who have presently disobeyed   31

has resulted in your being shown mercy

in order that now they too might be shown mercy.

For God bound all into disobedience   32

in order that he might show mercy to all.

After having summarized the first two midrashic forms (in 11:28 with respect to 9:6-29 and 9:30—10:21), Paul in 11:30-31 summarizes the mystery revealed, 11:11-24. And in verse 32, he brings together the argument as a whole, 9:6—11:24, by completing a circular argument that he began in 9:6-12.

Significantly, "mercy" here is not synonymous with universal salvation. Rather, Paul is making a final statement about the merciful and elective character of God in the context of disobedience. In a similar way that Paul emphasized the disobedience of one man, Adam, working through all (5:12f), and righteousness through Jesus Christ to the many (5:15), so also Paul reasons that disobedience of the gentiles and of Israel results in God's mercy to all (11:31-32)—an elective decision of God. This use of "all" shows Paul's consistent movement toward gentile inclusiveness—God's mercy to all nations.[77]

---

77. This composite thinking can be observed in the use οὕτως (v. 30) and the accompanying ἵνα clause (v. 31). Concerning God's mercy, Paul has both gentiles and Jews in mind.

Summary

Because Paul's integrated themes and poetic structure continue his narrative through argument, a summary of this literary unit, 11:1-11:32, is given. After this, relevant insights are discussed relating the theological truths in this section to the rest of the body of Paul's argument, 9:6—10:21, and to the rest of his letter.

Narrative Summary

God has revealed his wise decisions to Paul in the present. God chooses Jacob, the twin in the "lesser" position, requiring the descendant nations of both brothers to serve in humble obedience to God. Yet both nations rebel. While God shows his wrath to Esau's descendants as a merciful warning to Israel, the people remain obstinate. Upon Israel's disobedience, God shows his mercy to gentile nations, resulting in jealousy. In the end, some of Israel, a full number, will come back to God. Thus, God's initial decision of the election of "Israel" was not partial, but one that bound men unto disobedience so that all might have the opportunity to receive mercy.

Relevant Insights

In 11:1-10, Paul transitions from his two previous midrashic sections, 9:6-29 and 9:30—10:21, to prepare his readers for the revealed mystery, 11:11-24. Using olive tree grafting imagery, Paul warns the gentile Christians against pride. After these imperatives, he concludes and summarizes his argument, 11:25-32. Relevant insights from each of these individual units—11:1-10, 11-24, and 25-32—are discussed below.

Romans 11:1-10

Paul weaves his own context of grieving for Israel with Elijah's context in interceding against Israel, 11:1-10, in order to strengthen his identification as a "remnant" Israelite. By doing so, Paul contrasts Elijah's attitude with God's compassionate character in response to Israel. God reserves for himself a "remnant" by grace in the present, not according to "works" (11:6; see also 3:20, 27-28; 4:2, and 6). This reference to Elijah reveals Paul's intimate understanding of God's heart for Israel—for in this lament-argument, Paul identifies with the intercession of Moses, David, Hosea, Isaiah, and Elijah (9:3, 25, 27; 11:1-5 and 9).

In 11:5-7, Paul brings together two sets of themes: "not by works" in relation to "hardened" Israel, and the "called grace of God" in relation to the "remnant."

> Therefore, in this same manner and in this present time there is a remnant
>> according to the called grace of God,
> but if by grace, it is not by works
>> otherwise grace would no longer be grace.
> Why therefore? What Israel sought, they did not achieve
>> but the called achieved and the rest were hardened.

These themes summarize the first two major sections of his argument—gentiles are "called" by God and are part of the "remnant," 9:6-29, and Israel has pursued justification by "works," becoming "hardened," 9:30–10:21. Paul's purpose in this transition section, 11:1-10, is to move the reader from thinking in terms of the representative groups of "Israel" and the "gentiles"—which was for the purpose of highlighting Israel's misguided pursuit of righteousness by works—to a different set of representative groups: "hardened Israel" and the "remnant called by grace." This is an important literary distinction needed in order to make sense of the revealed mystery that follows, 11:11-24.

It is also worth repeating that the context of Paul's Old Testament verse list, 11:8-10, gives evidence against Israel for her disobedience, and the context of the verse list also validates God's wrath to be carried out against those who reject the Messiah (11:10 and Ps. 69). But Paul does not directly answer the question that he raises at the beginning of this section, 11:1: "Has God rejected His people?" This limited explanation of God's wrath effectively builds suspense in the "narrative" by withholding the final verdict concerning God's sentencing of "hardened" Israel (see 11:7 and 9:30—10:21; and it also allows Paul the opportunity to emphasize God's bestowing of grace upon the remnant; see 11:5 and 9:6-29.)

Form, 11:11-24

Paul weaves together logical patterns, metaphors, and imperatives in a style different from any of his previous paragraphs, 11:11-24. He begins with two synonymous stanzas built around a "jealousy" theme and then reveals the sequence of God's plan using "how much more" language concerning the future "fullness" of Israel, 11:11-12. Paul then parallels this truth by demonstrating how he participates in Israel's reconciliation, 11:13-15.

Paul employs agricultural imagery—"first fruits" and "root" (v. 16)—to transition from the topic of Israel's future fullness, 11:11-15, into the practical imperatives addressed to the gentiles, imperatives that are embedded within an extended olive tree metaphor, 11:17-22. The olive tree metaphor imagery illustrates the kindness of God toward the gentiles as a result of Israel's disobedience, framing Paul's bold command to the church in Rome: "Be humble!" In the final verses, Paul summarizes this whole section, 11:11–24, by integrating similar form and elements from 11:11–15 and 11:17–22, particularly the "how much more" language from verses 11–15 with the olive tree imagery of verses 17–22.

Future "fullness," 11:11–15

Concerning the phrase future "fullness" of Israel, 11:11–15, Paul's point is clear: on account of Israel's sins, God mercifully blesses the gentiles, which then causes jealousy, resulting in Israel's fullness. Ironically, Israel does not remember their low position from which God called them (see 9:11–13), but they persist in disobedience, which puts them in a position of weakness and need to call upon God. Paul reasons that since Israel's failure results in riches to the gentiles, Israel's repentance will result in a "greater" or "full" return of Israel to God (an allusion to the resurrection power of God). One of Paul's primary motivations is revealed here, for as his ministry among the gentiles is magnified, his ethnic people become jealous, resulting in the salvation of some of them (a truth more explicitly stated in 15:19).

This explanation of God's response to sin concerning Israel's disobedience mirrors his earlier discussion in his letter concerning God's response to sin entering the world through Adam, 5:18–21. Paul uses three different words for Israel's disobedience in 11:11–12—trespass, failure, and casting away—that results in salvation, riches, and reconciliation for the gentiles. And in describing how sin entered through one man affecting all persons, 5:18–21, Paul reveals the result through Christ's obedience of how grace abounds more, resulting in life, 5:18–19. Paul sees himself participating in this hope for Israel.

"First Fruits," 11:16

In 11:16, Paul's agricultural phrases—"first fruits" and "root"—accent God's plan in bringing about holiness. Paul's "how much more" language in verses 11-15 emphasizes the degree of Israel's repentance and salvation, but the "how much more language" in verse 16, implies Israel's holiness (paraphrase): "If the first fruits [gentiles] are holy, *how much more* will Israel be made holy!" God's mercy to the gentiles reveals his merciful and wise character, for God uses the gentiles (not Jewish converts) to provoke "Israel" to jealousy, causing Israel's repentance. With this in mind, Paul uses the "root" imagery to introduce the patriarchs into the olive tree metaphor that follows, 11:17f. In other words, Paul's words in 11:16 give the reader assurance concerning Israel's salvation (paraphrase): "If the patriarchs are holy and if the gentiles are also made holy how much more will Israel be holy?"

"Kindness-Severity," 11:17-24

In the olive tree metaphor, Paul enlightens his recipients concerning the kindness and severity of God in election—the cutting and engrafting—in order to prevent pride among them, 11:17-21. Paul warns the gentile Christians to choose humility to avoid judgment: "*Do not be high minded but fear, for if God did not spare the natural branches neither in any way will he spare you*," 11:20-21. This underscores Paul's purpose in writing his letter: to engender fertile, "humble" soil among the gentile believers in the Roman congregation, 1:13; to renew their minds in Christ's likeness, 12:1-3, and to give a sound theological basis for warning them against judging the weak in faith, 14:1—15:7.

Paul uses two synonyms—"kindness" (χρηστότης) and "severity" (ἀποτομίαν)—within the olive tree metaphor for God's wrath and mercy, affirming the continuous and impartial nature of God in his elective purposes. In the first main section of his letter, 2:3-4, Paul expresses God's kindness in contrast to coming wrath, that God's enduring patience leads to repentance. Only here, 11:22, does Paul use the term "severity" in reference to being "cut out" (ἐκκόπτω) of the olive tree. These actions contribute to the understanding of Paul's other discussions in his letter concerning God's wrath and righteousness revealed from heaven (see 1:17-18, 2:1-11, and 13:1-4). Paul ends the olive tree metaphor by emphasizing the grace of God, 11:23-24.

The content of Paul's poetic parallels and structure in 11:1-24 reveal that God does not show favoritism in his election of Israel. Sequence and order do not mean superiority or less in significance. God is the God of the Jew and the gentile, 3:29; and there is no distinction between Jew or Greek, for the Lord is Lord of all, 10:12. The focus of Paul's argument is on God's character—he chooses those in humble circumstances. According to the olive tree imagery, a reversal has occurred. Gentiles Christians (as a group) repent and turn to God before the Jews do (as a group). Paul is not arguing that the gentiles replace the Jews in God's order of election; rather, Paul uses the olive tree imagery to emphasize God's *impartiality*, that whether Jew or gentile, humility is God's desire. At the same time, Paul does not eliminate ethnic distinctions but honors God's order (e.g., "first to the Jew and then to the gentile," 1:16). Thus, the whole argument has less to do with an emphasis on "equality" and more to do with an emphasis on God's character in election (e.g., choosing the son in the humble situation and blessing those who remain in faith).

Romans 11:25-32

In this final section, 11:25-32, Paul brings together all of the elements thus far. He begins by summarizing the purpose in revealing the mystery, 11:25, "*to not think of yourselves too highly*" (see also 11:18, 21; 9:13-14; 10:2-9; 12:1-3; 13:1-6; 14:1—15:7). Yet Paul adds new phrases—"partial" (ἀπὸ μέρους) hardening and "fullness of the gentiles"—in his summary to further elaborate on God's character, 11:25-26.

By clarifying that a "partial" hardening of Israel has happened, 11:25, Paul eliminates concern about a permanent hardening of Israel. (After the olive tree metaphor, Paul no longer uses the term "Israel" in relation to "works," but returns to the defined identity of "hardened" Israel, 11:7-10, referring to the Israelites who have rejected Christ, whose disobedience God uses to bless the gentiles.) And when Paul uses the phrase "fullness of the gentiles," he refers to believers who are called (10:13 and 11:5). The mystery, then, consists of God's temporary hardening of Israel until God's full number of called gentiles come in. But more specifically, Paul contrasts "partial" and "fullness" to accent God's ability: a *temporary* hardening of Israel results in *eternal* blessing of the gentiles. This brings hope in that God can take what is "partial" and negative (disobedience) and work out what is "eternal" and positive (blessing—a supernatural work confirmed elsewhere in the letter [4:18-20; 5:15-21; 6:22-23; 8:11; and 11:28]—"For God works all things together for good for those . . . who are called according to his purpose"). This reasoning begs the question as to how much more, with God, will "fullness result in fullness?"

Concerning the phrase, "all Israel," it seems likely that based on several factors—Paul's parallel thought, the Old Testament support, and the meaning of Paul's particular phrases, such as "partial hardening," "fullness of the gentiles" and the adverb "likewise"—Paul refers to a full number of "hardened" Israelites who return to God. But taking into account Paul's inclusion of the gentile in his interpretation of what it means to be a Jew, 2:29, in his definition of *who* "Israel" is, 9:6 and 24, as well as in his clarification of the "remnant," 11:5-6, he may intend an emphasis for "all Israel" to include Jews and gentiles. It is Paul's use of the "remnant" theme, his lament elements, as well as his agricultural imagery in verse 16 that tip the balance in favor of the latter interpretation that "all Israel" refers to a remnant comprised of Jews and gentiles.

What also adds to this conclusion is Paul's omission of the "how much more" language, instead choosing the adverb-conjunction "and likewise." Earlier in the letter Paul uses this adverb to accent the nature of God's grace through Christ concerning sin (see 5:9, 10, 15, and 17), and here in 11:26, Paul's also uses the adverb "likewise" (οὕτως) to accent the result of the "whole," (see also the context of 11:16). Whereas the emphasis of "how much more" in verse 11:12 and 24 concern "repentant" Israel, the adverb "likewise" moves the focus away from an ethnic emphasis for "all Israel" and stresses *how* God is faithful to a people who believe in the Messiah by faith. In other words, Paul adjusts an old idiom to communicate new understanding.

It is important to see that Paul bases his reasoning on God's character in his election of Jacob and seeks to defend God's faithfulness by showing that God's *impartial* decision results in a plan for "all Israel" to return—the repentant Jews and gentiles who obey the word of Christ. This meaning is confirmed by the content and arrangement in Romans 9–11 where Paul follows the pattern of an Old Testament lament—an address, lamenting, turning to God, petitioning, and a final praise—with new significance. After establishing his right to speak and after listing God's covenantal gifts to Israel, 9:1-5, Paul *does not directly invoke God to act on Israel's behalf*. In this way, Paul places the responsibility on the nation of Israel for their loss, 9:6—10:21.

In Romans 11:28-29, Paul summarizes his two previous midrashic forms with respect to Israel. When Paul writes, "according to the gospel, [they are]enemies on account of us," he restates the sum of his second midrashic form, 9:30—10:21, where Israel rejected the gospel and remains obstinate. When Paul writes, "according to the elect, [they are] beloved on account of the fathers," the "beloved" refers to those of ethnic Israel in his first midrashic form, 9:6-29, who do not believe in the promised seed (the "elect" in 9:6-29 refers to both Jew and Gentile believers, not the nation of Israel). Therefore, the phrase "beloved on account of the fathers" emphasizes God's covenantal faithfulness and compassion to an obstinate Jewish nation. More specifically, God's choosing of Israel as His son, 9:4-5, does not mean that he withdraws his love when they reject the Messiah. Rather, Paul's use of "irrevocable" (ἀμεταμέλητα) refers to God's *mercy* in that God's hands are continually extended to them. Paul does not imply that all Israel will be saved due to their calling as an ethnic nation.

In Romans 11:30-31, Paul completes his circular argument that he began in 9:6-12. Significantly, "mercy" here is not synonymous with universal salvation. Paul is making a final statement about the merciful and elective character of God in the context of disobedience. In a similar way that Paul emphasized the disobedience of one man, Adam, working through all (5:12f), and righteousness through Jesus Christ to the many (5:15), so also Paul reasons that disobedience of the gentiles and the disobedience of Israel result in God's showing mercy to all (11:31-32)—a wise decision of God affecting all nations.

5

Paul's Praise to God, 11:33-36

Oh the depths of the riches and wisdom and knowledge of God. How unsearchable His judgments and untraceable His ways. Who has known the mind of the Lord, or who has been His counselor? Or who has first given to Him that He should repay? For from Him and through Him and in Him are all things. To Him be the glory into the ages, amen.

Paul's lament ends with praise to God for his merciful and wise plan for Israel. God elects the son of lower status, Jacob (and his descendants), and demonstrates his love to Israel by showing wrath to the older, rebellious son, Esau (and his descendants, the Edomites). Yet despite this warning, Israel continues to disobey, even to the point of rejecting the Messiah; they place confidence in "works" rather than in a relationship with Christ through faith. Does Israel's failure suggest that God's Word or his decision is flawed in any way? Not at all. God's order of election—to the Jew first and then the gentile—evidences his faithfulness to his promise, a covenant first made with Abraham based on an obedience by faith and then a covenant faithfully maintained with the children of promise, a called remnant by grace, comprised of Jew and gentile believers.[1]

In his midrashic arguments, Paul proves God's merciful character in his righteous decision by supporting and stressing several main points: first, the goodness and sovereignty of God are apart from man's efforts, 9:12 and 16. Second, God's wrath (e.g., against Pharaoh) results in the proclamation of his Name, his goodness, to "all of the earth," 9:17-18. Third, the failure of the elect people results in riches of God's mercy to the nations, 9:24. Fourth, despite Israel's disobedience—9:32 and 11:7f—God's compassionate character remains. The blessing of the gentiles results in jealousy, an expression of God's continuous mercy to his people, 11:11-24. In figurative terms, God molds "Israel" with gentile clay—a purposed result of his elective decision of Jacob. Therefore since God can work blessing from disobedience, the natural progression of thought is "how much more will God utilize the blessing of the gentiles to cause blessing for Israel!" In 11:33-36, Paul praises God for His immeasurable wisdom.

Poetic Form, 11:33-36

Oh the depths of the riches and wisdom and knowledge of God

how unsearchable His judgments and untraceable His ways.

Who has known the mind of the Lord,

or who has been His counselor?

Or who has first given to Him

that He should repay?

For from Him and through Him and in Him are all things—

To Him be the glory into the ages, amen.

---

1. In this way, the order of election does not negate God's impartiality.

Paul expresses himself with simple symmetry of thought in four parallel verses—the theme of God's "wisdom," 11:33-36.

A	Wisdom	v.33,	Hellenistic Judaism
A	Wisdom	v.34,	Isaiah 40:13
A	Wisdom	v.35,	Job 41:3
A	Wisdom	v.36,	Hellenistic Judaism

This thought-rhyme sequence compares to Paul's other lists of four "stanzas"[2]—9:25-29, 10:18-21, and 11:7-11. Here Paul embeds two Old Testament quotations between sayings from nonbiblical sources. It is likely that Paul writes his beginning and ending stanzas adapting known expressions from Hellenistic Judaism for his own theological purpose:[3]

2. "Stanza" is not used in a strict poetical sense. Though "phrase" might be an appropriate term, "stanza" carries the connotation of a unit of thought beyond the limitation of a phrase or clause. And "verse" as a poetic unit becomes confusing when referring to the Bible because of the numbering system of verses.

3. Peter Stuhlmacher finds all of 11:33-36 to be modeled after Hellenistic Judaism, but his reference to 2 Baruch 14:8f seems to relate closer to 11:33 ("Who, O Lord, my God, understands your judgment, or who fathoms the depth of your ways, or who contemplates the difficult burden of your paths, or who is able to contemplate your inscrutable decree, or who from those who have born have ever found the beginning and end of your wisdom?"; *Paul's Letter to the Romans: A Commentary*, trans. Scott J. Hafemann (Louisville: Westminster John Knox, 1994), 175. C. E. B. Cranfield finds that common use of the exclamation ᾧ (v. 33) is common in Hellenistic Greek but used only here in 11:33 in the New Testament; *A Critical and Exegetical Commentary on the Epistle to the Romans* (Edinburgh: T & T Clark, 1975–79), 590. In addition, the noun ἀνεξεραύνητος is only used here in the New Testament and not in the LXX; ibid. Concerning Paul's last stanza (11:36), particularly his use of the prepositions (ἐκ . . . διὰ . . . εἰς) suggests that Paul draws from Jewish writers who attributed to Yahweh concepts from Stoic philosophers; Douglas Moo, *The Epistle to the Romans* (Grand Rapids: Eerdmans, 1996), 743; Cranfield, *Critical and Exegetical Commentary*, 591; Dunn, *Romans*, 701; also, Eduard Norden, *Agnostos Theos: Untersuchungen zur Formenschichte religiöser Rede* (Stuttgart: Tuebner, 1923; repr. Darstadt: Wissenschatliche Buchgesellschaft, 1956), 240f. More importantly, as mentioned in the Introduction, Paul's revelation from Jesus Christ drives his theology, and based on his understanding of Christ, he sees the truth in Old Testament Scripture and in Hellenistic Judaism as well. In other words, as one who speaks "in Christ" he adapts and writes 11:33 and 11:36 to emphasize the wisdom of God and, indirectly, the compassion of Christ (see also Col. 1:16 and 1 Cor. 8:6).

Hellenistic Judaism	Oh the depths of the riches and wisdom and knowledge of God;
	how untraceable His judgments and unsearchable His ways.
Isaiah 40:13	Who has known the mind of the Lord,
	or who has been His counselor?
Job 41:3 (or 35:7)	Or who has first given to Him
	that He should repay?
Hellenistic Judaism	For from Him and through Him and in Him, all things.
	To Him the glory into the ages, amen.

It is probable that Paul intended a simple chiastic arrangement with the center receiving primary emphasis. By placing Hebrew Scripture at the heart of this praise, it seems that Paul subtly stresses specific revelation—Isaiah 40:13 and Job 41:3—in contrast to the general incalculableness of God's decisions.[4]

To the degree that Paul feels unending grief, 9:1-5, he now rejoices in his God's infinite wisdom, 11:33-36.[5]

---

4. Other and more elaborate chiastic forms have been presented. Norden argues for nine lines in this praise. The first three are exclamations; the next four are questions (two are OT quotations); the last two are a declaration and a doxological acclamation. In this way, there are three divine attributes, three questions, and three relations of things to God; Norden, *Agnostos Theos*, 240–50. Also, see G. Harder, 51–55.

Another possible chaistic arrangement signifies a Trinitarian emphasis, hinting at Christ (B) and the Father (A)—the Spirit overlays the entire set of quotations. The parallel would be based on themes: (A) v. 32, the depths of God, his infiniteness; (B) v. 33, the mind of Christ, his counsel; (B) "Christ" has been given, security; and (A) v. 34, "for from him . . ."

5. In this way, Paul experiences the heart of God for his people—God's compassion and wisdom are not mutually exclusive.

Grief for Israel	9:1-5
God's election	9:6-29
Israel's failure	9:30–10:21
God's plan of salvation	11:1-32
Praise for God's Wisdom	11:33-36

The initial lament passage and Paul's ending praise section frame the midrashic arguments, forming an *inclusio*.

The Spirit's Wisdom, 11:33-36

God through his Spirit reveals salvation history. Paul explains the faithful character of God through argument, support, and reason—particularly illustrating the compassionate and wise "mind of God." As Paul speaks as one "in Christ," 9:1f, he expresses Christ's compassion and the heart of the Father, and in Paul's arguments, God's Spirit enlightens Paul, giving him logical perspective as to God's decisions concerning Israel. God's election of Jacob, 9:13, leads the reader to better understand "who" God is. Thus Paul expresses amazement for what has been revealed to him and awe at what cannot be grasped.

Unsearchable Wisdom, 11:33

Paul first summarizes the infiniteness of God's compassion and wisdom, for which he has been given insight—"O the depths of the riches and the wisdom and the knowledge of God," 11:33a. While Paul previously described his "unceasing" grief in Christ, he is careful here to accent the Spirit's role. In other words, whereas God through Christ reveals his infinite compassion, now God through his Spirit reveals his infinite wisdom. The content of Paul's arguments—the

227

illustrations, proofs, reasoning and logic—direct the attention of the reader to the source of wisdom—the mind of God.

Paul's word choice demonstrates this. "Depths" applies to the whole of Paul's argument, 9:1—11:32,[6] and in the present sentence describes three substantives: "riches," "wisdom," and "knowledge." The wisdom language[7] along with the infinite emphasis, without directly mentioning God's compassion, gives primary import to God's Spirit.[8] God has revealed himself, a *spiritual* gift to Paul and the Roman believers. Yet paradoxically, this manifested knowledge cannot be fully comprehended. For while the midrashic reasoning and support have shown God's involvement and purpose, a precise tracing of *how* God governs with wrath and mercy is not fully known. But some of God's decisions—particularly his actions of mercy—have been made known to Paul (and the Roman believers) so that God receives the glory for his judgments. And at the same time, the impossibility of comprehending the full detail and number of these decisions—the unsearchable nature of God's wisdom—moves Paul to adoration.[9]

While "riches" may refer to both God's mercy and his wisdom, the emphasis here, based on Paul's use of the term "riches" in his argument, indirectly references mercy. It is the "riches" of God's kindness, tolerance, and patience that leads men to repentance, 2:4. God made known the "riches" of his glory on his vessels of *mercy,*

---

6. All three are dependent as in 1 Cor. 2:10; Rev. 2:24; *Aj.* 9.23; see also 1 Cor. 1:19-21; 2:7, 10; Col. 2:3; Eph. 3:8, 10; Vaughan, 214.

7. Joseph Fitzmyer notes the other uses of "inscrutable judgments" in wisdom literature; see 2 Apoc. Bar. 14:8-9; Ws. 17:1; Job 9:10; Ps. 77:20; and Prov. 25:3; *Romans* (New York: Doubleday, 1993), 634. The phrase "knowledge of God" does not seem to have a close parallel; ibid.

8. John Calvin expresses the inability to investigate the secrets of God, but we come to clear and certain knowledge of them by the grace of the Holy Spirit; *The Epistles of Paul the Apostle to the Romans and the Thessalonians*, eds. Ross Mackenzie, David W. Torrance, and Thomas F. Torrance (London: Oliver & Boyd, 1961), 260.

9. See Isa. 55:8-9 and Ps. 95:10.

9:23; and in 11:23, the disobedience of Israel, their failure, results in "riches" to the gentiles—a merciful action of God.

In the larger context, Paul's use of the term "riches" in 11:33 summarizes the compassion of Christ that Paul has experienced. Paul introduces lament language by stating that he speaks the truth "in Christ" in reference to his grief that he feels for his people. As Paul explains God's purposes for Israel, the tremendous sorrow expressed in an intercessory manner soon results in a more hopeful expression from his heart for Israel's salvation, 10:1. Furthermore, in Paul's other letters, mercy is often related to the knowledge of Christ (Eph. 1:7, 18; 2:7; 3:8, 16; Phil. 4:19; Col. 1:27; 2:2).[10] Not surprisingly, Paul begins the next major section of his letter to the Romans, 12:1—15:13, with the thematic phrase to the Roman believers: "by the mercies of God" offer your bodies as a living sacrifice. Yet in 11:33, Paul does not directly accent "mercy," allowing the focus of his praise be unto God for his wisdom.[11]

Whereas the first line of verse 33 glorifies God for what has been revealed, the second half—"how unsearchable his judgments and untraceable his ways"—expresses wonder at the infinite paths of knowledge leading to the mind of God, his Person.[12] Paul pairs "unsearchable" (ἀνεξεραύνητος)[13] with God's "judgments" intending

---

10. For "Riches of God," see M. Dion, "*La Notion paulinienne de `richese de Dieu' et ses sources,* " *ScEccl* 18 (1966): 139–48. Marcus Barth sees two semantic domains in the "riches of God": the Ephesians family, which signify the depth and power of God, and God as giver of wisdom; "Theologie—ein Bebet (Rom 11,33-36)," *TZ* 41 (1985): 335. He also understands the knowledge of God to refer to an intimate, knowing of God; ibid.

11. The term "wisdom" used only here in Romans concerns the Spirit (see 1 Cor. 2:13; 12:18) but could also indirectly refer to Christ (Col. 2:3 and Eph. 1:17).

12. "Throne" would be an appropriate biblical term for where God is and governs, but this imagery is not specifically mentioned in Romans 9–11.

13. The "judgments" (τὰ κρίματα) of God concern acts of revealing; Barth, "Theologie," 335. This is relevant for both Old and New Testament contexts. See also Psalm 36:6. Mehlmann investigates the adjective ἀνεξιχνίαστος where it is translated "investigabilis" in two places in the Latin Vulgate (11:33 and Eph. 3:8). The article is focused on the value of the different Latin terms (*investigare, vestigare, investigabilis*) and their textual history. Conclusively, the best

a meaning of governance, and follows this phrase with a synonymous adjective that rhymes in thought and initial sound—"how 'untraceable' (ἀνεξιχνίαστος) his ways." The word "untraceable" is used in the New Testament only in Ephesians 3:8 to describe the "riches of Christ." But in the LXX, "untraceable" refers to the glorious things of God without number (Job 5:9, 9:10, and 34:24),[14] and again this undetectable characteristic of God's wisdom in Job is related to divine administration (οἰκονομία). Furthermore, the phrase "his ways" is often used in wisdom literature to describe the decisions a person makes over time, a pattern or lifestyle (e.g., Prov. 4:18-19), but more often in the Old Testament, "his ways" refers to the righteous judgments of God that are unlike human thought (e.g., Deut. 32:4; Hos. 14:9; Isa. 40:8 and 55:8).

It is interesting that this paradox—between understanding specific revelation (as explained in Paul's logical progression of thought in his arguments) and not fully comprehending *how* God carries out his wise decisions and workings[15]—is similar to another of Paul's statements. At the end of his second major section, 5:12—8:39, Paul describes how the resurrection power of the Spirit is at work in the life of the believer, and he makes a summary statement that "God works all things together for the good for those who love him and are called according to his purpose," 8:28. He supports this truth with proof and reasoning. But the specifics as to how God works these things out is not known. Thus God's character is evidenced in his decisions. In Romans 9–11, his election reveals that he works

translation for ἀνεχιξίαστος is *investibabilis* (unsearchable); Mehlmann, "*Investigabilis*," 902–14. For a view of gnostic source, see Norden, *Agnostos Theos*, 243.

14. Thus far the word has been found only in biblical and biblically dependent usage. In the LXX, the word ἀνεξιχνίαστος is found only in Job 5:9; 9:10; 34:24, which indicates a common point of origin. For word history, see *TDNT* 1:358.

15. "The sum of the agreement in whole order of nature would be inverted unless the same God, who is the beginning of all things, is also the end"; Karl Barth, *The Epistle to the Romans*, trans. Edwyn C. Hoskyns (London: Oxford University Press, 1968), 422.

all things together among the nations—whether disobedience or faithfulness—for the good for those who are called by grace. This reality brings Paul to worship God, 11:33-36, for the knowledge received and glory for the infiniteness that cannot be fully known.

The Mind of the Lord, 11:34

Paul quotes two questions from Isaiah in the middle verses of his praise—11:34-35. Each question is rhetorical in nature and draws upon the Old Testament context. From his previous arguments, it has become important to ask: "What 'statement' is Paul making behind his selective Old Testament question?" And more specifically, "What meaning does Paul add to the Old Testament quotation context in light of the mystery he has explained?"

Paul quotes Isaiah 40:13—"Who has known the mind of the Lord, or who has been his counselor?" But in the first clause he apparently uses the LXX translation, "Who has known the *mind* [νοῦς] of the Lord?" (11:33a) rather than a translation of the MT: "Who has known the *Spirit* [רוח] of the Lord?" The context of the Isaiah quotation is the unfathomableness of God's righteous judgments in his powerful and caring deliverance of his people at the end of the age, in contrast to the insignificance of the nations—who are "a drop in the bucket" and as "dust on scales" (Isa. 40:15). But if Paul sees the reference of "Lord" as Christ rather than the primary emphasis of Yahweh, he rhetorically suggests that through Christ the mind of God (or the Spirit of God) is known. In other words, Paul conveys the general truth of Isaiah's message and, at the same time, he uses the quotation to summarize that the "mystery" *has been revealed*. But this nuance should not be overly stressed, for the following phrase, "who has been His counselor?" reaffirms the inability to know the mysteries of God.[16]

From an overall perspective, it is important to see that Paul praises God at the end of each major section—5:1-11, 8:31-39, 11:33-36, and 15:8-13.[17] These "praise" sections all have transitional qualities. For example, just as the themes of "grace," "death," "reconciliation," and "Spirit" foreshadow the content of 5:12—8:39, and just as the themes of "Christ's and the Spirit's intercession" and the "inseparableness of Christ's love" directly contrast the separation and grief discussed in 9:1—11:32, so also Paul's praise for the "mind of the Lord" leads believers into the practical application of choosing this mindset, 12:1—15:13. Interestingly, Paul follows his praise of 11:33-36 with the imperative to the Roman believers to offer themselves sacrificially, which involves a renewing of their *minds*—a corporate Christ-like behavior, 3:21f.

While Paul indirectly references "Christ" in his praise section of the lament, it is important to again make clear that God's wisdom—God's Spirit—is the primary import. Paul, then, intelligently and inconspicuously incorporates a Trinitarian emphasis.

God's Righteousness, 11:35

Paul paraphrases a question from the book of Job when he writes, "Or who has first given to Him, that He should repay?" (Job 35:7). In the Old Testament context, Job's friend Elihu speaks to Job about the righteousness of God. In particular, Elihu confronts Job about Job's own claim that he is righteous by asking, "If you are righteous, what does God receive from this? What benefit does God receive from

---

16. For "Christ"; see Barth, "Theologie," 335; Ernst Käsemann stresses that no one knows the mind of the Lord; *A Commentary on Romans*, trans. and ed. Geoffrey W. Bromiley (Grand Rapids: Eerdmans, 1980), 320.

17. For interrelated themes for 5:1-11, see Dahl, "A Synopsis of Romans 5:1-11 and 8:1-39," in *Studies in Paul: Theology for the Christian Mission*, ed. G. W. Bromiley (Minneapolis: Augsburg Publishing House, 1977), 88–91.

your hand?" The context ties in with one of the main reasons why Paul writes his argument—to defend God's righteousness.

Earlier in his letter, Paul asks the rhetorical question as to whether God's righteousness is made "more glorious" because of sin, 3:5, which raises a logical concern as to whether God is *unrighteous* for judging (does God gain an advantage because of sin—accenting his holiness—and then judge people for that sin?). Paul delays his answer until 9:14-18 where he places the responsibility of Israel's failure upon Israel, and shows how God's choice of the son in the lesser position was a merciful act, a context of God's goodness (9:15-16; Exod. 33:19). In this way, Paul's quotation from Job thematically and creatively summarizes one of the main points that began his argument—God's gift of mercy is a free and impartial gift, separate from a person's decisions, 9:11 and 16. For no one gives first to God; He is obligated to no one.[18]

The Job quotation also serves an additional thematic purpose—it introduces a "suffering" aspect to this praise section, just as the other preceding praise sections have done. In 5:1-12, after pronouncing that justification comes by faith and supporting this theme with support from Abraham's experience, 1:18—4:28, Paul rejoices in hope and in suffering (θλῖψις), 5:3. He explains how the love of God is poured into the hearts of believers because of Christ's unselfish death, 5:5f. Mysteriously, the believer perseveres and participates sacrificially. In 8:31-39, after describing the intimacy that the children of God share in Christ, 5:12—8:30, Paul rejoices in God's gracious gift of his son, a life in which there is no condemnation, 8:31-35. But before expressing the security that comes with not ever being separated from God's love, 8:37-39, Paul interjects a quotation from the Psalms that seems to shift the mood in an odd way: "For

---

18. Calvin, *Epistles of Paul*, 260; Also, Fitzmyer, "God owes us nothing . . . goodness is not a payment of services"; *Romans*, 357.

your sake we are being exposed to death all day long; we are considered as sheep to be slaughtered," (8:36; Ps. 44:22). Paul instructs that the love of Christ does not exclude participation in suffering and perseverance. Likewise, after explaining God's wise and merciful plan for Israel, 9:1—11:32, he gives praise to God and quotes from a passage in which Job suffers righteously, while his friend Elihu questions him. It is as though Paul, in a subtle way, communicates that receiving wisdom and revelation from God does not exempt a believer from participating in the suffering for righteousness in Christ.

Doxological Praise, 11:36

In the final sentences of his praise, Paul gives glory to God, "*For from Him and through Him and in Him are all things.*"[19] From one perspective, this phrase describes the whole process of salvation due to the working of God.[20] But from a literary perspective, it is possible that Paul borrows phrases from a common saying in Judaism, which depends upon Stoic influence.[21] This type of phrase with the repetitious pronoun "Him" and with alternating pronouns seems to have been known to Philo and others. It does not appear, however, that Paul's words are drawn from the mystic language of the Hellenistic world.[22] Consistent with Paul's style, he adapts his sources

19. Exegetically and homiletically, Florentinus Ogara understands the three prepositions to refer to the Trinity: the depth of the Father, the wisdom of the Son through whom all has been created, and the wisdom of the Holy Spirit through whom we come to all knowledge; Ogara's commentary on 11:33-36 (*Notae Exegeticae* and *Usus Homileticus*) was written for the first Sunday after the feast of Pentecost.
20. C. K. Barrett suggests a connection with the themes in 8:21, 28, and 11:32; *The Epistle to the Romans* (London: Hendrickson, 1991), 163f.
21. Marcus Barth sees a likely referent to "Almighty Jesus" in Paul's use of an Orphic Stoic phrase to Zeus; Barth, "Theologie," 338. The unity and variety are not contradictions, for the "ἐν" is not pantheistic or some esoteric missionary statement; ibid—"Sum of the agreement in whole order of nature would be inverted unless the same God, who is the beginning of all things, is also the end."

for his own theological purpose,[23] and based on Paul's use of a similar phrase in his other letters, it is likely that Paul has the Person of Christ in mind (e.g., 1 Cor. 8:6 and Col. 1:16)[24]—though the primary emphasis is praise to God.

Paul ends his lament with a doxological phrase—"To Him be the glory," 11:36b—a phrase with Jewish roots that is common in his letters (1:25; 16:27; Gal. 1:5; 1 Cor. 10:31; 2 Cor. 4:15; Phil. 1:11; Eph. 3:21; 1 Tim. 1:17; and 2 Tim. 4:18).[25] Initially in the lament, Paul addresses his readers by establishing his right to speak as an intercessor and emphasizing the covenant, 9:1-5. In the body of his argument, 9:6—11:32, Paul accuses Israel for her distress and then shifts the attention to God's faithfulness and a turning back to God. So it is not surprising that Paul follows the pattern of an Old Testament lament by bringing the listener to a heightened praise for God's actions and character, 11:33-36. Faithful and righteous—God is to be praised!

Summary

Paul praises God for his merciful and wise plan for Israel, 11:33-36 (one of four ending praise passages in the letter—5:1-11, 8:31-39, and 15:8-13). This ending forms an *inclusio* with the initial lament passage, 9:1-5. Just as Paul describes the infinite compassion of Christ, the heart of the Father, so too Paul illumined by the Spirit explains God's decisions concerning Israel. And while his infinite decisions

22. Philo, *The Special Laws*, 1.208: "The division of the animal into its limbs [allegorizing sacrificial regulations] indicates either that all things are one or that they come from one and return to one"). See also contra E. Norden, *Agnostos Theos*, 240–50. M. Barth expresses a similar stoic expression of Marcus Aurelius in *Meditation* 4:23, a hymn to Selene, which is inscribed as a charm upon a Gem; M. Barth, "Theologie," 423.

23. Paul's use appears to be more than the original source; Calvin, *Epistles of Paul*, 262.

24. Vaughan, 215.

25. See Sir. 39:14b-16; 1 Esdr. 4:40; 4 Macc. 18:24; 1QS 11:15-17; 1 QH 7:26-27. See also M. Dibelius, "Die Christianisierung einer hellenistichen Formel," *Neue Jarbucher für das klassische Altertum* 35 (1915): 22–36.

are unsearchable and his ways unfathomable, the mind of God—*who he is*—has been revealed to Paul, and now to the Roman church, concerning his election of the younger son, Jacob, and his merciful plan for the nations.

6

———

Conclusion

God's heart and mind has been made known to Paul. He grieves unceasingly for Israel, revealing God's infinite compassion through Christ working within him. And enlightened by the Spirit, Paul reveals the wisdom of God through integrated argument to show how God's election of Jacob—the son in the "lesser" position—is merciful and impartial to Jews and gentiles.

Paul's narrative sequence follows a logical pattern. God's elects Jacob in the womb when neither son had disobeyed. This merciful decision in electing Israel is also merciful to Esau, requiring both Jacob and his descendants, and Esau and his descendants, to choose humble service (mercy to Israel is merciful to gentiles). Neither of these groups pursues the kind of relationship of faith that God requires. God judges Esau's descendants for their disobedience as a merciful warning to Israel (wrath to gentiles results in mercy to Israel). Before the people of Israel were delivered from Egypt, with great patience God demonstrates his wrath to rebellious Pharaoh—wrath that proclaims God's name, his goodness, to the nations (wrath to a gentile nation results in mercy to gentile nations). In time, Israel proudly seeks righteousness through works of the law—choosing to reject the Messiah rather than believe. God then mercifully sends his call to the nations who respond (judgment to Israel for disobedience results in mercy to the gentiles). This mercy shown to the gentiles then serves as a catalyst for the Jews to become jealous and return to God ("how much more will God's mercy to the gentiles result in mercy to 'Israel'?"). In the end, God reserves for himself a remnant of Jews and gentiles.

Paul's argument in Romans 9–11 supports the above narrative, which is summarized below, section by section. (Romans 9–11 is a continuation of a topic began earlier concerning God's faithfulness and his righteousness—If God elected Israel, why did God's choice fail?) Relevant theological insights concerning the meaning and purpose of Paul's letter are also restated, but first a summary of contributions.

Literary Contributions

In working through Romans 9–11, the following literary findings are made: (a) Paul's use of the imperfect in his prayer, 9:3, makes more clear sense in light of God's heart working through Paul—8:27, 34; 3:21f; and 12:1-3; (b) Paul's intercessory nature is accented with more clarity concerning his identification with the prophets Isaiah, Jeremiah, and Elijah—9:21-23, 27; and 11:1-4—and in relationship with other intercessory passages in the letter—8:27, 34 and 12:1-3; (c) a close parallel between the vessel phrases, 11:22-23, and God's wrath to Pharaoh, 11:17 is made; (d) a more specific explanation of the difficult grammatical expression is given concerning God's wrath and the "vessel" phrases, 9:21-23; (e) dual-parallel verses in the chiastic arrangement of 9:30—10:3 are delineated; (f) a Roman suggestion is made for Jesus Christ as the "end of the Law," 10:4;

(g) additional thought rhymes and contrasts are outlined, 10:6-10 and 8-14; (h) the *hapax legomenon* of 11:11-24 is identified placing relevant semantic weight on the transitional verse 11:16 concerning the "first fruits" as gentiles; (i) Paul's literary use of the names "Israel" and the "gentiles," 9:30—10:3, are recognized, which gives import to the meaning of "All Israel," 11:26; (j) Paul arranges his "narrative-argument" in a logical sequence demonstrating that all of God's actions are merciful to both people groups—Israel and the gentiles; and (i) Paul's statements in the final verses of the body of the midrash reveal a specific summary of his previous sections, 11:28.

Romans 9:1-5

As one receiving revelation, Paul is moved to intercede on behalf of his people. Yet Paul's experience is different from his prophetic predecessors in that he speaks as one "in" Christ, 9:1. He grieves with overwhelming anguish, begging the question as to the source of his grief—either he speaks in a less sincere rhetorical manner or he speaks with genuine emotion. Evidently, Paul's words follow a natural progression from Christ and the Spirit's intercession for the believer (8:26-27, 34) to God's heart working through Paul in interceding for the nation of Israel. Paul's use of the imperfect tense affirms this *continual* sense of grief for those of rebellious Israel who have rejected the Messiah.

Romans 9:6-29

Paul's immediate focus turns to "who" comprises the called of "Israel" as he explains that some of the ethnic Jews are not part of "Israel." Paul's initial support comes from the Genesis story, highlighting God's character in his relationship with the patriarchs concerning the promised seed. Significantly, Paul points out that God chooses the "younger" (ἐλάσσων; 9:11b; Gen. 25:23)—Jacob, the son in the lesser position—revealing God's faithfulness, for his decisions are *merciful* and function apart from man's doing, 9:12 and 16. Paul's reference to Malachi (Rom. 9:12b; Mal. 1:1-2) gives historical proof of the disobedience of both nations—Esau's descendants, the Edomites, and Jacob's descendants, the Israelites—and how God's wrath serves as a merciful *warning* to the covenant people of Israel.

Paul continues narrating Israel's story with scriptural proof from the Exodus account. God's wrath against Pharaoh results in the proclamation of God's Name, which is *goodness*, a message reaching gentile nations, 9:17. By drawing upon Jeremiah's vision of the potter, Paul further establishes the truth that gentiles are included as part of God's elective plan, 9:19-23. In this context, God acts impartiality in desiring gentile nations to repent, yet the thrust of the Jeremiah passage accents God's impending judgment to Israel for their obstinate disobedience, even though they have received the blessings of election (a similar emphasis made with the Malachi quotation; 9:12b). Paul skillfully merges "vessel" statements, 9:21-23, with potter imagery from Isaiah to elaborate on the earlier Exodus context, 9:17, to narrate a "reversal" of Israel's status—that the descendants of Abraham by birth may not be the "children of promise."

Paul's argument in 9:6-23 is summarized as follows: God with great patience demonstrates his wrath against Pharaoh, a "vessel" of wrath prepared for destruction (1) for the purpose of making known his power, and (2) for the purpose of making known his Name, the riches of his glory, to the gentiles, who are "vessels of mercy," prepared for glory. In this way, God's wrath accomplishes destruction and *mercy*. Thus Paul concludes with the statement that God calls persons "not only from the Jews but also from the gentiles," 9:24, and supports his conclusion with an Old Testament verse list, 9:25-29.

Rhetorically speaking, suspense builds as the reader asks the question as to what will happen to rebellious Israel, the Jews who reject the Messiah—"will they be hardened . . . like Pharaoh?"

In practical terms, the election of Israel, 9:6-13, reveals the heart of God and his desire for *humility* from his people. God does not show favoritism, and the gentile believers in Rome must not become proud in their self-estimation—11:18, 21, and 12:3, and more specifically, they should not pass judgment on the "weak in faith," 14:1f, but bear the weaknesses of others, 15:1-3. They are to have the humble mind of Christ—3:21-26, 12:1-3, and 15:5.

Romans 9:30—10:21

In a dual-parallel poetic arrangement, 9:30—10:3, Paul contrasts two themes—"faith and law" with "pursuing righteousness"—and he contrasts two people groups—"Israel" and the "gentiles," 9:30—10:3. Israel pursues the "law of righteousness" but does not obtain the law nor know the righteousness of God. The gentiles do not pursue righteousness but receive righteousness by faith. (Paul uses these general labels—"Israel" and "gentiles"—for instruction purposes, and he is not implying that all Jews have rejected the Messiah nor that all gentiles have received righteousness). In essence, Paul personifies "Righteousness," drawing attention to a relational understanding of justification. At the center of the poetic arrangement, Israel stumbles on the "stone," the Messiah. Thus, Paul indicts Israel: the stone that they reject is the Person they did not know, 9:30—10:4. But did Israel "hear" the word of Christ?

Paul argues that Israel has heard the word of Christ but does not act in faith, 10:5-21. The "law" that Moses gave and the "word of faith" that Paul preaches carry the same message concerning Christ, 10:6-17, Paul associates "righteousness from the law" with "life," and not with selfish ambition, and then explains how torah speaks about this "righteousness" as personal and relational, revealing God's interest in the heart—10:6, 8, 9, 10, 11, 12, 13. Paul personifies the "word" as Christ, someone to be believed in inwardly and confessed openly, 10:9-13 (a fulfillment of righteousness and end to the law—see 3:21-28; 4:13-16; 6:14-15, 7:1—8:1f). In this way, an obedient faith comes by hearing the word of Christ, 10:14-17. Thus the Righteousness that Israel stumbles on is the Word that is sent into all of the world, a merciful action of God, 10:18-21.

This definition of faith—hearing the word of Christ—confirms Paul's interest in seeing the Roman Christians remain humble (see 1:5 and 16:19). Paul's repetitive use of words containing the root "hear/obey" (ακου- or ακοα- ; 10:14-17) leads to the conclusion that Paul makes an indirect statement concerning Israel's lack of hearing/ obeying. In other words, the "all" who are called, who believe, and who confess, 10:5-13, do not include some (of Israel) who disobey, 10:14-17. God's election of Jacob does not have any motivation of favoritism—he desires a humble response to "Righteousness" from Jew and gentile, 10:12.

Romans 11:1-10

Paul identifies with Elijah as a "remnant" Israelite in order to reveal God's compassionate character in his response to Israel's disobedience, 11:1-4. Paul brings together two sets of themes: "not by works" in relation to "hardened" Israel; and the "called grace of God" in relation to the "remnant," 11:5-7. These themes summarize the first two major sections of his argument—gentiles are "called" by God and are a part of the "remnant," 9:6-29, and Israel has sought justification by "works" becoming "hardened," 9:30—10:21. Paul's purpose in this transition section, 11:1-10, is to move the reader from thinking in terms of the representative groups of "Israel" and the "gentiles"—which was for the purpose of highlighting Israel's misguided pursuit of righteousness by works—to a different set of representative groups: "hardened Israel" and the "remnant called by grace." This distinction allows for "Jewish" Christians to be included in the meaning of "remnant," and it prepares the reader for the revealed "mystery" that follows, 11:11-24.

In Paul's supporting Old Testament verse list, 11:8-10, he gives evidence of Israel's disobedience and validates God's wrath to be carried out against those who reject the Messiah, 11:10. Paul does not directly answer his initial question concerning whether God has rejected His people? (11:1). This limited explanation of God's wrath effectively builds suspense in the "narrative" by withholding the final verdict concerning God's sentencing of "hardened" Israel.

Paul's argument underscores God's desire for humility in his election of Israel. The righteousness that Moses speaks about is the righteousness that Paul proclaims, which means that the nation of Israel has heard the "Word" and has rejected a relationship with him. In response to disobedience, God sends a call to the world bringing a message of salvation to all those who humbly confess that Jesus is Lord—whether Jew or Greek. Though Israel has stumbled, God continually extends his mercy to them.

Romans 11:11-24

Paul's poetic form is beautifully arranged, 11:11-24. In the first section, 11:11-15, Paul writes two synonymous stanzas built around a "jealousy" theme (which was introduced earlier: "*I will make you jealous by a nation that is not a nation*," 10:19). He then states the sequence of God's plan concerning the future "fullness" of Israel, 11:11-12, and demonstrates how he (Paul) himself participates in Israel's reconciliation, 11:13-15.

Paul employs agricultural imagery—"first fruits" and "root," 11:16—to transition from the topic of Israel's future fullness, 11:11-15, into the practical imperatives of the olive tree metaphor addressed to the gentiles, 11:17-22. For literary reasons, in order to make the olive tree metaphor work, Paul temporarily sets aside the identifications of "remnant" Israel and "hardened" Israel from 11:1-10, and returns to the more general terms—"gentiles" and "Israel" (from 9:30—10:3). By using the term "gentiles," Paul removes "Jewish Christians" from the metaphorical picture so that the term "gentiles" receives the semantic weight in the discussion. This means that verse 16 has great significance to the meaning of the whole section, for if the fathers [root] of the nation Israel are made holy and the gentile Christians [first fruits] who benefited from Israel's disobedience are made holy, "How much more according to the natural branches will Israel be made holy (engrafted into their own olive tree)?"

In this section, Paul reveals one of his motivations—to reach his ethnic people with the gospel. Concerning the future "fullness" of Israel, 11:11-15, Paul knows that God responds to Israel's disobedience by opening the door to the riches of God's grace to the gentiles, which then causes the Jewish people to become jealous, resulting in a "greater" or "full" return of Israel to God (where "sin abounds, grace abounds more," 5:18-19).

Paul explains through olive tree imagery the impartial and merciful character of God. "Cutting" and "engrafting" refer to God's "severity" and "kindness." Paul warns the gentile Christians to choose humility in order to avoid the severity of God: "*Do not be high minded but fear, for if God did not spare the natural branches neither in any way will he spare you*" (11:20-21). This underscores Paul's main purpose of his letter: to engender humility among the gentile believers in the Roman congregation, 1:13; in Christ's likeness,12:1-3, and more specifically, to give them a sound basis for not judging the weak in faith,14:1-15:7. The cutting and engrafting (severity and kindness) should also be understood in light of their synonyms—God's wrath and mercy—which are continuously carried out without favoritism (1:17-18; 2:1-11; and 13:1-4; God's wrath is also merciful, see 9:15-17; 13:4). Paul engenders hope for Israel as he ends the olive tree metaphor by emphasizing the grace of God, 11:23-24.

Romans 11:25-32

Paul summarizes the body of his argument. He begins by stating the purpose of revealing the mystery, 11:25, "*to not think of yourselves too highly*" (and the letter—11:18, 21; 9:13-14; 10:2-9; 12:1-3; 13:1-6; 14:1—15:7). And then Paul adds new phrases—"partial" hardening and "fullness of the gentiles" to restate God's plan for Israel: the mystery consists of God's partial hardening of Israel until God's full number of called gentiles comes in. Paul's contrast of "partial" and "fullness" accents God's ability: a *temporary* hardening of Israel results in *eternal* blessing of the gentiles. This brings hope in that God can take what is "partial" and negative (disobedience) and work out what is "eternal" and positive (blessing; see also 4:18-20; 5:15-21; 6:22-23; 8:11; and 11:28). How much more, with God, will "fullness result in fullness?"

Concerning the phrase, "all Israel," two views can be argued with confidence. Paul's parallel thought, Old Testament support, and particular phrases—such as "partial hardening," "fullness of the gentiles" and the adverb "likewise"—suggest that Paul intends a full number of "hardened" Israelites return to God. But taking into account Paul's inclusion of the gentile in his interpretation of what it means to be a Jew, 2:29, his definition of *who* "Israel" is, 9:6 and 24, as well as his clarification of the "remnant," it is more likely that "all Israel" refers to a remnant comprised of Jews and gentiles. This "remnant" interpretation is also supported by Paul's literary style, such as his use of: lament elements, the adverb "likewise" rather than "how much more language," and the agricultural imagery in 11:16.

In the final verses of the body of the argument, 11:28-31, Paul summarizes his two previous midrashic forms with respect to Israel, and he completes his circular argument that he began in 9:6-12, concerning God's election of Jacob. The phrase "beloved on account of the fathers" emphasizes God's covenantal faithfulness and compassion to an obstinate Jewish nation. More specifically, God's choosing of Israel as His son, 9:4-5, does not mean that he withdraws his love when they reject the Messiah. Rather, Paul's use of "irrevocable" (ἀμεταμέλητα) refers to God's *mercy* in that God's hands are continually extended to them. Paul does not equate "mercy" with universal salvation, but he makes a final statement about the merciful and elective character of God in the context of disobedience. This parallels Paul's earlier discussion concerning the disobedience of one man, Adam, and how through Jesus Christ righteousness results to the many, 5:12-15. In this way, Paul reasons that the disobedience of the gentiles and the disobedience of Israel result in God's showing mercy to all, 11:31-32.

Romans 11:33-36

Paul's unceasing anguish, 9:1-5, changes to praise, 11:33-36 (one of four ending praise passages in the letter—5:1-11, 8:31-39, and 15:8-13). Just as Paul describes the infinite compassion of Christ, the heart of the Father, so too Paul illumined by the Spirit explains God's decisions concerning Israel. On the one hand, Paul praises God for his infinite and unsearchable ways, and on the other hand, he exalts God for revealing his wise and merciful plan in electing Israel.

Paul's Purpose

Paul's theme verse, 1:16, creates an apparent paradox, "For I am not ashamed of the gospel for it is the power of God to *all* who believe—*first* the Jew and then the gentile." This study on Romans 9–11 sheds light on how God can elect Israel from among the nations without showing favoritism to Israel. Paul clarifies God's merciful decision in that he chooses Jacob, the son in the lesser position, which requires a humble decision of faith from all. While Paul writes in a general manner on the topic of disobedience of all persons—e.g., 2:12, 3:28, 5:12—and the mercy that comes through faith in Jesus Christ—e.g., 5:17-19 and 11:28—it is in Romans 9–11 where he explains the specific actions of God that reveal God's heart and mind for Israel.

For Paul, sequence and order do not mean either superiority or lesser significance. God is the God of the Jew and the gentile, 3:29; and there is no distinction between Jew or Greek, for the Lord is Lord of all, 10:12. According to the olive tree imagery, a reversal occurs in which gentiles Christians (as a group) repent and turn to God before the Jews do (as a group). Paul does not argue that the gentiles replace the Jews in God's order of election; rather, Paul uses the olive tree imagery to emphasize God's *impartiality*, that whether Jew or gentile, humility is what God desires. At the same time, Paul does not eliminate ethnic distinctions but honors God's order (e.g., "first to the Jew and then to the gentile," 1:16). In this way, Paul's argument has less to do with an emphasis on "equality" and more to do with an emphasis on God's character in election (e.g., choosing the son in the humble situation and blessing those who remain in faith).

An example of this humble mindset is seen in Paul's informal discussion of his plans to travel to Jerusalem, 15:14-33. Paul aims to bring an offering from the gentile Christians to the "poor" Jewish Christians in Jerusalem as a physical demonstration of the gospel. This sacrificial act from the gentile Christians shows respect for God's order of election ("to the Jew first") and it affirms acceptance of God's plan for the Jews in the re-grafting of the "natural olive branches" (11:11f). Paul describes this "fruitful gift" as an obligation from the gentile Christians, since the gentile Christians now share in the spiritual blessings of the Jews, 15:27-28.

Thus Paul sees himself as serving in a priestly role unto God on behalf of the gentiles (1:1, 9; and 15:15-16) to guide the Romans believers to be Christ-like in their *humble* service to God (11:25-26; 12:1-3; and 15:16). Without corrupting pride among the Roman church, a harvest of fruit can be born to the neighboring territories—particularly Spain. A successful outreach to the world—a full number of converts—will bring about jealousy from the disobedient Jews who rejected the Messiah, which will then result in some of them returning to God. Not only does Paul want to remind them of the humble and sacrificial love of God through atonement, 3:21-26, but he also demonstrates God's humble character in electing the son in the lesser position, 9:12. It is not surprising, then, that the climactic points in Paul's arguments give imperatives concerning "humility"—such as in the olive tree metaphor, "Be humble," 11:17-21; at the beginning of his admonition section: "Do not think of yourselves more highly than you ought," 12:1-3; and in his practical admonitions to the "strong" in faith to bear the weaknesses of others and not judge, 14:1—15:7.

What Paul seeks to achieve among the Roman believers—humility—is a decision that God has always desired from his people—righteousness through faith. God warns Israel before entering the promised land not to boast in their own righteousness, for it is because of God's faithfulness—to his covenant with Abraham,

Isaac, and Jacob—and it is because of the disobedience of the nations that he drives Israel's enemies out before them (Deut. 9:4). In this sense, the Lord is not "for" or "against" Israel or the nations, but he acts to fulfill his merciful plan for all (Josh. 5:13-14). God loves Israel because of his faithful covenant and because of their low position (Deut. 7:7). When God elects Jacob, he reveals his power through weakness so that all might be shown mercy.

Bibliography

Aageson, James W. "Typology, Correspondence, and the Application of Scripture in Romans 9-11." *JSNT* 31 (1987): 51–72.

———. "Scripture and Structure in the Development of the Argument in Romans 9-11." *CBQ* 48 (1986): 265–89.

———."Paul's Use of Scripture: A Comparative Study of Biblical Interpretation in Early Palestinian Judaism and the New Testament, with Special Reference to Romans 9-11." DPhil thesis., University of Oxford, 1983.

Abaelard, Peter, and Rolf Peppermüller. *Expositio in Epistolam ad Romanos: Römerbriefkommentar.* Fontes Christiani. Freiburg im Breisgau: Herder, 2000.

Abasciano, Brian J. "Corporate Election in Romans 9: A Reply to Thomas Schreiner." *JETS* 49, no. 2 (2006): 351–71.

———. *Paul's Use of the Old Testament in Romans 9:1-9: An Intertextual and Theological Exegesis.* Library of New Testament Studies. London: T & T Clark, 2005.

Abernathy, C. David. *An Exegetical Summary of Romans 1-8.* Dallas: SIL International, 2006.

Agamben, Giorgio. *The Time That Remains: A Commentary on the Letter to the Romans.* Translated by Patricia Dailey. Stanford, CA: Stanford University Press, 2005.

Aletti, Jean-N. *Israël et la Loi dans la Lettre Aux Romains*. Lectio Divina. Paris: Cerf, 1998.

———. "L'Argumentation Paulinienne en Rm 9." *Bib* 68 (1987): 41–46.

Allison, Dale C. "The Background of Romans 11.11-15: A Suggestion." *PRSt* 12, no. 1 (1985): 23–30.

Althaus, Paul. *Der Brief an die Römer, Übersetzt und Erklärt von Paul Althaus*. NTD. Göttingen: Vandenhoeck & Ruprecht, 1953.

Ambrosiaster. *Commentaries on Romans and 1-2 Corinthians*. Translated and edited by Gerald L. Bray. Ancient Christian Texts. Downers Grove, IL: InterVarsity Press, 2009.

Anderson, Erik. *Der Brief an die Römer*. Ausgewöhlte Schriften. Wörzburg: Echter, 1997.

Anderson, R.D. *Ancient Rhetorical Theory and Paul*. Louvain: Kok Pharos, 1996.

Angers, Dominque. "The Pauline Expressions 'Until This Very Day' and Until Today' (Rom 11,8 and 2 Cor 3,14-15) in the Light of the Septuagint." In *Voces Biblicae*, edited by Jan Joosten and Peter J. Tornson, 115–54. Dudley, MA: Peeters, 2007.

Aus, Roger. "Paul's Travel Plans to Spain and the 'Full Number of the Gentiles' of Rom XI 25." *Novum Testamentum* 21 (1979): 251–52.

Baaij, Pieter K. *Israël en de Volken: Exegetische Studie van Romeinen 9-11*. Heerenveen: Groen, 2003.

Badenas, Robert. *Christ: The End of the Law: Romans 10.4 in Pauline Perspective*. JSNT. Sheffield: JSOT, 1985.

Bailey, J. L., and Lyle D. Vander Broek. *Literary Forms in the New Testament: A Handbook*. Louisville: Westminster John Knox, 1992.

Baker, Murray. "Paul and the Salvation of Israel: Paul's Ministry, the Motif of Jealousy, and Israel's Yes." *CBQ* 67, no. 3 (2005): 469–84.

Baldwin, Joyce. *Haggai, Zechariah, Malachi: An Introduction and Commentary.* Tyndale Old Testament Commentaries 24. Downers Grove, IL: InterVarsity, 1972

Barrett, C. K. *The Epistle to the Romans.* Black's New Testament Commentaries. London: Hendrickson, 1991.

Barth, Karl. *The Epistle to the Romans.* Translated by Edwyn C. Hoskyns. London: Oxford University Press, 1968.

Barth, Marcus. "Theologie—ein Bebet (Rom 11,33-36)." *TZ* 41 (1985): 330–48.

Bartlett, David L. *Romans.* Westminster Bible Companion. Louisville: Westminster John Knox, 1995.

Bassi, Karen. *Acting Like Men: Gender, Drama, and Nostalgia in Ancient Greece.* Ann Arbor: University of Michigan Press, 1998.

Battle, John A. "Paul's Use of the Old Testament in Romans 9:25:26." *GTJ* 2, no. 1 (1981): 115–29.

Baxter, A. G., and John A. Ziesler. "Paul and the Arboriculture: Romans 11:17-24." *JSNT* 7, no. 24 (1985): 25–32.

Beale, G.K. "An Exegetical and Theological Consideration of the Hardening of Pharaoh's Heart in Exodus 4-14 and Romans 9." *Trinity Journal* 5 (1984): 129–54.

Bechtler, Steven Richard. "Christ, the Telos of the Law: The Goal of Romans 10:4." *CBQ* 56 no. 2 (1994): 288–308.

Beker, J. Christiaan. "Romans 9-11 in the Context of the Early Church." *PSBSup* 1 (1990): 40–55.

———. *Paul the Apostle: The Triumph of God in Life and Thought.* Philadelphia: Fortress Press, 1980.

Bekken, Per Jarle. "Paul's Use of Deut 30.12-14 in Jewish Context." In *The New Testament and Hellenistic Judaism,* edited by Søren Giversen and Peder Borgen, 183–203. Aarhus: Aarhus University Press, 1995.

————. *The Word is Near You: A Study of Deuteronomy 30:12-14 in Paul's Letter to the Romans in a Jewish Context*. Beihefte Zur Zeitschrift für die Neutestamentliche Wissenschaft und die Kunde der älteren Kirche 144. New York: Walter de Gruyter, 2007.

Bell, Richard H. *The Irrevocable Call of God: An Inquiry into Paul's Theology of Israel*. WUNT. Tübingen: Mohr Siebeck, 2005.

————. *No One Seeks for God: An Exegetical and Theological Study of Romans 1.18-3.20*. WUNT. Tübingen: Mohr Siebeck, 1998.

————. *Provoked to Jealousy: The Origin and Purpose of the Jealousy Motif in Romans 9-11*. WUNT Tübingen: Mohr Siebeck, 1994.

Benko, Stephen. *Pagan Rome and the Early Christians*. Bloomington: Indiana University Press, 1984.

Berger, K. "Abraham in den paulinishen Hauptbriefen," *Münchener theologishe Zeitschrift* 17 (1966): 47–89.

Bergmeier, Roland. *Das Gesetz im Römerbrief und andere Studien zum Neuen Testament*. WUNT. Tübingen: Mohr Siebeck, 2000.

Berkley, Timothy W. *From a Broken Covenant to Circumcision of the Heart: Pauline Intertextual Exegesis in Romans 2:17-29*. SBL Dissertation Series 175. Atlanta: Society of Biblical Literature, 2000.

Best, Ernest. *The Letter of Paul to the Romans*. Cambridge Bible Commentary. Cambridge: Cambridge University Press, 1967.

Biays, Paul M. *Parallelism in Romans*. Fort Hays Studies 5. Hays: Fort Hays Kansas State College, 1967.

Birnbaum, Ellen. *The Place of Judaism in Philo's Thought: Israel, Jews, and Proselytes*. Brown Judaic Studies. Atlanta: Scholars Press, 1996.

Black, David Alan. *Paul, Apostle of Weakness: Astheneia and Its Cognates in the Pauline Literature*. American University Studies 3. New York: Lang, 1984.

Black, Matthew. *Romans*. New Century Bible. London: Oliphants, 1973.

Blass, F., and A. Debrunner. *A Greek Grammar of the New Testament and Early Christian Literature*. Edited and translated by Robert Funk. Chicago: Chicago University Press, 1961.

Blomberg, Craig. "Elijah, Election, and the Use of Malachi in the New Testament. *Criswell Theological Review* 2 (1987): 99–117.

Boers, Hendrikus. *The Justification of the Gentiles: Paul's Letters to the Galatians and Romans*. Peabody, MA: Hendrickson, 1994.

Boguslawski, Steven C. *Thomas Aquinas on the Jews: Insights into His Commentary on Romans 9-11*. Studies in Judaism and Christianity. New York: Paulist, 2008.

Bonda, Jan. *The One Purpose of God: An Answer to the Doctrine of Eternal Punishment*. Translated by Reinder Bruinsma. Grand Rapids: Eerdmans, 1998.

Bonhard, P. E. "Les Tresors de la misericorde (Rm 11,33-36)." *AsSeign* 53 (1964): 13–19.

Bormann, Lukas, Kelly Del Tredici, and Angela Standhartinger, eds. *Religious Propaganda and Missionary Competition in the New Testament World: Essays in Honor of Dieter Georgi*. Supplements to Novum Testamentum. Leiden: Brill, 1994.

Bornkamm, Günther. "The Letter to the Romans as Paul's Last Will and Testament." In *The Romans Debate*, edited by Karl P. Donfried, 16–28. Minneapolis: Augsburg Publishing House, 1977.

———. "The Praise of God: Romans 11.33-36." *Early Christian Experience* (1976): 105–11.

Bosman, Philip. *Conscience in Philo and Paul: A Conceptual History of the Synoida Word Group*. WUNT. Tübingen: Mohr Siebeck, 2003.

Bourke, Myles. *A Study of the Metaphor of the Olive Tree in Romans XI*. Studies in Sacred Theology 2. Washington: Catholic University of America Press, 1947.

Bowker, John W. "Merkabah Visions and the Visions of Paul." *Journal of Semitic Studies* 16, no. 2 (1971): 157–73.

Brackett, James Kristian. "Paul's Use of the Old Testament in Romans 9–11." Th.M. thesis, the Master's Seminary, 1998.

Brändle, Rudolf, and Ekkehard W. Stegemann. "The Formation of the First 'Christian Congregations' in Rome in the Context of Jewish Congregations." In *Judaism and Christianity in First-Century Rome*, edited by Karl P. Donfried and Peter Richardson, 117–27. Grand Rapids: Eerdmans, 1998.

Bratsiotis, Panagiotis. "Eine Exegetische Notiz zu Röm 9:3 and 10:1." *Novum Testamentum* 5, no. 4 (1962): 299–300.

Brent, Allen. *The Imperial Cult and the Development of Church Order: Concepts and Images.* Leiden: Brill, 1999.

Brodeur, Scott. *The Holy Spirit's Agency in the Resurrection of the Dead: An Exegetico-Theological Study of 1 Corinthians 15,44b-49 and Romans 8,9-13.* Rome: Gregorian University Press, 1996.

Bruce, F. F. *Romans.* Tyndale New Testament Commentaries. Grand Rapids: Eerdmans, 1985.

Bryan, Christopher. *A Preface to Romans: Notes on the Epistle in Its Literary and Cultural Setting.* Oxford: Oxford University Press, 2000.

Bryne, Brendon. *Romans.* Collegeville, MN: Liturgical Press, 1996.

———. *'Sons of God' – 'Seeds of Abraham': A Study of the Idea of Sonship of God of All Christians in Paul against the Jewish Background.* Rome: Biblical Institute Press, 1979.

Bultmann, Rudolf Karl. *Theology of the New Testament.* Translated by Kendrick Grobel. New York: Scribner, 1951–55.

Burkes, Shannon. *God, Self, and Death: The Shape of Religious Transformation in the Second Temple Period.* Supplements to the Journal for the Study of Judaism. Leiden: Brill, 2003.

Burnett, Gary W. *Paul and the Salvation of the Individual*. Biblical Interpretation Series. Leiden: Brill, 2001.

Calvin, John. *The Epistles of Paul the Apostle to the Romans and the Thessalonians*. Edited by Ross Mackenzie, David W. Torrance, and Thomas F. Torrance. London: Oliver & Boyd, 1961.

Campbell, Constantine R. *Paul and Union with Christ: An Exegetical and Theological Study*. Grand Rapids: Zondervan, 2012.

Campbell, Douglas A. *The Deliverance of God: An Apocalyptic Rereading of Justification in Paul*. Grand Rapids: Eerdmanns, 2009.

———. "Determining the Gospel through Rhetorical Analysis in Paul's Letter to the Roman Christians." *In Gospel in Paul: Studies in Corinthians, Galatians, and Romans for Richard N. Longenecker*, edited by L.A. Jervis and P. Richardson. Sheffield: Shefflield Academic Press, 1994.

Campbell, William S. *Paul and the Creation of Christian Identity*. London: T & T Clark, 2006.

———."'All God's Beloved in Rome!': Jewish Roots and Christian Identity." In *Celebrating Romans: Template for Pauline Theology: Essays in Honor of Robert Jewett*, edited by Sheila E. McGinn, 67–82. Grand Rapids: Eerdmans, 2004.

———. "Divergent Images of Paul and His Missions." In *Reading Israel in Romans: Legitimacy and Plausibility of Divergent Interpretations*, edited by Cristina Grenholm and Daniel Patte, 187–211. Harrisburg, PA: Trinity Press International, 2000.

———. "The Rule of Faith in Romans 12.1-15.13: The Obligation of Humble Obedience to Christ as the Only Adequate Response to the Mercies of God." In vol. 3 of *Pauline Theology: Romans*, edited by D. M. Hay and E. E. Johnson, 259–86. Minneapolis: Fortress Press, 1995.

———. "Israel." In *Dictionary of Paul and His Letters*, edited by Gerald F. Hawthorne and Ralph P. Martin, 441–42. Downers Grove, IL: InterVarsity Press, 1993.

———. *Paul's Gospel in an Intercultural Context: Jew and Gentile in the Letter to the Romans.* Studies in the Intercultural History of Christianity. New York: Lang, 1991.

———. "The Freedom and Faithfulness of God in Relation to Israel." *JSNT* 13 (1981): 27–45.

Capes, David B. "YHWH and His Messiah: Pauline Exegesis and the Divine Christ." *Horizons in Biblical Theology* 16, no. 2 (1994): 121–43.

Carson, D. A., Peter T. O'Brien, and Mark A. Seifrid, eds. *Justification and Variegated Nomism.* Grand Rapids: Baker Academic, 2001–2004.

Chae, Daniel Jong-Sang. *Paul as Apostle to the Gentiles.* Carlisle: Paternoster, 2007.

Charles, Gary W. "Romans 11:1-10." *Interpretation* 58, no. 3 (2004): 283–86.

Charlesworth, James Hamilton. *The Old Testament Pseudepigrapha and the New Testament: Prolegomena for the Study of Christian Origins.* Society for New Testament Studies. Cambridge: Cambridge University Press, 1985.

Chibici-Revneanu, Nicole. "Leben im Gesetz: Die Paulinische Interpretation von Lev 18:5 (Gal 3:12; Röm 10:5)." *Novum Testamentum* 50, no. 2 (2008): 105–19.

Childs, Brevard. "On Reading the Elijah Narratives." *Interpretation* 34 (1980): 134–35.

Chilton, Bruce D. "Romans 9-11 as Scriptural Interpretation and Dialogue with Judaism." *Ex Auditu* 4 (1988): 27–37.

Cohen, J. "The Mystery of Israel's Salvation: Romans 11:25-26 in Patristic and Medieval Exegesis." *Harvard Theological Review* 98 (2005): 247–81.

Cohn, Robert L. "The Literary Logic of 1 Kings 17-19." *JBL* 101 (1982): 341–42.

Cook, J. R. Daniel. *Unlocking Romans: Resurrection and the Justification of God.* Grand Rapids: Eerdmanns, 2008.

Corbett, E.P.I. *Classical Rhetoric for the Modern Student.* New York: Oxford University Press, 1990.

Cook, Michael J. "Paul's Argument in Romans 9-11." *Review & Expositor* 103, no. 1 (2006): 91–111.

Corley, Bruce. "Significance of Romans 9-11: A Study in Pauline Theology." DPhil thesis, Southwestern Baptist Theological Seminary, 1975.

Cosgrove, Charles H. *Elusive Israel: The Puzzle of Election in Romans.* Louisville: Westminster John Knox, 1997.

———. "Rhetorical Suspense in Romans 9-11: A Study in Polyvalence and Hermeneutical Election." *JBL* 115, no. 2 (1996): 271–87.

Cotterell, Peter, and Max Turner. *Linguistics & Biblical Interpretation.* Downers Grove, IL: InterVarsity Press, 1989.

Coxhead, Steven R. "Deuteronomy 30:11-14 as a Prophecy of the New Covenant in Christ." *Westminster Theological Journal* 68, no. 2 (2006): 305–20.

Cranfield, C. E. B. *A Critical and Exegetical Commentary on the Epistle to the Romans.* 2 vols. Edinburgh: T & T Clark, 1975–79.

Cranford, Michael. "Election and Ethnicity: Paul's View of Israel in Romans 9.1-13." *JSNT* 15, no. 50 (1993): 27–41.

Dahl, N. A. "The Future of Israel." In *Studies in Paul: Theology for the Early Christian Mission*, edited by G. W. Bromiley, 137–58. Minneapolis: Augsburg Publishing House, 1977.

———. "A Synopsis of Romans 5:1-11 and 8:1-39." In *Studies in Paul: Theology for the Christian Mission*, edited by G. W. Bromiley, 88–91. Minneapolis: Augsburg Publishing House, 1977.

Daly-Denton, Margaret. "David the Psalmist: Jewish Antecedents of a New Testament Datum." *Australian Biblical Review* 52 (2004): 32–47.

Das, A. Andrew. *Solving the Romans Debate.* Minneapolis: Fortress Press, 2007.

de Villiers, J. L. "The Salvation of Israel According to Romans 9-11." *Neotestamentica* 15 (1981): 199–221.

Demson, David. "John Calvin."In *Reading Romans through the Centuries: From the Early Church to Karl Barth*, edited by Jeffrey Greenman and Timothy Larsen, 137–48. Grand Rapids: Brazos, 2005.

Dewey, Arthur J. "A Re-Hearing of Romans 10:1-15." *Semeia* 65 (1994): 109–27.

———. "Eis tēn Spanian: The Future and Paul." In *Religious Propaganda and Missionary Competition in the New Testament World: Essays in Honor of Dieter Georgi*, edited by Lukas Bormann, Kelly Del Tredici, and Angela Standhartinger, 321–49. Supplements to Novum Testamentum. Leiden: Brill, 1994.

Dibelius, M. "Die Christianisierung einer hellenistichen Formel." *Neue Jarbucher für das klassische Altertum* 35 (1915): 224–36.

Di Lella, A. A. "Tobit 4,9 and Roman 9,18: An Intertextual Study." *Biblica* 90, no. 2 (2009): 260–63.

Dinter, Paul E. *The Remnant of Israel and the Stone of Stumbling in Zion according to Paul (Romans 9-11)*. DPhil thesis, Union Theological Seminary, 1980.

Dion, M. "*La Notion paulinienne de 'Richese de Dieu' et ses sources*." *ScEccl* 18 (1966): 139–48.

Dodd, C. H. *The Epistle of Paul to the Romans*. Moffatt New Testament Commentary. London: Harper & Brothers, 1954.

Dodson, Joseph R. *The "Powers" of Personification: Rhetorical Purpose in the Book of Wisdom and the Letter to the Romans*. Beihefte zur Zeitschrift für die Neutestamentliche Wissenschaft und die Kunde der älteren Kirche. Berlin: Walter de Gruyter, 2008.

Donaldson, Terence L. "Jewish Christianity, Israel's Stumbling and the *Sonderweg* Reading of Paul." *JSNT* 29, no. 1 (2006): 27–54.

———. *Paul and the Gentiles: Remapping the Apostle's Convictional World*. Minneapolis: Fortress Press, 1997.

———. "Riches for the Gentiles (Rom 11:12): Israel's Rejection and Paul's Gentile Mission." *JBL* 112 (1993): 81–98.

Donfried, Karl P., ed. *The Romans Debate*. Minneapolis: Augsburg Publishing House, 1977.

——— and Peter Richardson, eds. *Judaism and Christianity in First-Century Rome*. Grand Rapids: Eerdmans, 1998.

Driver, S.R. *The Book of Exodus*. Cambridge: Cambridge University Press, 1911.

Dumbrell, William J. "What Are You Doing Here? Elijah at Horeb." *Crux* 22 (1986): 15–17.

Dunn, James D. G. *Paul and the Mosaic Law*. WUNT. Tübingen: Mohr, 1996.

———. *Romans*. WBC. Dallas: Word Books, 1988.

———. "'Righteousness from the Law' and 'Righteousness from Faith': Paul's Interpretation of Scripture in Rom 10:1-10." In *Tradition and Interpretation in the New Testament*, edited by Gerald F. Hawthorne and Otto Betz, 216–28. Grand Rapids: Eerdmans, 1987.

Eckert, Jost. "Das Letzte Wort des Apostels Paulus über Israel (Röm 11:25-32) – eine Korrektur seiner bisherigen Verkündigung?" In *Schrift und Tradition*, edited by Kristen E. Skydsgaard and Lukas Vischer, 57–84. Paderborn: Ferdinand Schöningh, 1996.

Edwards, James. *Romans*. New International Biblical Commentary 6. Peabody, MA: Hendrickson, 1992.

Ehrensperger, Kathy. *That We May Be Mutually Encouraged: Feminism and the New Perspective in Pauline Studies*. London: T & T Clark, 2004.

———, and R. Ward Holder, eds. *Reformation Readings of Romans*. Romans through History and Cultures Series 8. London: T & T Clark, 2008.

Ekem, John David K. "A Dialogical Exegesis of Romans 3.25a." *JSNT* 30, no. 1 (2007): 75–93.

Elass, Mateen Assaad. "Paul's Understanding and Use of the Concept of Election in Romans 9-11." DPhil thesis, University of Durham, 1996.

Ellingworth, Paul. "Translation and Exegesis: A Case Study (Rom 9:22ff)." *Biblica* 59, no. 3 (1978): 396–402.

Elliott, Mark A. "Romans 9-11 and Jewish Remnant Theology." ThM diss, Toronto School of Theology, University of Toronto, 1986.

Elliott, Neil. *The Arrogance of Nations: Reading Romans in the Shadow of Empire.* Paul in Critical Contexts. Minneapolis: Fortress Press, 2008.

———. *The Rhetoric of Romans: Argumentative Constraint and Strategy and Paul's Dialogue with Judaism.* JSNT. Sheffield: JSOT, 1990.

Ellis, E. Earle. *The Old Testament in Early Christianity: Canon and Interpretation in the Light of Modern Research.* WUNT. Tübingen: Mohr Siebeck, 1991.

———. *Prophecy and Hermeneutic in Early Christianity: New Testament Essays.* Tübingen, J.C.B. Mohr, 1978.

———. "Exegetical Patterns in 1 Corinthians and Romans." In *Grace Upon Grace*, edited by James I. Cook, 137–42. Grand Rapids: Eerdmans, 1975.

———. *Paul and His Recent Interpreters.* Grand Rapids: Eerdmans, 1961.

———. *Paul's Use of the Old Testament.* Edinburgh: Oliver & Boyd, 1957.

Ellison, H. L. *The Mystery of Israel: An Exposition of Romans 9-11.* Grand Rapids: Eerdmans, 1966.

Esler, Philip F. "Ancient Oleiculture and Ethnic Differentiation: The Meaning of the Olive-Tree Image in Romans 11." *JSNT* 26, no. 1 (2003): 103–24.

———. *Conflict and Identity in Romans: The Social Setting of Paul's Letter.* Minneapolis: Fortress Press, 2003.

Evans, Craig A., and James A. Sanders, eds. *The Function of Scripture in Early Jewish and Christian Tradition.* JSNT. Sheffield: Sheffield Academic Press, 1998.

———. *Paul and the Scriptures of Israel.* JSNT. Sheffield: JSOT, 1993.

Fears, J.R. "Cult of Virtues and Roman Imperial Ideology," *ANRW* 2, 17, 2 (1981): 827–948.

Fee, Gordon D. *Pauline Christology: An Exegetical-Theological Study.* Peabody, MA: Hendrickson, 2007.

———. *God's Empowering Presence: The Holy Spirit in the Letters of Paul.* Peabody, MA: Hendrickson, 1994.

Ferguson, Everett. *Backgrounds of Early Christianity.* Grand Rapids: Eerdmanns, 2003.

Fitzmyer, Joseph A. *Romans.* AB. New York: Doubleday, 1993.

Flebbe, Jochen. *Solus Deus: Untersuchungen zur Rede von Gott im Brief des Paulus an die Römer.* Beihefte zur Zeitschrift für die Neutestamentliche Wissenschaft und die Kunde der älteren Kirche 158. New York: Walter de Gruyter, 2008.

Gaca, Kathy, and L. L. Welborn, eds. *Early Patristic Readings of Romans.* Romans through History and Cultures Series. New York: T & T Clark, 2005.

Gadenz, Pablo T. *Called from the Jews and from the Gentiles: Pauline Ecclesiology in Romans 9-11.* WUNT. Tübingen: Mohr Siebeck, 2009.

———. "'The Lord Will Accomplish His Word': Paul's Argumentation and Use of Scripture in Romans 9:24-29." *Letter & Spirit* 2 (2006): 141–55.

Gager, John. *Reinventing Paul.* New York: Oxford University Press, 2000.

Gamble, Harry. *The Textual History of the Letter to the Romans: A Study in Textual and Literary Criticism.* Grand Rapids: Eerdmans, 1977.

Garlington, Don. *Faith, Obedience, and Perseverance: Aspects of Paul's Letter to the Romans.* WUNT. Tübingen: Mohr Siebeck, 1994.

Gaston, Lloyd. *Paul and the Torah.* Vancouver: University of British Columbia Press, 1987.

Gianoulis, George C. "Is Sonship in Romans 8:14-17 a Link with Romans 9?" *Bibliotheca Sacra* 166, no. 661 (2009): 70–83.

Glancy, Jennifer A. "Israel vs. Israel in Romans 11:25-32." *Union Seminary Quarterly Review* 45, no 3-4 (1991): 191–203.

Glenny, W. Edward. "The 'People of God' in Romans 9:25-26." *Bibliotheca Sacra* 152, no. 605 (1995): 42–59.

Godet, Frédéric Louis. *Commentary on Romans*. Grand Rapids: Kregel, 1977.

Goodman, Martin. *The Roman World: 44 BC—AD 180.* London: Routledge, 1997.

Gorday, Peter. *Principles of Patristic Exegesis: Romans 9-11 in Origen, John Chrysostom, and Augustine.* Studies in the Bible and Early Christianity 4. New York: E. Mellen, 1983.

Gordon, T. David. "Why Israel Did not Obtain Torah-Righteousness: A Translation Note on Rom 9:32." *Westminster Theological Journal* 54, no. 1 (1992): 163–66.

Grayston, Kenneth. *The Epistle to the Romans.* Epworth Commentaries. Peterborough: Epworth, 1997.

Greenman, Jeffrey P., and Timothy Larsen, eds. *Reading Romans Through the Centuries: From the Early Church to Karl Barth.* Grand Rapids: Brazos, 2005.

Grenholm, Cristina, and Daniel Patte, eds. *Gender, Tradition and Romans: Shared Ground, Uncertain Borders.* Romans through History and Cultures Series. New York: T & T Clark, 2005.

———, eds. *Reading Israel in Romans: Legitimacy and Plausibility of Divergent Interpretations.* Romans through History and Cultures Series 1. Harrisburg, PA: Trinity Press International, 2000.

Grieb, A. Katherine. *The Story of Romans: A Narrative Defense of God's Righteousness.* Louisville: Westminster John Knox, 2002.

Griffith, Mark. "The King and Eye: The Rule of the Father in Greek Tragedy." *Proceedings for the Cambridge Philological Society* 44 (1998): 22–86.

Guerra, Anthony J. "Romans 3:29-30 and the Apologetic Tradition." Ann Arbor: University Microfilms, , 1986.

———. *Romans and the Apologetic Tradition: The Purpose, Genre and Audience of Paul's Letter.* Society for New Testament Studies. Cambridge: Cambridge University Press, 1995.

Güting, Eberhard W., and David L. Mealand. *Asyndeton in Paul: A Text-Critical and Statistical Enquiry into Pauline Style.* Studies in the Bible and Early Christianity 39. Lewiston, NY: E. Mellen, 1998.

Haacker, Klaus. *The Theology of Paul's Letter to the Romans.* New Testament Theology. Cambridge: Cambridge University Press, 2003.

———. *Der Brief des Paulus an die Römer.* Theologischer Handkommentar zum Neuen Testament. Leipzig: Evangelische Verlagsanstalt, 1999.

———. "Die Geschichtstheologie von Röm 9-11 im Lichte Philonischer Schriftauslegung." *NTS* 43, no. 2 (1997): 209–22.

Hafemann, Scott. *Paul, Moses, and the History of Israel: The Letter/Spirit Contrast and the Argument from Scripture in 2 Corinthians 3.* WUNT. Tübingen: Mohr Siebeck, 1995.

———. "The Salvation of Israel in Romans 11.25-32." *ExAud* 4 (1988): 38–58.

Hahn, Roger Lee. *Pneumatology in Romans: Paul's Christological and Eschatological Interpretation of Pneuma Traditions and Its Significance for the Letter's Structure.* DPhil thesis, Duke University, 1984.

Hahne, Harry Alan. *The Corruption and Redemption of Creation: Nature in Romans 8:19-22 and Jewish Apocalyptic Literature.* Library of New Testament Studies. London: T & T Clark, 2006.

Hanson, Anthony T. "Vessels of Wrath or Instruments of Wrath? Romans 9:22-23." *Journal of Theological Studies* 32, no. 2 (1981): 433–43.

Harder, G. *Paulus und das Bebet.* NTF 10. Gütersloh: Bertelsmann, 1936.

Harris, Murray. "Prepositions and Theology in the Greek New Testament." In *New International Dictionary of New Testament Theology*, edited by Colin Brown, 3:1171–215. Carlisle: Paternoster, 1976.

Hartung, Matthias. "Die Kultische Bzw Agrartechnisch-Biologische Logic der Gleichnisse von der Teighebe und Vom Ölbaum in Röm 11.16-24 und die Sich Daraus Ergebenden Theologischen Konsequenzen." *NTS* 45, no. 1 (1999): 127–40.

Harvey, Graham. *The True Israel: Uses of the Names Jew, Hebrew, and Israel in Ancient Jewish and Early Christian Literature*. Arbeiten zur Geschichte des antiken Judentums und des Urchristentums. Leiden: Brill, 1996.

Havemann, J. C. T. "Cultivated Olive – Wild Olive: The Olive Tree Metaphor in Romans 11:16-24." *Neotestamentica* 31, no, 1 (1997): 87–106.

Hawthorne, Gerald, and Otto Betz, eds. *Tradition and Interpretation*. Grand Rapids: Eerdmans, 1987.

Haynes, S. R. "Recovering the Real Paul: Theology and Exegesis in Romans 9-11." *Ex Auditu* 4 (1988): 70–84.

Hays, Richard B. *The Conversion of the Imagination: Paul as Interpreter of Israel's Scripture*. Grand Rapids: Eerdmans, 2005.

———. *The Letter to the Galatians*. NIB. Nashville: Abington, 2000.

———. *Echoes of Scripture in the Letters of Paul*. New Haven, CT: Yale University Press, 1989.

Heckel, Theo K. *Der Innere Mensch: Die paulinische Verarbeitung eines platonischen Motivs*. WUNT. Tübingen: Mohr Siebeck, 1993.

Heil, John Paul. "From Remnant to Seed of Hope for Israel: Romans 9:27-29." *CBQ* 64, no. 4 (2002): 703–20.

———. *Paul's Letter to the Romans: A Reader-Response Commentary*. New York: Paulist, 1987.

Heliso, Desta. *Pistis and the Righteous One: A Study of Romans 1:17 against the Background of Scripture and Second Temple Jewish Literature*. WUNT. Tübingen: Mohr Siebeck, 2007.

Hendriksen, William. *Exposition of Paul's Epistle to the Romans*. Grand Rapids: Baker Book House, 1981.

Hillert, Sven. *Limited and Universal Salvation: A Text-Oriented and Hermeneutical Study of Two Perspectives in Paul*. Coniectanea Biblica. Stockholm: Almqvist & Wiksell, 1999.

Hock, R.F. "Paul and Greco-Roman Education." In *Paul in the Greco-Roman World: A Handbook*, edited by J.P. Sampley, 198–227. London: Trinity Press International, 2003.

Hofius, Otfried. "'All Israel Will be Saved': Divine Salvation and Israel's Deliverance in Romans 9-11." *PSBSup* 1 (1990): 19–39.

———. "Las Evangelium und Israel. Erwägungen zu Röm 9-11." *ZTK* 83 (1986): 297–324.

Horne, C. M. "The Meaning of the Phrase 'And Thus All Israel Will be Saved' (Romans 11:26)." *JETS* 21 (1978): 329–34.

van der Horst, Pieter W. "'Only Then Will All Israel be Saved': A Short Note on the Meaning of Kai Outos in Romans 11:26." *JBL* 119, no. 3 (2000): 521–25.

Huang, Yong Suk. "Die Vervendung des Wortes πᾶς in den paulinischen Briefen." Ph.D. diss., Friedrich-Alexander Universtät, 1985.

Hübner, Hans. *Gottes Ich und Israel: Zum Schriftgebrauch Des Paulus in Römer 9-11*. Forschungen zur Religion und Literatur des Alten und Neuen Testaments. Göttingen: Vandenhoeck & Ruprecht, 1984.

Hultgren, Arland J. *Paul's Gospel and Mission: The Outlook from His Letter to the Romans*. Philadelphia: Fortress Press, 1985.

Hvalvik, Reidar. "A 'Sonderweg' for Israel: A Critical Examination of a Current Interpretation of Romans 11.25-27." *JSNT* 38 (1990): 87–107.

Iovino, Paolo. "'The Only Wise God' in the Letter to the Romans: Connections with the Book of Wisdom." In *Deuterocanonical and Cognate Literature*, 283–305. Berlin: De Gruyter, 2005.

Ito, Akio. "The Written Torah and the Oral Gospel: Romans 10:5-13 in the Dynamic Tension between Orality and Literacy." *Novum Testamentum* 48, no. 3 (2006): 234–60.

Jeffers, James S. *Conflict at Rome: Social Order and Hierarchy in Early Christianity.* Minneapolis: Fortress Press, 1991.

Jegher-Bucher, Verena. "Erwählung und Verwerfung im Römerbrief? Eine Untersuchung von Röm 11,11-15." *TZ* 47 (1991): 326–36.

Jeremias, Joachim. "Einige Vorwiegend sprachliche Beobachtungen zur Römer 11,25-36." In vol. 3 of *Die Israelfrage Nach Röm 9-11*, edited by Werner Georg Kümmel and Lorenzo De Lorenzi, 193–203. Rome: Abbazia S. Paolo, 1977.

———. "Chiasum in den Paulusbreifen." *ZNW* 49 (1958): 145–56.

Jervell, Jacob. "Letter to Jerusalem." In *The Romans Debate*, edited by Karl P. Donfried, 61–74. Minneapolis: Augsburg Publishing House, 1977.

Jervis, L. Ann. *At the Heart of the Gospel: Suffering in the Earliest Christian Message.* Grand Rapids: Eerdmans, 2007.

———. *The Purpose of Romans: A Comparative Letter Structure Investigation.* JSNT. Sheffield: JSOT, 1991.

———, and Peter Richardson, eds. *Gospel in Paul: Studies on Corinthians, Galatians and Romans for Richard N. Longenecker.* JSNT. Sheffield: Sheffield Academic Press, 1994.

Jewett, Robert. *Romans: A Commentary.* Edited by Eldon Jay Epp. Hermeneia. Minneapolis: Fortress Press, 2007.

———. "Paul, Phoebe, and the Spanish Mission." In *The Social World of Formative Christianity and Judaism*, edited by Jacob Neusner, Ernest S. Frerichs, Peder Borgen, and Richard Horsley, 142–61. Philadelphia: Fortress: Fortress Press, 1988.

———. "The Law and the Coexistence of Jews and Gentiles in Romans." *Interpretation* 39, no. 4 (1985): 341–56.

———. "Romans as an Ambassadorial Letter." *Interpretation* 36, no. 1 (1982): 5–20.

Jobes, Karen H. "Distinguishing the Meaning of Greek Verbs in the Semantic Domain for Worship." *Filologia Neotestamentaria* 4, no. 8 (1991): 183–92.

Johnson, Dan G. "The Structure and Meaning of Romans 11." *CBQ* 46 (1984): 91–103.

Johnson, E. Elizabeth. *The Function of Apocalyptic and Wisdom Traditions in Romans 9-11.* SBL Dissertation Series. Atlanta: Scholars Press, 1989.

Johnson, Luke Timothy. *Reading Romans: A Literary and Theological Commentary.* Reading the New Testament Series. New York: Crossroad, 1997.

Johnson, S. Lewis. "Paul and 'The Israel of God': An Exegetical and Eschatological Case-Study." *Master's Seminary Journal* 20, no. 1 (2009): 41–55.

Jolivet, Ira. "Christ the TELOS in Romans 10:4 as Both Fulfillment and Termination of the Law." *Restoration Quarterly* 51, no. 1 (2009): 13–30.

Juncker, Günther H. "'Children of Promise': Spiritual Paternity and Patriarch Typology in Galatians and Romans." *Bulletin for Biblical Research* 17 (2007): 131–60.

Kammler, Hans-Christian. "Die Prädikation Jesu Christi als 'Gott' und die paulinische Christologie: Erwägungen zur Exegese von Röm 9,5b." *Zeitschrift für die neutestamentliche Wissenshaft und die Kunde der älteren Kirche* 94, no. 3–4 (2003): 164–80.

Karris, Robert J. *Galatians and Romans.* New Collegeville Bible Commentary, New Testament 6. Collegeville, MN: Liturgical Press, 2005.

———. "Romans 14:1—15:13 and the Occasion of Romans." *CBQ* 25 (1973): 155–78.

Käsemann, Ernst. *A Commentary on Romans*. Translated and edited by Geoffrey W. Bromiley. Grand Rapids: Eerdmans, 1980.

———. "Justification and Salvation History in the Epistle to the Romans." In *Perspectives on Paul*, 60–78. Philadelphia: Fortress Press, 1971.

Kaylor, R. David. *Paul's Covenant Community: Jew and Gentile in Romans*. Atlanta: John Knox, 1988.

Keck, Leander E. *Romans*. Abingdon New Testament Commentaries. Nashville: Abingdon, 2005.

———. "Pathos in Romans? Mostly Preliminary Remarks." In *Paul and Pathos*, edited by Thomas Olbricht and Jerry Sumney, 71–96. Society of Biblical Literature Symposium 16. Atlanta: Scholar Press, 2001.

Keesmaat, Sylvia C. *Paul and His Story: (Re)interpreting the Exodus Tradition*. JSNTSup. Sheffield: Sheffield Academic Press, 1999.

Keller, Winfrid. *Gottes Treue, Israels Heil: Röm 11, 25-27: Die These vom "Sonderweg" in der Diskussion*. Stuttgarter Biblische Beitrage. Stuttgart: Katholisches Biblewerk, 1998.

Kennedy, G.A. *New Testament Interpretation through Rhetorical Criticism*. Chapel Hill: University of North Carolina Press, 1984.

Kertelge, Karl. *Der Brief an die Römer*. Geistliche Schriftlesung. Düsseldorf: Patmos-Verlag, 1971.

Khiok-Khng, Yeo, ed. *Navigating Romans through Cultures: Challenging Readings by Charting a New Course*. Romans through History and Culture Series. New York: T & T Clark, 2004.

Kim, Johann D. *God, Israel, and the Gentiles: Rhetoric and Situation in Romans 9-11*. SBL Dissertation Series. Atlanta: SBL, 2000.

Kim, Jung Joo. *The Spirit of God as Witness to the Redemption in Christ: A Tradition-Historical Analysis of Paul's Pneumatology in Romans 8*. ThD thesis, Harvard University, 1989.

Kim, Seyoon. *Christ and Caesar: The Gospel and the Roman Empire in the Writings of Paul and Luke*. Grand Rapids: Eerdmans, 2008.

———. *Paul and the New Perspective: Second Thoughts on the Origin of Paul's Gospel.* Grand Rapids: Eerdmans, 2001.

———. "The 'Mystery' of Rom 11:25-26 Once More." *NTS* 43, no. 3 (1997): 412–29.

———. *The Origin of Paul's Gospel.* WUNT. Tübingen: Mohr, 1981.

Kimball, Charles A. "Jesus' Exposition of the Old Testament in Luke's Gospel." PhD diss., Southwestern Baptist Theological Seminary, 1991.

Kirk, J. R. Daniel. *Unlocking Romans: Resurrection and the Justification of God.* Grand Rapids: Eerdmans, 2008.

Klein, Günter. "Paul's Purpose in Writing the Epistle to the Romans." In *The Romans Debate*, edited by Karl P. Donfried, 29–43. Minneapolis: Augsburg Publishing House, 1977.

Klein, William W. *The New Chosen People: A Corporate View of Election.* Grand Rapids: Academie, 1990.

Klumbies, Paul-Gerhard. "Israels Vorzüge und das Evangelium von der Gottesgerechtigkeit in Römer 9-11." *WD* 18 (1985): 135–57.

Kocur, Miroslav. *National and Religious Identity: A Study in Galatians 3, 23-29 and Romans 10, 12-21.* Osterreichische Biblische Studien 24. Frankfurt am Main: Lang, 2003.

Kotansky, R. "Note on Romans 9,6: *Ho logos tou Theou* as the Proclamation of the Gospels." *Studia Biblica* 7 (1977): 24–30.

Kraus, Wolfgang. *Der Tod Jesu als Heiligtumsweihe: Eine Untersuchung zum Umfeld der Sühnevorstellung in Römer 3, 25-26a.* Wissenschaftliche Monographien zum Alten und Neuen Testament 66. Neukirchen-Vluyn: Neukirchener Verlag, 1991.

Kühl, Ernst. *Der Brief des Paulus an die Römer.* Leipzig: Quelle & Meyer, 1913.

Kümmel, Werner Georg. *Die Israelfrage nach Röm 9-11.* Rome: Abtei von St. Paul vor den Mauern, 1977.

Kuss, Otto. *Der Römerbrief.* Regensburg: Pustet, 1957.

Kuyper, Lester Jacob. "Hardness of Heart According to Biblical Perspective." *Scottish Journal of Theology* 27, no. 4 (1974): 459–74.

Kyrychenko, Alexander. "The Consistency of Romans 9-11." *Restoration Quarterly* 45, no. 4 (2003): 215–27.

Lambrecht, Jan. "Grammar and Reasoning in Romans 11,27." *Ephemerides Theologicae Lovanienses* 79, no. 1 (2003): 179–83.

————, and Richard William Thompson. *Justification by Faith: The Implications of Romans 3:27-31*. Zacchaeus Studies. Wilmington, DE: Glazier, 1989.

Lane, W. L. "Social Perspectives on Roman Christianity during the Formative Years from Nero to Nerva: Romans, Hebrews, 1 Clement." In *Judaism and Christianity in First-Century Rome*, edited by Karl P. Donfried and Peter Richardson, 196–244. Grand Rapids: Eerdmans, 1998.

Lenski, R. C. H. *The Interpretation of St. Paul's Epistle to the Romans*. Columbus, OH: Wartburg, 1945.

Lim, Timothy H. "Midrash Pesher in the Pauline Letters." In *The Scrolls and the Scriptures: Qumran Fifty Years After*, edited by Stanley E. Porter and Craig A. Evans, 280–92. Sheffield: Sheffield University Press, 1997.

Litwak, Kenneth D. "One or Two Views of Judaism: Paul in Acts 28 and Romans 11 on Jewish Unbelief." *Tyndale Bulletin* 57, no. 2 (2006): 229–49.

Loader, William. "Apocalyptic Model of Sonship: Its Origin and Development in New Testament Tradition." *JBL* 97, no. 4 (1978): 525–54.

Lodge, John G. *Romans 9-11: A Reader-Response Analysis*. University of South Florida International Studies in Formative Christianity and Judaism 6. Atlanta: Scholars Press, 1996.

Lohse, Eduard. *Rechenschaft vom Evangelium: Exegetische Studien zum Römerbrief*. Beihefte zur Zeitschrift für die neutestamentliche Wissenschaft und die Kunde der älteren Kirche 150. New York: Walter de Gruyter, 2007.

————. *Theologische Ethik im Römerbrief des Apostels Paulus.* Göttingen: Vanderhoeck & Ruprecht, 2004.

Longenecker, Bruce W. *Eschatology and the Covenant: A Comparison of 4 Ezra and Romans 1-11.* JSNTSup. Sheffield: JSOT, 1991.

————. "Different Answers to Different Issues: Israel, the Gentiles and Salvation History in Romans 9-11." *JSNT* no. 36 (1989): 95–123.

Lübking, Hans-Martin. *Paulus und Israel im Römerbrief: Eine Untersuchung zu Romer 9-11.* Europäische Hochschulschriften, Reihe XXIII, Theologie 260. New York: Lang, 1986.

Lund, N. W. *Chiasmus in the New Testament: A Study in Formgeschichte.* Peabody, MA: Hendrickson, 1942.

Lung-kwong, L. *Paul's Purpose in Writing Romans: The Upbuilding of a Jewish and Gentile Christian Community in Rome.* Bible and Literature 4. Jian Dao Dissertation Series 6. Hong Kong: Alliance Bible Seminary, 1998.

Luther, Martin. *Lectures on Romans.* Translated and edited by Wilhelm Pauck. Library of Christian Classics 15. Philadelphia: Westminster, 1961.

Lyonnet, S. "Le role d'Israel dans l'histoire du salut selon Rom. 9-11." In *Etudes sur l'epître aux Romains*, 264–73. Rome: Gregorian University Press, 1989...

Maartens, Pieter J. "A Critical Dialogue of Structure and Reader in Romans 11:16-24." *Hervormde Teologiese Studies* 53 (1997): 1030–51.

————. "Inference and Relevance in Paul's Allegory of the Wild Olive Tree." *Hervormde Teologiese Studies* 53 (1997): 1000–29.

MacGorman, J. W. *Romans: Everyman's Gospel.* Nashville: Convention Press, 1976.

Machura, Jacek. *Die paulinische Rechtfertigungslehre: Positionen deutschsprachiger katholischer Exegeten in der Römerbriefauslegung des 20. Jahrhunderts.* Eichstätter Studien 49. Regensburg: Pustet, 2003.

Magda, Ksenija. *Paul's Territoriality and Mission Strategy: Searching for the Geographical Awareness Paradigm behind Romans.* WUNT. Tübingen: Mohr Siebeck, 2009.

Marquardt, Friedrich-Wilhelm. *Die Juden im Römerbrief.* Theologische Studien. Zürich: Theologischer Verlag, 1971.

Martin, Brice. *Christ and the Law in Paul.* Leiden: Brill, 1989.

———. "Paul on Christ and the Law." *JETS* 26, no. 3 (1983): 271–82.

Martin, Ralph P. *Reconciliation: A Study of Paul's Theology.* New Foundations Theological Library. Atlanta: John Knox, 1981.

Martin, Thomas F. *Rhetoric and Exegesis in Augustine's Interpretation of Romans 7:24-25a.* Studies in Bible and Early Christianity 47. Lewiston, NY: E. Mellen, 2001.

McGinn, Sheila E., ed. *Celebrating Romans: Template for Pauline Theology: Essays in Honor of Robert Jewett.* Grand Rapids: Eerdmans, 2004.

Mehlmann, J. "anexichniastos= *investigabilis* (Rom 11:33; Eph. 3:8)." *Bib* 40 (1959): 902–14.

Merkle, Benjamin L. "Romans 11 and the Future of Ethnic Israel." *JETS* 43, no. 4 (2000): 709–21.

Metzger, Bruce. *A Textual Commentary on the Greek New Testament.* New York: American Bible Society. 1994.

———. "The Punctuation of Rom 9:5." In *Christ and Spirit in the New Testament,* edited by Barnabus Lindars, Stephen S. Smalley, and C. F. D. Moule, 95–112. Cambridge: Cambridge University Press, 1973.

Michel, Otto. *Der Brief an die Römer.* Göttingen: Vandenhoeck & Ruprecht, 1963.

Miller, James C. "The Jewish Context of Paul's Gentile Mission." *Tyndale Bulletin* 58, no. 1 (2007): 101–15.

———. *The Obedience of Faith, the Eschatological People of God, and the Purpose of Romans.* SBL Dissertation Series. Atlanta: SBL, 2000.

Minear, Paul S. *The Obedience of Faith: The Purposes of Paul in the Epistle to the Romans.* Studies in Biblical Theology 19. London: SCM, 1971.

Moo, Douglas J. *The Epistle to the Romans.* NICNT. Grand Rapids: Eerdmans, 1996.

Morris, Leon. *The Epistle to the Romans.* Grand Rapids: Eerdmans, 1988.

Moule, H. C. G. *Romans.* Edited by Philip Hillyer. Classic New Testament Commentary. London: Mashall Pickering, 1992.

Mounce, Robert H. *Romans.* New American Commentary 27. Nashville: Broadman & Holman, 1995.

Moxnes, Halvor. *Theology in Conflict: Studies in Paul's Understanding of God in Romans.* Supplements to Novum Testamentum 53. Leiden: Brill, 1980.

Moytyer, Alec. *The Prophecy of Isaiah: An Introduction and Commentary.* Downers Grove, IL: InterVarsity Press, 1998.

Munck, Johannes. *Christ & Israel: An Interpretation of Romans 9-11.* Translated by Ingeborg Nixon. Philadelphia: Fortress Press, 1967.

———. *Paul and the Salvation of Mankind.* Atlanta: John Knox, 1959.

Murphy-O'Conner, Jerome. *Paul and the Letter-Writer: His World, His Opinions, His Skills.* Good News Studies 46. Collegeville, MN: Liturgical, 1995.

Murray, John. *The Epistle to the Romans.* 2 vols. Grand Rapids: Eerdmans, 1968.

Mussner, Franz. "'Ganz Israel wird gerettet werden' (Röm 11.26): Versuch einer Auslegung." *Kairos* 18 (1976): 241–55.

Nanos, Mark D. "God, Israel, and the Gentiles: Rhetoric and Situation in Romans 9-11." *CBQ* 63, no. 1 (2001): 152–54.

———. "Challenging the Limits That Continue to Define Paul's Perspective on Jews and Judaism." In *Reading Israel in Romans: Legitimacy and Plausibility of Divergent Interpretations*, edited by Cristina Grenholm and Daniel Patte, 212–24. Harrisburg, PA: Trinity Press International, 2000.

————. *The Mystery of Romans: The Jewish Context of Paul's Letter*. Minneapolis: Fortress Press, 1996.

Neusner, Jacob, ed. *Judaism and Christianity in the First Century*. Origins of Judaism 3. New York: Garland, 1990.

Nock, A.D. "Religious Attitudes of the Ancient Greeks." *Proceedings of the American Philosophical Society* 85 (1942): 472–82.

Norden, Eduard. *Agnostos Theos: Untersuchungen zur Formenschichte religiöser Rede*. Stuttgart: Tuebner, 1923; repr. Darstadt: Wissenschatliche Buchgesellschaft, 1956.

Novakovic, Lidija. "The Decalogue in the New Testament." *Perspectives in Religious Studies* 35, no. 4 (2008): 373–86.

Nwachukwu, Mary Sylvia Chinyere. *Creation-Covenant Scheme and Justification by Faith: A Canonical Study of the God-Human Drama in the Pentateuch and the Letter to the Romans*. Tesi Gregoriana. Rome: Gregorian University Press, 2002.

Nygren, Anders. *Commentary on Romans*. Philadelphia: Fortress Press, 1949.

Odell-Scott, David W., ed. *Reading Romans with Contemporary Philosophers and Theologians*. Romans through History and Culture Series. New York: T & T Clark, 2007.

Ogara, Florentinus. "'Ex ipso et per ipsum et in ipso sunt omnia': Notae in Rom. 11, 33-36." Verbum domini 15 (1935): 164–71.

Origen. *Commentary on the Epistle to the Romans*. Books 1-5. Translated by Thomas P. Scheck. Fathers of the Church. Washington, DC: Catholic University of America Press, 2001.

Oropeza, B. J. "Paul and Theodicy: Intertextual Thoughts on God's Justice and Faithfulness to Israel in Romans 9-11." *NTS* 53, no. 1 (2007): 57–80.

Ortland, Dane. "The Insanity of Faith: Paul's Theological Use of Isaiah in Romans 9:33." *Trinity Journal* 30, no. 2 (2009): 369–88.

Osborne, Grant R. *Romans*. IVP New Testament Commentary Series. Downers Grove, IL: InterVarsity, 2004.

Oss, Douglas A. "Paul's Use of Isaiah and Its Place in His Theology with Special Reference to Romans 9-11." PhD diss. Westminster Theological Seminary, 1993.

Österreicher, J. M. "Israel's Misstep and Her Rise: The Dialectic of God's Saving Design in Rom. 9-11." In *Studiorum Paulinorum Congressus Internationalis Catholicus 1961.* Analecta Biblica, 317–27. Rome: Pontifical Biblical Institute, 1963.

Park, Doo. "The Salvation of All Israel by the Mercy of God in the Apocalyptic Era: An Analysis of Romans 11: 25-32 and the Context of Romans 9-11." PhD diss., Southwestern Baptist Theological Seminary, 1998.

Pidock-Lester, Karen. "Romans 10:5-15." *Interpretation* 50 (1996): 288–92.

Piper, John. *The Justification of God: An Exegetical and Theological Study of Romans 9:1-23.* Grand Rapids: Baker Books, 1993.

Plag, Christoph. *Israels Wege zum Heil; eine Untersuchung zu Römer 9 Bis 11.* AT 40. Stuttgart: Calwer Verlag, 1969.

Porter, Stanley E., ed. *Paul: Jew, Greek, and Roman.* Pauline Studies 5. Leiden: Brill, 2008.

———,ed. *Paul's World.* Pauline Studies 4. Leiden: Brill, 2008.

———, ed. *The Messiah in the Old and New Testaments.* McMaster New Testament Studies. Grand Rapids: Eerdmans, 2007

———, ed. *Paul and His Opponents.* Pauline Studies 2. Leiden: Brill, 2005.

———, ed. *Handbook of Classical Rhetoric in the Hellenistic Period (330 B.C.-A.D. 400).* New York: Brill, 1997.

———, and Christopher D. Stanley, eds. *As it is Written: Studying Paul's Use of Scripture.* Society of Biblical Literature Symposium Series 50. Atlanta: Society of Biblical Literature, 2008.

———, and Jacqueline C. R. De Roo, eds. *The Concept of the Covenant in the Second Temple Period.* Supplements to the Journal for the Study of Judaism 71. Leiden: Brill, 2003.

Quesnel, Michel. "La Figure de Moïse en Romains 9-11." *New Testament Studies* 49, no. 3 (2003): 321–35.

Räisänen, H. "Romans 9-11 and the 'History of Early Christian Religion.'" In *Text and Contexts: Biblical Texts in Their Textual and Situational Contexts: Essays in Honor of Lars Hartman,* edited by Tord Fornberg and David Hellholm, 743–65. Oslo: Scandinavian University Press, 1995.

———. *Paul and the Law.* WUNT 29. Tübingen: Mohr Siebeck, 1983.

———. "Römer 9-11: Analyse eines geistigen Ringens." *ANRW II* 25, no. 4 (1987): 2891–939.

Ramsay, William M. "The Olive Tree and the Wild Olive." *Expositor* 11 (1905): 152–60.

Rapa, Robert Keith. *The Meaning of "Works of the Law" in Galatians and Romans.* Studies in Biblical Literature 31. New York: Lang, 2001.

Reasoner, Mark. *Romans in Full Circle: A History of Interpretation.* Louisville: Westminster John Knox, 2005.

———. *The Strong and the Weak: Romans 14.1—15.13 in Context.* Society for New Testament Studies Monograph Series. Cambridge: Cambridge University Press, 1999.

Reed, Jeffrey. "The Epistle." In *Handbook of Classical Rhetoric in the Hellenistic Period: 330 B.C.-A.D. 400,* edited by Stanley E. Porter, 171–94. Boston: Brill, 2001.

Reichert, Angelika. *Der Römerbrief als Gratwanderung: Eine Untersuchung zur Abfassungsproblematik.* Forschungen zur Religion und Literatur des Alten und Neuen Testaments. Göttingen: Vandenhoeck & Ruprecht, 2001.

Reinbold, Wolfgang. "Paulus und das Gesetz: Zur Exegese von Röm 9,30-33." *Biblische Zeitschrift* 38, no. 2 (1994): 253–64.

Rese, M. "Israel und Kirche in Römer 9." *NTS* 34 (1988): 208–17.

Rhyne, C. Thomas. *Faith Establishes the Law.* SBL Dissertation Series 55. Chico, CA: Scholars Press, 1981.

———. "Nomos Dikaiosynēs and the Meaning of Romans 10:4." *CBQ* 47, no. 3 (1985): 486–99.

Rhys, Howard. *The Epistle to the Romans.* New York: Macmillan, 1961.

Richardson, Peter, and Stephen Westerholm. With A. I. Baumgarten, Michael Pettem, and Cecilia Wassén. *Law in Religious Communities in the Roman Period: The Debate Over Torah and Nomos in Post-Biblical Judaism and Early Christianity.* Studies in Christianity and Judaism. Waterloo, Ontario: Wilfrid Laurier University Press, 1991.

Ridderbos, Herman. *Paul: An Outline of His Theology.* Translated by John Richard de Witt. Grand Rapids: Eerdmans, 1975.

Riesner, Rainer. *Paul's Early Period.* Grand Rapids: Eerdmans, 1998.

Robinson, D. W. B. "The Distinction between Jewish and Gentile Believers in Galatians." *ABR* 13 (1965): 29–48.

Robinson, John A. T. *Wrestling with Romans.* Philadelphia: Westminster, 1979.

Roetzel, C. J. "'Διαθῆκαι' in Romans 9,4." *Bib* 51 (1970): 377–90.

Rutgers, Leonard. "Roman Policy toward the Jews: Expulsions from the City of Rome during the First Century C.E." In *Judaism and Christianity in First-Century Rome,* edited by Karl P. Donfried and Peter Richardson, 93–116. Grand Rapids: Eerdmans, 1998.

Sanday, William, and Arthur C. Headlam. *A Critical and Exegetical Commentary on the Epistle to the Romans.* International Critical Commentary. Edinburgh: T & T Clark, 1898.

Sanders, E. P. *Paul, the Law, and the Jewish People.* Philadelphia: Fortress Press, 1993.

———. *Judaism: Practice and Belief 63 BCE–66 CE.* London: SCM, 1992.

———. *Paul.* Oxford: Oxford University Press, 1991.

———. "Paul's Attitude toward the Jewish People." *Union Seminary Quarterly Review* 33, no. 3–4 (1978): 175–87.

———. *Paul and Palestine Judaism: A Comparison of Patterns of Religions.* Philadelphia: Fortress Press, 1977.

Schlatter, Adolf. *Romans: The Righteousness of God.* Translated by Sigfried S. Schatzmann. Peabody, MA: Hendrickson, 1995.

Schlier, Heinrich. *Der Römerbrief: Kommentar.* Herders theologischer Kommentar zum Neuen Testament. Freiburg im Breisgau: Herder, 1979.

Schmithals, Walter. *Der Römerbrief: Ein Kommentar.* Gütersloh: Mohn, 1988.

Schneider, Nélio. "Die 'Schwachen' in der christlichen Gemeinde Roms: Eine historisch-exegetische Untersuchung zu Röm 14,1-15, 13." D. Theol. Dissertation, Kirchliche Hochschule Wuppertal, 1989.

Schnelle, Udo, ed. *The Letter to the Romans.* Bibliotheca Ephemeridum Theologicarum Lovaniensium. Leuven: Peeters, 2009.

Scholem, Gershom Gerhard. *Major Trends in Jewish Mysticism.* New York: Schocken Books, 1954.

Schreiner, Thomas R. "Corporate and Individual Election in Romans 9: A Response to Brian Abasciano." *JETS* 49, no. 2 (2006): 373–86.

———. "Does Romans 9 Teach Individual Election Unto Salvation? Some Exegetical and Theological Reflections." *JETS* 36, no. 1 (1993): 25–40.

———. "Paul's View of the Law in Romans 10:4-5." *Westminster Theological Journal* 55, no. 1 (1993): 113–35.

———. *Romans.* Baker Exegetical Commentary on the New Testament. Grand Rapids: Baker Books, 1998.

Schwindt, Rainer. "Mehr Wurzel als Stamm und Krone: Zur Bildrede vom Ölbaum in Röm 11,16-24." *Biblica* 88, no. 1 (2007): 64–91.

Scott, James M. "Paul's Use of Deuteronomic Tradition." *JBL* 112 (1993), 645-665.

———. *Adoption as Sons of God: An Exegetical Investigation into the Background of Yiothesia in the Pauline Corpus.* WUNT. Tübingen: Mohr Siebeck, 1992.

————. "The Function of Apocalyptic and Wisdom Traditions in Romans 9–11." *Journal of Biblical Literature* 110, no. 4 (1991): 742–44.

Scroggs, Robin. "Paul as Rhetorician: Two Homilies in Romans 1–11." In *Jews, Greeks, and Christians; Religious Cultures in Late Antiquity: Essays in Honor of William David Davies*, edited by Robert Hamerton-Kelly and Robin Scroggs, 271–98. Leiden: Brill, 1976.

Seewann, Maria-Irma. "Semantische Untersuchung zu Porosis, Veranlasst durch Röm 11,25." *Filologia Neotestamentaria* 10, no. 19–20 (1997): 139–56.

Segal, Alan F. *Paul the Convert: The Apostolate and Apostasy of Saul the Pharisee.* New Haven, CT: Yale University Press, 1990.

————.*Rebecca's Children: Judaism and Christianity in the Roman World.* Cambridge, MA: Harvard University Press, 1986.

Seifrid, M. A. "Righteousness Language in the Hebrew Scriptures and Early Judaism." In *Justification and Variegated Nomism*, edited by D. A. Carson, Peter T. O'Brien, and Mark A. Seifrid, 1:415–42. WUNT 181. Tübingen: Mohr Siebeck, 2001–2004.

————. *Justification by Faith: The Origin and Central Development of a Pauline Theme.* Leiden: Brill, 1998.

————. "Paul's Approach to the Old Testament in Rom 10:6-8." *Trinity Journal* 6, no. 1 (1985): 3–37.

Shum, Shiu-Lun. *Paul's Use of Isaiah: A Comparative Study of Paul's Letter to the Romans and the Sibylline and Qumran Sectarian Texts.* WUNT 156. Tübingen: Mohr, 2002.

Siegert, Folker. *Argumentation bei Paulus, Gezeigt an Röm 9–11.* WUNT. Tübingen: Mohr, 1985.

Sievers, Joseph. "'God's Gifts and Call are Irrevocable': The Reception of Romans 11:29 through the Centuries and Christian-Jewish Relations." In vol. 1 of *Reading Israel in Romans: Legitimacy and Plausibility of Divergent Interpretations*, edited by Cristina Grenholm and Daniel Patte, 127–73.

Romans through History and Cultures Series. Harrisburg, PA: Trinity Press International, 2000.

———. "'God's Gifts and Call are Irrevocable': The Interpretation of Rom. 11:29 and Its Uses." *Society of Biblical Literature Papers* 36 (1997): 337–57.

Siker, Jeffrey S. *Disinheriting the Jews: Abraham in Early Christian Controversy.* Louisville: Westminster John Knox, 1991.

Simpson, John W. *The Future of Non-Christian Jews: I Thessalonians 2:15-16 and Romans 9-11.*" Ph.D. diss., Fuller Theological Seminary, 1988.

Sloyan, Gerard. *Is Christ the End of the Law?* Tübingen: Mohr, 1983.

Smart, James D. *Doorway to a New Age: A Study of Paul's Letter to the Romans.* Philadelphia: Westminster, 1972.

Smiles, Vincent M. "The Concept of 'Zeal' in Second-Temple Judaism and Paul's Critique of It in Romans 10:2." *CBQ* 64, no. 2 (2002): 282–99.

Smith, Philip C. "God's New Covenant Faithfulness in Romans." *Restoration Quarterly* 50, no. 4 (2008): 235–48.

Soderlund, Sven K., and N. T. Wright, eds. *Romans and the People of God: Essays in Honor of Gordon D. Fee on the Occasion of His 65th Birthday.* Grand Rapids: Eerdmans, 1999.

Song, Changwon. *Reading Romans as a Diatribe.* Studies in Biblical Literature. New York: Lang, 2004.

Southall, David J. *Rediscovering Righteousness in Romans: Personified Dikaiosyneē Within Metaphoric and Narratorial Settings.* WUNT 2. Tübingen: Mohr Siebeck, 2008.

Spencer, F. Scott. "Metaphor, Mystery and the Salvation of Israel in Romans 9-11: Paul's Appeal to Humility and Doxology." *Review & Expositor* 103, no. 1 (2006): 113–38.

Stamps, Dennis L. "Rhetorical Criticism of the New Testament: Ancient and Modern Evaluations of Argumentation." In *Approaches to New Testament Studies,* edited by Stanley E. Porter and David Tombs, 129–60. Sheffield: Sheffield Academic Press, 1995.

Stanley, Christopher D. "'Pearls before Swine': Did Paul's Audiences Understand His Biblical Quotations?" *Novum Testamentum* 41, no. 2 (1999): 124–44.

———. "'Neither Jew nor Greek': Ethnic Conflict in Graeco-Roman Society." *JSNT* 64 (1996): 101–24.

———. "The Significance of Romans 11:3-4 for the Text History of the LXX Book of Kingdoms." *JBL* 112 (1993): 43–54.

———. "'The Redeemer Will Come ek Ziōn': Romans 11.26-27 Revisited." In *Paul and the Scriptures of Israel*, edited by Craig A. Evans and James A. Sanders, 118–42. Sheffield: JSOT, 1993.

———. *Paul and the Language of Scripture: Citation Technique in the Pauline Epistles and Contemporary Literature*. Cambridge: Cambridge University Press, 1992.

Starnitzke, Dierk. *Die Struktur paulinischen Denkens im Römerbrief: Eine linguistisch-logische Untersuchung*. Beiträge zur Wissenschaft vom Alten und Neuen Testament. Stuttgart: Kohlhammer, 2004.

Stegner, William. "Romans 9:6-29 – A Midrash." *JSNT* 22, no. 1 (1984): 37–52.

Steinbrenner, David. *Paul the Jew: Reconfigured Israelite Identity Construction in Romans 9:1-8 & 11:1-2*. PhD diss., Duke University, 2008.

Stendahl, Krister. *Final Account: Paul's Letter to the Romans*. Minneapolis: Fortress Press, 1995.

———. "In No Other Name." In *Christian Witness and the Jewish People*, edited by A. Sovik, 48–53. Geneva: Lutheran World Federation, 1976.

———. *Paul among Jews and Gentiles*. Philadelphia: Fortress Press, 1976.

Stowers, Stanley. *A Rereading of Romans: Justice, Jews, and Gentiles*. New Haven, CT: Yale University Press, 1994.

———. "Paul on the Use and Abuse of Reason." In *Greeks, Romans, and Christians: Essays in Honor of Abraham J. Malherbe*, edited by David L.

Balch, Everett Ferguson, and Wayne A. Meeks, 253–86. Minneapolis: Fortress Press, 1990.

———. *Letter Writing in Greco-Roman Antiquity*. Library of Early Christianity. Philadelphia: Westminster, 1986.

———. *A Critical Reassessment of Paul and the Diatribe: The Dialogical Element in Paul's Letter to the Romans*, Ph.D diss., Yale University, 1979.

———. *The Diatribe and Paul's Letter to the Romans*. SBL Dissertation Series 57. Chico, CA: Scholars Press, 1981.

Stuhlmacher, Peter. *Paul's Letter to the Romans: A Commentary*. Translated by Scott J. Hafemann. Louisville: Westminster John Knox, 1994.

———. "Genesis 12:1-3 und die Urgeschichte des Jahwisten. Zur Interpretation von Römer 11.25-32." In *Probleme biblischer Theologie*, edited by H. W. Wolff, 555–70. Munich: Kaiser, 1971.

Suggs, M. Jack. "'The Word is Near You': Romans 10:6-10 within the Purpose of the Letter." In *Christian History and Interpretation*, edited by W. R. Farmer, C. F. D. Moule, and R. R. Niebuhr, 289–312. Cambridge: Cambridge University Press, 1967.

Sumney, Jerry. "Paul's 'Weakness': An Integral Part of His Conception of Apostleship." *JSNT* 52 (1993): 71–91.

Suter, Ann, ed. *Lament: Studies in the Ancient Mediterranean and Beyond*. New York: Oxford University Press, 2008.

———. "Male Lament in Greek Tragedy." In *Lament: Studies in the Ancient Mediterranean and Beyond, edited by Ann Suter*, 156–80. New York: Oxford University Press, 2008.

Swancutt, Diana Marie. *Pax Christi: Romans as Protrepsis to Live as Kings*. PhD diss., Duke University, 2001.

Tabor, James D. *Things Unutterable: Paul's Ascent to Paradise in Its Greco-Roman, Judaic, and Early Christian Contexts*. Studies in Judaism. Lanham, MD: University Press of America, 1986.

Talbert, Charles H. *Romans*. Macon, GA: Smyth & Helwys, 2002.

Tanner, J. Paul. "The New Covenant and Paul's Quotations from Hosea in Romans 9:25-26." *Bibliotheca Sacra* 162, no. 645 (2005): 95–110.

Taubes, Jacob. *The Political Theology of Paul.* Stanford, CA: Stanford University Press, 2004.

Taylor, Vincent. *The Epistle to the Romans.* London: Epworth, 1955.

Theissen, Gerd. "Röm 9-11 eine Auseinandersetzung des Paulus mit Israel und mit sich selbst: Versuch einer psychologischen Auselgung." In *Fair Play: Diversity and Conflicts in Early Christianity: Essays in Honour of Heikki Räisänen,* edited by Ismo Dunderberg, Christopher Tuckett, Kari Syreeni, 311–41. Boston: Leiden, 2002.

Theobald, Michael. *Studien Zum Römerbrief.* WUNT. Tübingen: Mohr Siebeck, 2001.

Thielman, Frank. *From Plight to Solution: A Jewish Framework for Understanding Paul's View of the Law in Galatians and Romans.* Leiden: Brill, 1989.

———. "Unexpected Mercy: Echoes of a Biblical Motif in Romans 9-11." *Scottish Journal of Theology* 47, no. 2 (1994): 169–81.

Thompson, Michael. *Clothed with Christ: The Example and Teaching of Jesus in Romans 12.1-15.13.* JSNTSup 59. Sheffield: JSOT, 1991.

Thyen, Hartwig. "Das Mysterium Israel (Röm 11,25-32)." In *Gesetz im frühen Judentum und im Neuen Testament,* 304-18. Göttingen: Vandenhoeck & Ruprecht, 2006.

Tobin, Thomas. *Paul's Rhetoric in Its Contexts: The Argument of Romans.* Peabody, MA: Hendrickson, 2004.

Toews, John E. *Romans.* Believers Church Bible Commentary. Scottdale, PA: Herald, 2004.

Toit, Andrie du. *Focusing on Paul: Persuasion and Theological Design in Romans and Galatians.* Edited by Cilliers Breytenbach and David S. du Toit. Beihefte zur Zeitschrift für die Neutestamentliche Wissenschaft und die Kunde der älteren Kirche 151. Berlin: Walter de Gruyter, 2007.

Toney, Carl N. *Paul's Inclusive Ethic: Resolving Community Conflicts and Promoting Mission in Romans 14-15.* WUNT 2. Tübingen: Mohr Siebeck, 2008.

Uddin, Mohan. "Paul, the Devil and 'Unbelief' in Israel (with Particular Reference to 2 Corinthians 3-4 and Romans 9-11)." *Tyndale Bulletin* 50, no. 2 (1999): 265–80.

Udoh, Fabian, E., ed. with Susannah Heschel, Mark Chancey, and Gregory Tatum. *Redefining First-Century Jewish and Christian Identities: Essays in Honor of Ed Parish Sanders.* Christianity and Judaism in Antiquity Series 16. Notre Dame, IN: University of Notre Dame Press, 2008.

Vanlaningham, Michael G. "Paul's Use of Elijah's Mt. Horeb Experience in Rom 11:2-6: An Exegetical Note." *Master's Seminary Journal* 6, no. 2 (1995): 223–32.

Vaughan, Curtis, and Bruce Corley. *Romans.* Grand Rapids: Zondervan, 1976.

Wagner, J. Ross. *Heralds of the Good News: Isaiah and Paul "in Concert" in the Letter to the Romans.* Supplements to Novum Testamentum 101. Leiden: Brill, 2002.

———. *"Who Has Believed Our Message?": Paul and Isaiah "in Concert" in the Letter to the Romans.* Ph.D. diss., Duke University, 1999.

Walker, Rolf. *Studie zu Römer 13, 1-7.* Theologische Existenz Heute. Munich: Kaiser, 1966.

Wallace, Daniel B. *Greek Grammar beyond the Basics: An Exegetical Syntax of the New Testament.* Grand Rapids: Zondervan, 1996.

Wallace, David R. *The Gospel of God: Romans as Paul's Aeneid.* Eugene, OR: Pickwick, 2008.

Walters, James. "Romans, Jews, and Christians: The Impact of the Roman on Jewish/Christian Relations in First-Century Rome." In *Judaism and Christianity in First-Century Rome,* edited by Karl P. Donfried and Peter Richardson, 175–95. Grand Rapids: Eerdmans, 1998.

————. *Ethnic Issues in Paul's Letter to the Romans: Changing Self-Definitions in Earliest Roman Christianity*. Valley Forge, PA: Trinity Press International, 1993.

Wasserberg, Günter. "Romans 9-11 and Jewish Christian Dialogue." In vol. 1 of *Reading Israel in Romans: Legitimacy and Plausibility of Divergent Interpretations*, eds. Cristina Grenholm and Daniel Patte, 174–211. Romans through History and Cultures Series. Harrisburg, PA: Trinity Press International, 2000.

Watson, Duane, and Alan J. Hauser. *Rhetorical Criticism of the Bible*. Biblical Interpretation Series 4. Leiden: Brill, 1994.

Watson, Francis. *Paul and the Hermeneutics of Faith*. London: T & T Clark, 2004.

————. *Paul, Judaism, and the Gentiles: A Sociological Approach*. Cambridge: Cambridge University Press, 1998.

Waymeyer, Matt. "The Dual Status of Israel in Romans 11:28." *Master's Seminary Journal* 16, no. 1 (2005): 57–71.

Weaver, Joel A. *Theodoret of Cyrus on Romans 11:26: Recovering an Early Christian Elijah Redivivus Tradition*. American University Studies 249. New York: Lang, 2007.

Wedderburn, A. J. M. *The Reasons for Romans*. Studies of the New Testament and Its World. Edinburgh: T & T Clark, 1988.

Weima, Jeffrey A. D. "Preaching the Gospel in Rome: A Study of the Epistolary Framework of Romans." In *Gospel in Paul: Studies on Corinthians, Galatians and Romans for Richard N. Longenecker*, edited by L. Ann Jervis and Peter Richardson, 337–66. Sheffield: Sheffield Academic Press, 1994.

Wengst, Klaus. *"Freut Euch, Ihr Völker, mit Gottes Volk!": Israel und die Völker als Thema des Paulus – ein Gang Durch Den Römerbrief*. Stuttgart: Kohlhammer, 2008.

Westerholm, Stephen. *Understanding Paul: The Early Christian Worldview of the Letter to the Romans*. Grand Rapids: Baker Academic, 2004.

———. "Paul and the Law in Romans 9-11." In *Paul and the Mosaic Law*. Edited by James D. G. Dunn. WUNT, 215–37. Tübingen: Mohr, 1996.

Wilckens, Ulrich. *Der Brief an die Römer*. Vol. 2. Evangelisch-Katholischer Kommentar Zum Neuen Testament. Zürich: Neukirchen-Vluyn, 1997.

Wiles, G. P. *Paul's Intercessory Prayers*. Cambridge: Cambridge University Press, 1974.

Winger, Michael. *By What Law?: The Meaning of Nomos in the Letters of Paul*. SBL Dissertation Series 128. Atlanta: Scholars Press, 1992.

———. "Unreal Conditions in the Letters of Paul." *JBL* 105, no. 1 (1986): 110–12.

Witherington, Ben, III. *Paul's Letter to the Romans: A Socio-Rhetorical Commentary*. Grand Rapids: Eerdmans, 2004.

———. *Grace in Galatia: A Commentary on Paul's Letter to the Galatians*. Grand Rapids: Eerdmans, 1998.

Worgul, G. S. Jr. "Romans 9-11 and Eccesiology." *BTB* 7 (1977): 99–109.

Wright, N. T. *Paul: In Fresh Perspective*. Minneapolis: Fortress Press, 2005.

———. "The Letter to the Romans: Introduction, Commentary, and Reflection." In *The New Interpreter's Bible*. Edited by Leander Keck, 393–770. Nashville: Abingdon Press, 2002.

Young, B. "The Ascension Motif of 2 Corinthians 12 in Jewish, Christian and Gnostic Texts." *Grace Theological Journal* 9 (1988): 73–103.

Young, Edward J. *The Book of Isaiah*. 3 vols. New International Commentary on the Old Testament. Grand Rapids: Eerdmanns, 1972.

Zeller, Dieter. *Der Brief an die Römer*. Regensburger Neues Testament. Regensburg: Pustet, 1985.

———. *Juden und Heiden in der Mission des Paulus; Studien Zum Römerbrief*. Forschung zur Bibel. Stuttgart: Verlag Katholisches Bibelwerk, 1973.

Ziesler, John. *Paul's Letter to the Romans*. TPI New Testament Commentaries. London: SMC, 1989.

Zoccali, Christopher. "'And So All Israel Will be Saved': Competing Interpretations of Romans 11.26 in Pauline Scholarship." *JSNT* 30, no. 3 (2008): 289–318.

Index of Scripture References

Index of Subjects

79, 81, 148, 166, 213, 223, 237,
240. *See also* Edomites

faithfulness of God, 1, 6, 12, 15,
41, 48, 58–62, 65, 67–68,
72–73, 79, 86n47, 100n66, 106,
168, 171, 188, 205, 209–11,
220–21, 223, 231, 235, 238,
240, 246, 248
favoritism. *See* impartiality
full number. *See* fullness
fullness: of the Gentiles, 17, 154,
190–91, 193–96, 198–99, 203,
206–8, 219, 245, 248; of Israel,
122, 153, 168, 173–77, 187,
188n40, 195, 198–201, 208,
213, 215–16, 219, 243–45

gentiles: general reference of, 1–2,
4, 6, 10, 14, 17–21, 23, 25, 51,
58n5, 63–66, 70–71, 73n34,
77–79, 83, 85, 88, 90, 93–98,
101, 103–4, 119–21, 129n25,
138, 143–49, 151, 153–55, 161,
163–64, 169–70, 173, 175–76,
178–79, 181, 190–91, 194–201,
203, 206–7, 212–13, 216–17,
219, 221, 224, 229, 237–38,
240–41, 244–46, 248; Paul's
literary use of the term, 4,
105–15, 119–20, 133–34,

146–47, 149–51, 163, 172n15,
181, 193n43, 194, 196, 214,
239, 241–42, 244; specific
reference to believing, 3–4,
14n14, 19n21, 20n23, 21,
23–25, 27, 63, 69, 95, 98–99,
102–4, 106, 153–54, 162–64,
168, 170, 172–74, 176–77,
180–88, 193, 195–203, 206–8,
210–11, 213–18, 219, 221, 224,
238, 240–42, 244–48
goodness of God, 48, 73, 75–76,
84, 94, 103–4, 224, 233, 237,
240
grace of God, 8, 15, 18, 20, 25, 51,
99n64, 104, 122, 132n26, 151,
153, 155–56, 158, 161–64, 168,
176, 177, 180, 186, 188, 196,
200, 202, 207–9, 214–16, 218,
220, 224, 228n8, 231–32,
243–45

humility, 2, 4, 14n14, 16n17,
17–21, 23–24, 27, 69n26,
79–80, 101–3, 148, 184, 188,
191, 192, 196, 218, 241,
243–44, 247–48

impartiality, 1–2, 4, 72, 78n41, 80,
89, 102, 104, 129n25, 137, 150,
188, 196n50, 210, 213, 218,

Spain, 2, 16n17, 22–23, 103, 178,
248

Spirit, 8, 19, 29–37, 39, 40n20, 41,
48–49, 52, 53n54, 64, 119,
143n41, 178, 180, 186n38, 202,
205, 208n69, 226n4, 227–32,
234n19, 235, 237, 239, 246

son, lesser (or younger), 1–2, 53,
55, 68–70, 72, 75, 79, 81, 101,
148, 149n48, 174n18, 192, 213,
233, 236–37, 240, 247–48

Stone of Stumbling, 105, 111,
112n4, 116–19, 133, 135, 143,
150, 165   .

stumble of Israel. *See* Israel's fall

unrighteousness, 55, 59–61,
73–76, 81, 104, 129n25

vessels: of honor and dishonor, 56,
82, 83–87, 89, 91–95, 99n64;
of mercy, 56, 82, 85–86,
92–95, 99, 228, 240; of wrath,
56, 82–83, 89, 92–95

wisdom of God, 6, 11–12, 31, 36,
121, 178, 184, 210n73, 223–34,
237

wrath of God, 20n23, 56, 61,
70–72, 77–78, 82–83, 86,
88–89, 91–99, 103–4, 129n25,
145–46, 148–49, 159, 165–67,
183, 185–86, 199n56, 204,
208n70, 213, 215, 217, 218,
223–24, 228, 237–38, 240,
243–45